Japan's Foreign Investment
and Asian Economic Interdependence

Japan's Foreign Investment and Asian Economic Interdependence

Production, Trade, and Financial Systems

Edited by Shojiro Tokunaga

UNIVERSITY OF TOKYO PRESS

Publication of this book was partially supported by a Grant-in-Aid for the Publication of Scientific Research Results from the Ministry of Education, Science and Culture of Japan.

ISBN 4-13-047053-1
ISBN 0-86008-486-8
Printed in Japan

Contents

Preface

Malaysian Prime Minister Mahathir, with his endorsement in December 1990, gave a powerful impetus to the proposal of an East Asia Economic Grouping (EAEG). He suggested that the EAEG (whose name was later changed to East Asia Economic Caucus (EAEC) should promote coordination of members' policies toward the Uruguay Round and foster trade liberalization and economic cooperation in the West Pacific. One of the group's functions would be to give its members leverage against intensifying protectionism in North America and the EC. The very proposal of a grouping, however, was indicative of changes in the economic situation in the region. During the 1980s, particularly the second half of the decade, Asian production and trading systems were revolutionized in ways that strengthened economic interdependence.

During the 1970s, on the heels of the Japanese economy's decade of rapid growth, the Asian newly industrializing economies (NIEs) emerged from the pack of developing countries by means of export-oriented strategies. Since the latter half of the 1980s, the ASEAN countries have stood out for their strong potential to become the next generation of NIEs.

Japan and the Asian NIEs have become major investors in the ASEAN countries, in response to structural changes in their own economies. The past two decades have produced a "flowering of hypotheses that purport to explain the international trade and direct investment activities of firms in terms of the so-called product cycle" (Vernon 1979).

Today, the Asian region has become synonymous with economic

dynamism. It consists of a core of developing counties (the ASEAN countries and China) and an outer circle of advanced economies (Japan and the NIEs). In the process of industrialization, the developing core countries are becoming more economically interdependent with Japan and the Asian NIEs, forming various types of economic linkages, both public and private, in investment, production, R&D, technology transfer, trade and distribution, financing, information, transport, official aid, and other areas.

Vernon's product cycle theory is useful for explaining the intra-Asian trade and investment activities of Japanese and Asian NIEs firms, although it is of only limited use in analyzing their investment operations in the EC and the USA. First, Japanese firms' foreign direct investment (FDI) in Asia is focused on manufacturing rather than on the services sector, to a greater extent than their investments in Europe and the US. According to a 1990 survey by the Toyo Keizai Shimposha, the ratio of manufacturing investment to the total (in terms of number of cases) was 50.4% in the Asian NIEs, 59.1% in ASEAN, and 57.3% in China. The same ratio in the EC and North America was 21.2% and 30.2%, respectively, while the ratio of commerce to the total investment activity was 51.8% and 37%, respectively. Japanese firms' main activities in the EC and the U.S. are internal market-oriented, as Figure 1 illustrates.

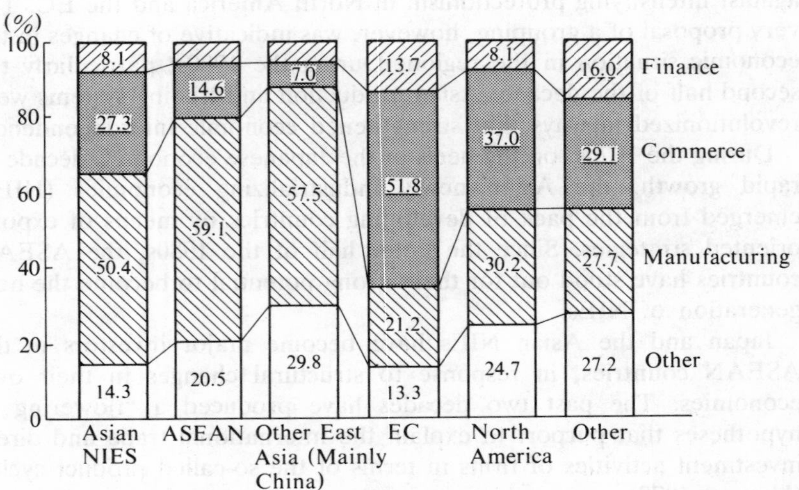

Fig. 1. Share of manufacturing, commercial, and financial businesses in total Japan-oriented firms (% of total by region)

Second, according to the product cycle hypothesis, firms that set up production facilities overseas characteristically do so because of some real or imagined monopolistic advantages. Some threat or promise in the market, in other words, which occurs in the process of developing a new product, typically provides the stimulus to innovation. Japanese firms, for example, are at a competitive disadvantage in terms of labor costs, and this drives them to develop new products and establish production facilities overseas.

The product cycle theory is also inadequate for explaining the dynamic economic development of the Asian countries themselves, or how intra-Asian economic networks are organized. Both the ASEAN countries and China have successfully pursued an outward-oriented growth strategy and introduced export-oriented industries. Partially as a result of intra-Asian linkages, not only the Asian NIEs but also the ASEAN countries are on the way to successfully establishing their own self-reliant economies.

These phenomena are among those that we have studied, and that are investigated and discussed in this book.

References

Toyo Keizai Shimposha (ed.). 1990. *Gyoshu-betsu Kaigai Shinshutsu Kigyo 1990* (Survey of Japanese Firms' Overseas Investment by Industry, 1990 edition).

Vernon, Raymond. 1979. The product cycle hypothesis in a new international environment. *Oxford Bulletin of Economics and Statistics*.

Acknowledgments

This book would not exist without the sponsorship of the Ministry of Education, Science and Culture, Japan, which provided a Grant-in-Aid for the Publication of Scientific Research Results. The Ministry also financially supported the 1989-90 international research project entitled "Japan's Investment and the Changing Structures in Thailand and Malaysia: Comparative Investigation of the Asian Economy."

The editor wishes to thank the Murata Science Foundation, Kyoto, which financed the 1990-91 research project on the evolution of international physical distribution and Asian trading networks, and the editorial staff of the University of Tokyo Press.

Japan's Foreign Investment
and Asian Economic Interdependence

Part I
Asian Economic Networks

1 Japan's FDI-Promoting Systems and Intra-Asia Networks: New Investment and Trade Systems Created by the Borderless Economy

Shojiro Tokunaga

Faculty of Economics, Kyushu University

INTRODUCTION: JAPAN AS A MATURE ECONOMY

A Mature Economy without Unemployment

One of the important phrases in Keynes's *The General Theory* is the "paradox of poverty in the midst of plenty," which implies a gap between actual and potential gross domestic product (GDP):

> The richer the community, the wider will tend to be the gap between its actual and its potential production.... A wealthy community will have to discover much ampler opportunities for investment if the saving propensities of its wealthier members are to be compatible with the employment of its poor members. If in a potentially wealthy community the inducement to invest is weak, then, in spite of its potential wealth, the working of the principle of effective demand will compel it to reduce its actual output, until, in spite of its potential wealth, it has sufficiently diminished to correspond to the weakness of the inducement to invest.

Japan already has a mature economy. Figure 1 indicates that the rate of business income to compensation of employees has continued to decline since 1973. The growth rates of GNP, factor supplies, and factor productivity from 1980-1985 were much lower than in previous years (Fig. 2). These facts are evidence that the Japanese economy has been mature since the mid-1970s, when the days of rapid growth were over in Japan as well as in other advanced economies.

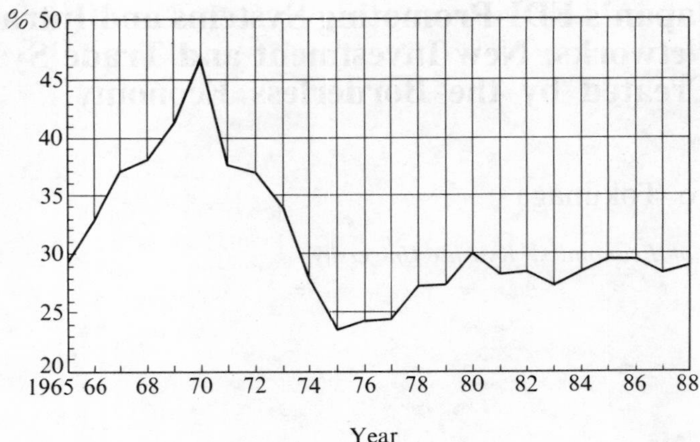

Fig. 1. Changing pattern of business profit share (ratio of returns on assets and business income to wage income)
Source: Based on annual National Accounts (*Kokumin Keizai Keisan*).

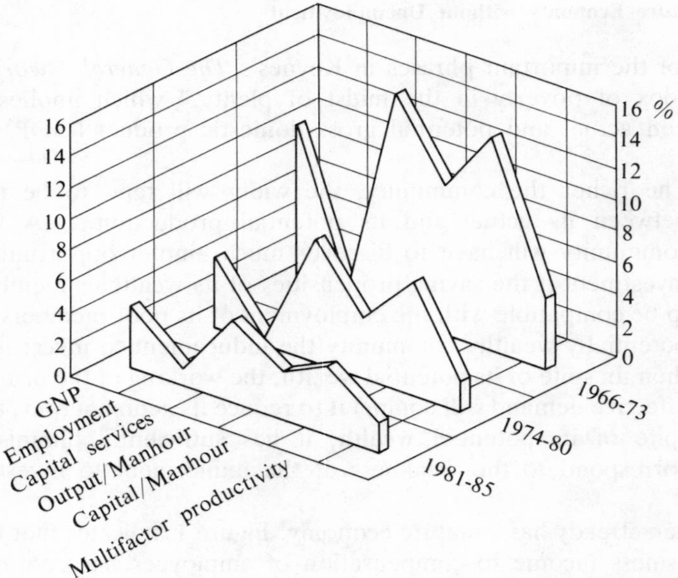

Fig. 2. General indicators of the Japanese economy (growth rate)
Source: OECD. Drawing courtesy of Mr. Sepel.

Another interesting phenomenon is the rapid increase in the propensity to save. The Japanese economy nominally expanded values of financial and stock assets and land in the 1980s, although not that of the net capital assets and housing (Fig. 3). Japan's current excess savings do not, however, indicate a weakness in inducement to invest, because during the 1980s (and early 1990s) Japan's unemployment rate was much lower than that in any other advanced or mature economy.

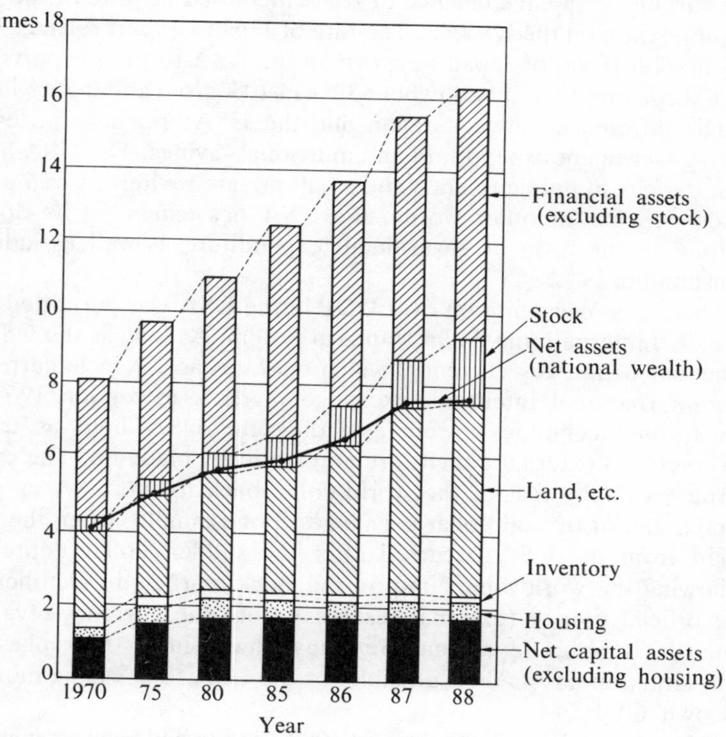

Fig. 3. National assets balances as ratio to GNP
Source: *White Paper on the Japanese Economy 1990* (Tokyo: BII).

Why has Japan maintained prosperity with excess savings? One of the main reasons, of course, is in the nature of an "export-led" economy. The Japanese economy has managed to maintain a high rate of growth even during the upsurge in the value of the yen following the Plaza Accord in September 1985, transforming its structure from an export-led base to a domestic demand-led one accompanied by aggressive foreign direct investment (FDI).

Heavy Reliance on the US Market: First Half of the 1980s

Japan has an economic structure that mainly relies on exports rather than domestic consumption, in contrast to the United States. In the five years from 1982 to 1986, productivity in the Japanese manufacturing sector rose rapidly compared with that in the USA. In the same period, the surplus of Japan's balance of trade increased in spite of the deficit accumulation on the US side. The rate of Japan's export reliance on the US market (ratio of Japan's exports to the USA to total exports) went up a surprising 14 points, to about 39% in 1986 from about 25% in 1980.

The difference between Japan and the USA appeared in terms of both government expenditure and individual savings. The USA has had vast deficits in public finance and small private savings as well as huge trade deficits. In other words, the USA has expanded its domestic market in the form of government expenditure as well as individual consumption.

The excess consumption over GDP in the USA was permitted by the so-called international dollar standard system. As long as the US dollar functions as the key currency, which operates as a vehicle currency in the international interbank exchange markets (Swoboda 1968) and which the economic powers excluding the USA hold as external reserves, US external deficits are automatically made up. The external surpluses of the rest of the world come back to the USA as private capital and/or official dollar exchanges. For example, when the capital flight from the USA occurred after the sudden dollar depreciation following the worldwide slump in the stock markets in October 1987, the official money (external reserves) from the currency-revaluating countries such as Japan and Germany flowed in as the replacement. This situation has made it possible for the USA to consume more than its own GDP.

On the other hand, until the mid-1980s, Japan had been strengthening its export reliance structure by utilizing improved productivity for cost reduction instead of expansion of domestic demand. This, backed up by the relative decrease in government expenditures, made the ratio of savings to domestic demand rise. The excess savings were absorbed in two main ways: (1) a rapid increase in (nominal) values of domestic financial assets and real estate; and (2) an increase in Japanese foreign investment, especially portfolio investment.

Domestic Demand-led Growth and FDI: After the Plaza Accord

In September 1985 the ministers of finance of the Group of Five (the USA, Japan, West Germany, the UK, and France) agreed to the devaluation of the US dollar, especially, in relation to the Japanese yen and German mark, to strengthen US competitiveness and reduce its cumulative current balance deficits. This was the so-called Plaza Accord.

Since the mid-1980s, economic friction between the US and Western Europe and Japan has simmered. The USA has preserved its ability to act unilaterally against "barriers to US exports" under section 301 of the Trade Act of 1974, which empowers the president to retaliate unilaterally against foreign practices perceived as detrimental to US commercial interests. The regular section 301 procedures and remedies were substantially strengthened to "super 301" by the Omnibus Trade and Competitiveness Act of 1988 (1988 Trade Act). Japan has been compelled to exercise voluntary restraints on exportable goods with comparative advantage such as automobiles, VCRs, semiconductors, and so on.

In addition, the Structural Impediments Initiative (SII) talks between Japan and the USA were launched in 1989 to solve structural problems in Japan which act as impediments to trade and to balance of payments adjustment outside the scope of Section 301 of the US Trade Act. As a result of SII, Japan has been pursuing appropriate policies to sustain solid economic growth led by strong domestic demand, especially to promote accumulation of social overhead capital (see the Ministry of International Trade and Industry's Final Report on the SII Talks [MITI 1990]).

With rising incomes and shifts in exchange rates, labor costs in Japan have also been much closer or almost the same as those in the USA. Moreover, since 1988 "labor shortage" issues have been seriously discussed. According to the Bank of Japan's "Short-term Economic Survey of All Enterprises," the employee judgment diffusion index (the ratio of those industries reporting a "surplus" against those reporting an "insufficiency" of labor) shows that the outlook in manufacturing as well as nonmanufacturing industry changed to one of insufficiency in February 1988 (Economic Planning Agency 1990) (see Fig. 3A).

According to the Economic Planning Agency of Japan (EPA), which circulated a questionnaire to the manufacturing sector in 1990, over 40% of responding corporations cited diversified production and entry into a different industry or type of manufacturing, development of new

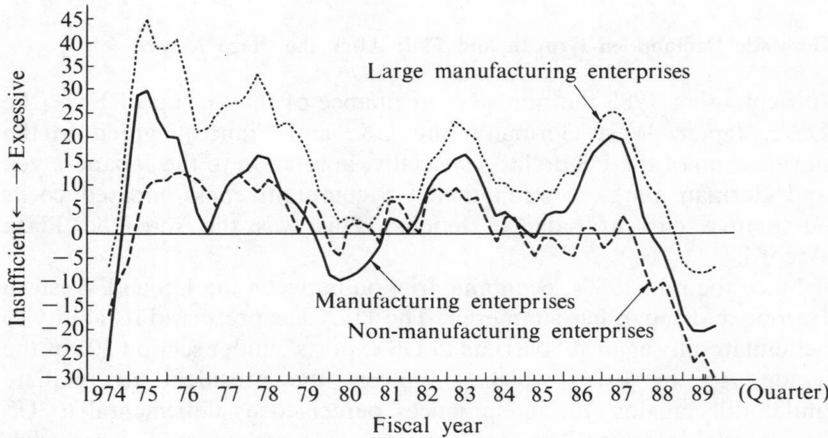

Fig. 3A. Transition in judgment D.I. on number of employees
Source: Economic Planning Agency, *Economic Survey of Japan 1988-89* (Tokyo: EPA, 1990).

products, and R&D as well as ordinary labor demand in a period of economic prosperity as reasons for labor shortage. This implies that Japanese manufacturing has become more sophisticated.

In the changing circumstances of yen appreciation, economic friction, and labor shortage (including rising labor costs), Japan has been converting from a traditional pattern of growth and investment to a new one based on a domestic demand- and FDI-led base. The transformation of an export-led economy to a domestic demand-led one implies at least three immediate issues: 1) reduction of massive external imbalances, especially with the USA; 2) creation of diverse lifestyles for a better quality of life; and 3) promotion of social overhead capital improvement for the smooth facilitation of industrial restructuring.

Japanese firms are pursuing various business strategies to adapt to the above-mentioned environmental changes. Among the major elements of these strategies are higher value-added products, sophistication and centralization of production technology (high-tech orientation), full use of information intensification, and diversification of business operations (rationalized operations). The concept of industry sophistication has been prevalent since the period of high economic growth, but at that time the emphasis in industry sophistication was mainly toward lowering costs through mass production. At present, however, the emphasis is on achieving a variety of orientations, such as small volumes or new types of products with high value added to satisfy a growing diversity of needs (Economic Planning Agency 1990, p. 64).

A large amount of FDI by Japanese firms is not in conflict with a sophisticated or domestic-led economy, because FDI contributes to the creation of new kinds of value-added products and therefore to the establishment of sophisticated social and economic infrastructure in Japan. At the same time it transfers Japan's mature industries to less competitive industrialized countries and newly industrializing economies.

In fact, in the changing economic circumstances outlined above, Japanese manufacturers' foreign investments have accelerated since 1986. Since 1985 the ratio of Japan's exports to gross national product (GNP) has been declining rapidly and, in contrast, the ratio of Japan's FDI to GNP has been rising. Japan is thus on the way to becoming an FDI- and domestic demand-led economy (see Fig. 4).

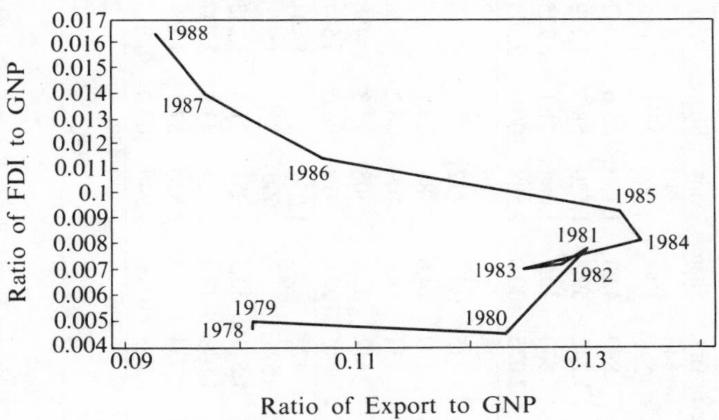

Fig. 4. Ratio of FDI and Exports to GNP
Source: EAG, *Nihon to Sekai o Kaeru Kaigai Chokusetsu Toshi* (Foreign Direct Investment and the Changing Role of Japan in the World) (Tokyo: EAG, 1990).

FDI BY JAPANESE MANUFACTURERS: CHARACTERISTICS AND FORMS

Production Facilities Abroad: Concept and Implications

Table 1 indicates the trends of Japan's FDI from 1981 to 1986 by three business types (manufacturing, exploitation of natural resources, and trade and services) and by form (acquisition of securities and money-lending).

Why does FDI include "money-lending" as one of the categories? Because FDI is for the purpose of "establishing lasting economic relations that give the possibility of exercising an effective influence of

Table 1. Japan's Overseas Direct Investment, 1981-86 (by industry and form of investment).

Industry	Form		1981 Amt.	1981 Share	1982 Amt.	1982 Share	1983 Amt.	1983 Share	1984 Amt.	1984 Share	1985 Amt.	1985 Share	1986 Amt.	1986 Share
Manufacturing	Securities Acquisition	New	298 (240)	13.1	343 (226)	16.5	340 (246)	13.1	817 (303)	32.6	489 (363)	20.8	1,185 (597)	32.7
		Existing	1,102	48.3	899	43.3	1,180	45.6	962	38.4	1,124	47.8	1,556	42.9
		Subtotal	1,400	61.4	1,242	59.8	1,520	58.7	1,779	71.0	1,614	68.6	2,741	75.6
	Lending		880	38.6	833	40.2	1,064	41.1	725	29.0	738	31.4	887	24.4
	Total		2,280	100.0	2,075	100.0	2,588	100.0	2,505	100.0	2,352	100.0	3,628	100.0
Natural Resources Exploitation	Securities Acquisition	New	50 (43)	1.9	25 (15)	3.4	26 (22)	6.1	12 (17)	2.2	73 (32)	11.2	117 (33)	16.6
		Existing	120	4.5	109	14.6	84	20.1	66	12.4	96	14.7	134	19.1
		Subtotal	171	6.5	134	18.0	109	26.2	78	14.6	168	25.8	251	35.7
	Lending		2,474	93.5	612	82.0	308	73.8	458	85.4	484	74.2	452	64.3
	Total		2,645	100.0	746	100.0	418	100.0	534	100.0	652	100.0	703	100.0
Commerce and other Services	Securities Acquisition	New	474 (465)	12.2	428 (524)	9.0	1,071 (600)	21.7	1,504 (508)	21.8	1,436 (627)	16.2	3,507 (789)	20.1
		Existing	1,178	30.4	1,571	33.2	1,053	21.3	1,233	17.9	2,745	30.9	6,047	34.7
		Subtotal	1,651	42.7	1,999	42.2	2,124	43.0	2,737	39.7	4,181	47.1	9,554	54.8
	Lending		2,220	57.4	2,734	57.8	2,820	57.1	4,157	60.3	4,702	52.9	7,869	45.2
	Total		3,861	100.0	4,733	100.0	4,940	100.0	6,895	100.0	8,883	100.0	17,423	100.0
New Securities Grand Total Acquired		Amt. (Cases)	822 (748)		796 (765)		1,437 (868)		2,333 (828)		1,998 (1,023)		4,809 (1,419)	

Note: Figures in parentheses are numbers of cases.

Source: K. Nakai, " 1986 Nendo no Wagakuni no Kaigai Chokusetsu Toshi Doko, " *Kaigai Toshi Kenkyuho.* Tokyo: Export-Import Bank of Japan, Oct. 1987.

the management." For example, according to the code of liberalization of capital movements adopted by the Organization for Economic Co-operation and Development (OECD), "overseas direct investment" is defined as "investment for the purpose of establishing lasting economic relations with an undertaking—such as, in particular, investments which give the possibility of exercising an effective influence of the management thereof:

1. creation or extension of a wholly-owned enterprise, subsidiary or branch, [or] acquisition of full ownership of an existing enterprise;
2. participation in a new or existing enterprise;
3. a long-term loan (five years and longer)."

Japan maintained extensive restrictions when it joined the OECD in 1964. The liberalization of FDI had been progressing during the period of rapid economic growth in Japan in phase I (October 1969), phase II (September 1970), phase III (July 1971), and phase IV (July 1972). During the period, the concept of a foreign juridical person substantially controlled by a Japanese corporation (in the OECD code, nonresidents who "exercise an effective influence on the management") which is a key term in FDI, changed remarkably.

Before phase I a juridical person meant a Japanese majority-owned (50% or more) corporation; in the case of joint ventures in developing countries, it was construed as 25% or more ownership, one or more full-time directors, and a minimum investment. After phase I and II, the concept of an overseas juridical person substantially controlled by a Japanese corporation was expanded to include majority-owned corporations without overseas directors.

After the phase III liberalization step, the limit to the investment amount was removed and the definition of the overseas juridical person was also greatly relaxed to include 1) a 10% or more Japanese-owned corporation accompanied by one of the following six requirements: dispatch of one or more full- or part-time directors, furnishing of technology, supply of raw materials and parts, purchasing of products, financial assistance, and execution of an exclusive agency agreement; and 2) a 25% or more Japanese-owned one. With the phase IV liberalization that took place in June 1972, the criteria for the approval of FDI were loosened.

The foreign exchange and foreign trade control law of Japan, which dramatically and basically changed the attitude toward capital movements to "liberalization in principle" from "prohibition in principle" in October 1980, follows the OECD's concept of FDI. Under the new foreign exchange law, a "direct foreign investment" means "acquisition of any securities issued by a juridical person established under foreign legislation, or any money lending to such a juridical person... as an act purporting to establish a long-term economic relationship therewith, or any payment of funds for establishment or expansion of a branch, factory, or other place of business in a foreign country, by a resident."

The acquisition of securities falling under FDI is as follows: 1) a transaction to acquire 10% or more of a foreign juridical person's equity; 2) a transaction to acquire less than 10% of the equity accompanying dispatch of one or more directors, furnishing technology, supplying raw materials or products, executing a sole agency contract, or establishing other lasting economic links.

Money-lending that falls under FDI is 1) long-term (over one year) loans for foreign juridical persons possessing more than 10% of equity; and 2) even with less than 10% or none at all, long-term loans to foreign juridical persons with whom some form of lasting economic relations is maintained.

Under the new foreign exchange law, there is a category of "FDI without ownership." Provision of loans exceeding one year to a foreign juridical person whose management is influenced by a Japanese firm through long-term contracts is construed to be FDI from Japan. Acquiring equity is a form of effective management control of a foreign corporation. The essence of FDI, therefore, is related not necessarily to acquiring the "ownership" but to exercising effective influence on the management of a foreign-located firm.

Production Facilities Abroad: Their Classification

When a production facility abroad is categorized as part of an international intracompany network, equity participation alone is not a sufficient criterion. Even though equity participation does exist, unless there is a way to share in management or marketing, there is little difference from a security investment for obtaining dividends or capital gains. On the contrary, if it is possible to have local firms substitute for the production of plants in Japan or to incorporate foreign firms in a Japanese corporation's intracompany production network by means of furnishing technology, capital equipment, parts, and so on, those local firms are obviously overseas production facilities of Japanese corporations.

The criterion for determining whether an organization is a production facility abroad or not is whether it supports a wing for research and development (R&D), production, marketing, and physical distribution systems of a Japanese firm as a base for taking charge of production activity or as one process in the intracompany production network. If such a sector abroad is an important segment of the main company's business activities, and, further, if it has strong bargaining power in the area of technology or other matters, the securing of management control must be sought by the Japanese firm. "Equity sharing" is an important measure to determine the relative position of an overseas production base, the bargaining power held by the local partner (or government), and/or the depth of the cooperative relationship, but it cannot be the absolute criterion for determining whether a local (foreign-located) firm is a production facility abroad or not.

Production facilities abroad are foreign juridical persons who are incorporated as a link in Japanese corporations' R&D, production, marketing, and physical distribution systems and, therefore, support the latter's international or borderless production processes. Parts and semifinished and final products manufactured by local firms are all subject to the control of the corporations that share equity or money-lending along with the establishment of lasting economic links by dispatching one or more directors, furnishing technology, supplying capital goods, etc.

If production facilities abroad are defined as above, FDI in the manufacturing sector is essentially internationalization of the production process. Acquisition of ownership is one of the methods of achieving an international production system. The visible and invisible intracompany networks or international R&D, production, and physical distribution systems of the parent corporations are key points.

Figure 5 illustrates the forms of establishment of production facilities abroad. They are divided broadly into two categories, acquisition of ownership and nonownership relations. The former would include a branch factory (expansion of a factory in a foreign country by a Japanese corporation), a partnership with local residents, a local stock company (foreign judicial body as a joint-stock company) including a wholly-owned subsidiary, a joint venture, and capital participation by means of stock acquisition. The latter, nonownership relations, are based on lasting economic connections such as dispatching directors, furnishing technology, and supplying raw materials, parts, and semifinished products. The forms of nonownership relations are production sharing or cooperative production, production consignment or compensation trade (providing capital equipment and material as rental and buying the products back), processing with supplied materials, processing on order, etc.

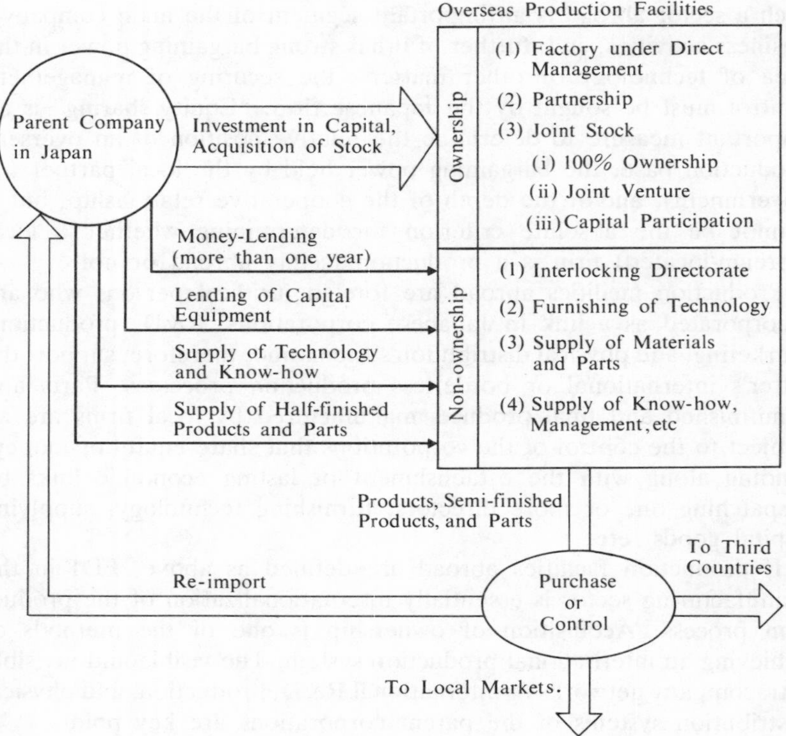

Fig. 5. Methods of establishing overseas production facilities

Asianization of Production and Forms of FDI

The three factors of yen appreciation, economic friction with the USA and the EC, and a blue-collar worker shortage have impelled Japanese businesses to undertake a global process of horizontal specialization, mainly in assembling and processing industries. Let us examine the current status of Japanese manufacturers' FDI on the basis of the "18th and 19th Surveys on Japanese Business Activity Abroad," conducted in 1988 and 1989 by the Ministry of International Trade and Industry (MITI).

As of the end of March 1989, there were 7,544 Japanese overseas subsidiaries in which Japanese corporations held more than 10% of the equity. Of the total abroad engaged in business activities 3,243 firms were manufacturers, of which about 33% or 1,028 firms had been established for only three years, from fiscal 1986. It is surmised that in the same period 53%, or 546 manufacturing subsidiaries, were located in Asia (Table 2). These consisted of 165 manufacturers of electrical machinery and appliances, 63 in chemicals, 57 in transportation equipment and parts, and others.

Today, Japanese manufacturers seeking comparatively low-cost production bases are attracted by ASEAN countries as substitutes for Asian NIEs, which have been becoming less competitive than before both in wage levels and in terms of exchange rates. For example, of 546 Asian production bases newly established in fiscal 1986, 261 were located in Asian NIEs. In fiscal 1989, however, 104 Japanese manufacturing facilities were set up in ASEAN countries excluding Singapore, one and a half times as many as those in Asian NIEs (74 units).

It is also interesting to consider the manufacturers' expanded FDI including industrial cooperation and technology transfer, joint ventures with minority ownership, and majority-owned subsidiaries. According to a 1989 survey by the Japan External Trade Organization (JETRO), the number of industrial cooperation and technology transfer agreements without any ownership numbered 1,958 cases, more than joint ventures (1,354) and three-fourths of 2,636 majority-owned subsidiaries. (See Appendix Table A at the end of this chapter.)

The ASEAN Promotion Center on Trade in Tokyo, with the cooperation of the Small Business Finance Corporation, sent questionnaires to 34,925 small- and medium-scale firms in Japan in 1989, focusing on manufacturers, with work forces of 30 to 1,000 and capital of ¥10 million to ¥300 million. The survey was conducted by mail, and 9,060 firms responded. Sixty percent of Japanese small- and medium-scale businesses covered by the survey were considering investing abroad, especially in the ASEAN area, and almost 30% were planning to do so within five years. In addition, a total of 1,141 companies, or about 13% of the respondents, had already set up businesses abroad, of which 411 firms or 36% had invested in the ASEAN countries. Businesses investing in the ASEAN area are mainly manufacturers of electrical machinery and appliances and other machinery.

Of the firms which had already invested in the ASEAN region, those citing the use of low-cost labor as their reason accounted for 61.2%, higher than in any other area. The second most common reason was the cultivation and maintenance of the local market (cited by 40.1%).

Among the firms planning to invest or interested in investing in the ASEAN region, the use of low-cost labor was also the main reason (58.8%). However, export back to Japan ranked second (36.9%),

Table 2. Japanese Manufacturing FDI to Asia, by Industry, through 1988.

(amounts in US $ millions)

Year(s)	Food		Textiles		Wood & pulp		Chemicals		Iron & non-ferrous metals		Machinery		Electronics		Transport equipment		Other		Subtotal	
	Cases	Amt.	Cases	Amt.	Cases	Amt.	Cases	Amt.	Cases	Amt.	Cases	Amt.	Cases	Amt.	Cases	Amt.	Cases	Amt.	Cases	Amt.
1951 – 70	43	23	170	107	23	15	122	19	70	34	85	15	152	45	20	14	230	48	915	320
1971	5	3	37	53	10	4	26	13	11	5	17	5	23	19	2	0	65	22	196	124
1972	24	9	46	132	24	14	20	9	48	31	23	10	86	36	9	19	76	17	356	277
1973	25	12	117	191	58	38	45	32	60	29	66	19	156	83	22	44	132	38	681	486
1974	23	21	46	118	38	23	54	34	41	38	26	18	43	30	15	19	78	57	364	358
1975	25	24	18	71	16	13	44	49	24	66	28	18	34	36	16	32	38	57	243	367
1976	23	7	16	47	10	6	32	44	26	67	31	12	38	44	14	8	29	51	219	285
1977	20	8	21	83	10	8	26	75	26	29	27	16	33	32	10	24	60	57	233	334
1978	26	14	25	35	9	2	32	189	41	389	62	64	95	93	16	43	58	28	364	858
1979	33	17	29	34	15	9	47	63	44	43	59	65	72	55	13	36	63	116	375	437
1980	40	10	30	50	11	10	53	193	50	299	43	31	37	71	11	29	46	32	321	724
1981	28	19	45	42	8	10	67	136	39	312	48	42	48	57	13	39	58	31	354	688
1982	20	9	35	40	20	9	69	132	30	144	30	52	42	43	19	45	57	68	322	542
1983	33	19	24	132	18	17	66	207	29	63	34	74	53	45	22	123	67	59	346	738
1984	33	27	24	39	11	8	35	56	20	111	35	63	65	93	30	66	57	54	310	516
1985	42	34	22	8	7	4	42	39	23	36	39	76	47	51	27	151	73	60	322	460
1986	50	28	18	21	13	9	43	47	32	61	52	95	111	262	36	130	107	150	462	804
1987	63	142	45	28	25	13	80	246	95	306	76	102	184	467	61	206	161	169	790	1,679
1988	78	90	106	149	53	177	88	200	102	205	118	259	164	852	35	155	191	284	935	2,370

Source: MITI, 1990.

followed by the cultivation and maintenance of the local market (33.6%) and the securing of inexpensive raw materials (27.2%).

JAPAN'S OFFICIAL DEVELOPMENT ASSISTANCE AND ESTABLISHMENT OF FDI-PROMOTING SYSTEMS

The Shift to Asian ODA and the Role of the Overseas Economic Cooperation Fund

According to the Economic Cooperation Bureau (ECB) of the Ministry of Foreign Affairs of Japan, the net outflow of official development assistance (ODA), other official funds (OOF), and private funds (PF) amounted to $8,965 million, $1,544 million, and $13,502 million, respectively, in 1989. The amount of the net official outflows of ODA and OOF was almost equal to that of FDI in the private sector.

Total worldwide Development Assistance Committee (DAC) country ODA in 1989 amounted to $46,498 million, of which Japan's ODA was about 19%, ranking first among world ODA contributors for the first time. Three-fourths of Japan's ODA was bilateral, over 60% of which concentrated in Asia.

The Overseas Economic Cooperation Fund of Japan (OECF) has supplied loans mainly for the development of developing countries' infrastructure since 1966. The OECF deals with virtually all bilateral ODA loans, which in 1989 amounted to $3,943 million, with the OECF's share accounting for 44.0% of Japan's total ODA and 58.2% of Japan's total bilateral ODA. The reason OECF loans to foreign governments constitute a significant part of Japan's ODA is attributed to the nature of the loans. Since 1975 loans to foreign governments with grant elements of 25% or more have been the focus of the OECF. Today, there is a clear demarcation between OECF loans and loans by the Export-Import Bank of Japan (EXIM Bank). The purpose of OECF loans to foreign governments is to provide assistance for the social and economic development of developing countries, and the loans are made on very concessional terms with the above-mentioned grant element.

In 1989, OECF loan commitments to Asian governments as a percentage of the total amounted to 77.5%. To the six Asian countries of Indonesia, the Philippines, Thailand, Myanmar, Sri Lanka, and South Korea, the OECF became the top assistance donor among nonprivate financial institutions (including the World Bank and Asian Development Bank) on a net-disbursement basis in 1988. Bangladesh, China, and Pakistan are countries to which the OECF, although not the largest aid donor, has provided the same volume of aid as the top donor institutions (OECF 1990, p.12).

The OECF has another function related to private loans and equity investment, i.e., loans to and equity investment in corporations registered both in Japan and in developing countries. In 1989, 79% of total loans to and equity investment in corporations were distributed in Asia.

Export-Import Bank of Japan as FDI Promoter

The OECF is a governmental financial institution established to promote Japan's economic cooperation with developing countries through the provision of loans usually referred to as ODA. The Export-Import Bank of Japan is also governmental. Today, its lending schemes fall into two main categories: (1) loans to domestic corporations such as supplier credits, technical service credits and import credits, and overseas investment credits; and (2) loans to foreign governments and corporations, including buyer credits, overseas investment credits, untied direct loans, public bond purchases, and refinancing loans. The bank's operational framework has fundamentally changed from promoting exports to encouraging foreign investment since the Export-Import Bank Act was amended in the latter half of the 1980s. In other words, the bank works as an FDI-promoting financial institute rather than as an export-promoting one.

Official export credits are divided into two categories, supplier credits and buyer credits. Supplier credits are extended to Japanese corporations for deferred-payment exports of plant, capital equipment, and technical services, and buyer credits are extended to foreign importers for their imports of plant, equipment, and technical services from Japan. The latter are called bank-to-bank loans when lending for the same purpose is channeled through intermediary financial institutions in buyer countries. Today, these official credits are closely related to the expanded concept of FDI in the form of joint ventures, cooperative production, buy-back agreements on the basis of technology transfer or of processing with supplied capital goods, etc.

Official import credits are primarily extended to Japanese corporations for their development and import of natural resources and other items which are deemed essential to the Japanese economy. Credits for the same purpose can also be extended to foreign firms. Following the Japanese government's announcement of its Comprehensive Economic Measures in 1983, however, the bank launched a finance scheme for promoting the import of manufactured goods from abroad. This scheme is used to do business with production facilities abroad such as subsidiaries, joint ventures, production cooperation, and buy-backs.

Under the amended Export-Import Bank Act of 1986, the bank extends overseas investment credits to Japanese entities to provide them with funds for overseas investment as follows:

a) credits to Japanese corporations for their equity participation in foreign corporations;

b) credits to Japanese corporations for their loans to foreign governments or corporations to provide them with long-term funds for ventures operating outside Japan;

c) credits to Japanese corporations to be extended as loans to foreign governments or corporations for their equity participation in foreign firms in which the Japanese corporations have equity shares;

d) credits to Japanese corporations for their equity participation in corporations established in Japan for the sole purpose of making overseas investment in the above-mentioned items (a), (b), and (c); and

e) credits to Japanese corporations to provide them with funds required for projects operating abroad.

These credits are principally extended in yen, but some in foreign currencies such as the US dollar are also available when justified. The bank extends those credits to foreign governments, foreign governmental institutions, etc., for funds for equity participation in or loans to corporations in which a Japanese company has an equity share. When the bank extends credits to foreign corporations indirectly through foreign governmental financial institutions, those are called "two-step loans."

Currently, the EXIM Bank mainly operates foreign investment schemes, i.e., overseas credits and overseas project loans, rather than original official export credits. As shown in Table 3, the share of overseas investment credits to disbursements of the bank's financing rose to 37% in 1990 from 25% in 1985, while the share of export credits to the same declined to 12% from 51% in the same period. Loans outstanding to East and Southeast Asia had 12% and 25% of the total, respectively, by the end of March 1990.

The New Trade Insurance System for Promoting FDI

In 1987 the Export Insurance Act was amended and renamed the Trade Insurance Act, under which MITI has established a new trade insurance system. Under the new system MITI provides protection against risks or losses from overseas investment, intermediary trade outside Japan, and prepaid imports as well as from exports.

Table 3. Disbursements, by Purpose of Financing (¥ billion).

	1985	1986	1987	1988	1989	Share (%)
Export Credits	394.0	259.1	224.3	175.6	148.0	12%
Import Credits	103.6	182.5	219.5	159.9	140.4	12
Overseas Investment Credits	190.8	116.5	230.5	374.2	451.1	37
United Direct Loans (Bonds)	79.6	124.2	192.5	277.1	474.4	39
Government Loans	7.9	10.0	7.5	—	0	0
Total	775.9	692.0	874.3	986.9	1213.9	100

Source: OECF, Annual Report 1990.

General Export Insurance is mainly to protect against preshipment losses. In cases such as exports of plants, ships, or technical services, Export Proceeds Insurance (Medium- and Long-term Export Credit Insurance) or Technical Services Supply Insurance is provided when export bills are settled on a deferred payment basis, or when Japanese banks provide foreign importers with credit in conjunction with the EXIM Bank. Export Proceeds Insurance is provided to cover any possible losses due to commercial risk such as bankruptcy as well as those due to political risk.

With the recent increase in the number of international consortia formed for plant exports, it has become necessary for export insurance agencies of the countries of the participating corporations to make joint insurance arrangements for assuring the appropriate coverage for both main contractors and subcontractors forming these consortia. Japan had concluded agreements for this purpose with eight countries—Belgium, France, Singapore, the UK, the Netherlands, Austria, Spain, and Canada—as of April 1989 (Export-Import Bank of Japan 1989).

It is natural that these export insurance schemes are used by Japanese corporations to supply plants, capital equipment, etc. to their overseas subsidiaries, joint ventures, and production-sharing firms, including project financing and cooperative production, technology transfer, etc. In other words, the traditional export insurance schemes also are deeply related to Japan's expanded-concept FDI.

As shown in Figure 6, MITI operates three new types of insurance schemes to provide protection against risks associated with FDI. Prepaid Insurance was created mainly to provide protection against risks associated with prepaid manufactured imports. These manufactured goods can be used as a means of repayment for previously supplied capital goods to offshore joint ventures, production participation, etc.

Intermediary Insurance aims at coping with intermediary trade between Japan and third countries in which there is risk of nonpayment. Japanese small and medium-scale manufacturers who have established

(A) Import-Prepayment Insurance System

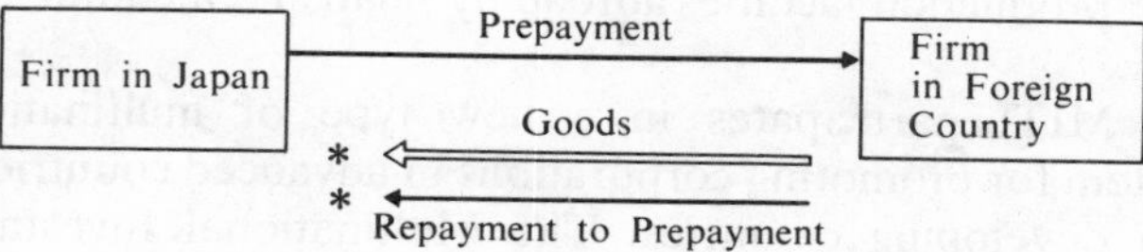

(B) Intermediary Insurance System

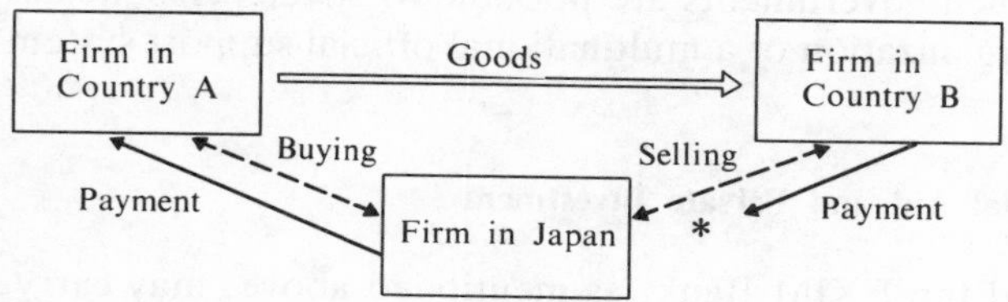

(C) Expanded Insurance System for Foreign Investment

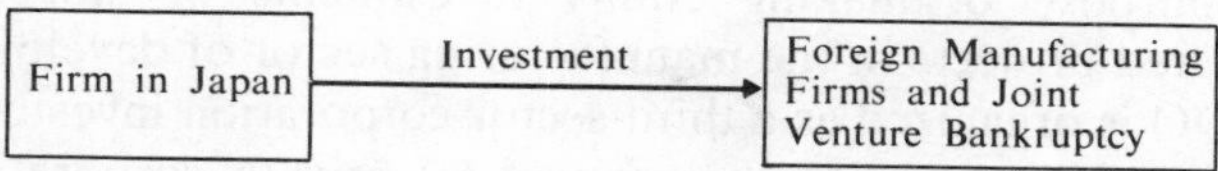

(D) Multilateral Investment Guarantee Agency (MIGA)

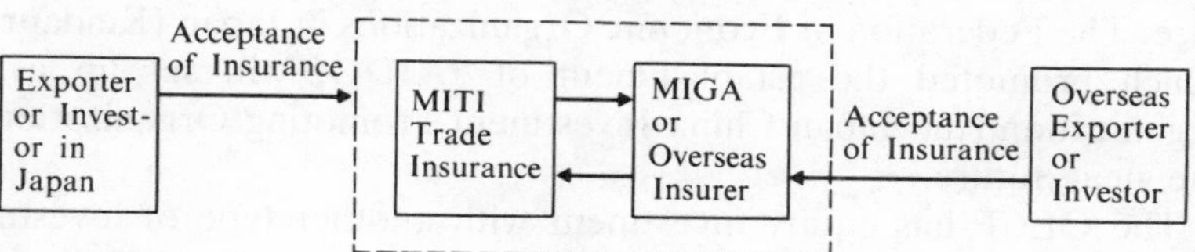

Fig. 6. MITI's new and expanded trade insurance system
Source: Shojiro Tokunaga et al., *Gendai no Boeki Torihiki to Kinyu* (Contemporary Foreign Trade and Financing) (Tokyo: Yuhikaku, 1988).

production facilities abroad for exporting products to third countries play an intermediary role in trade between third countries as operating headquarters of those subsidiaries, joint ventures, cooperative production facilities, etc. Intermediary Insurance promotes establishing these kinds of overseas production bases.

Before 1987, Overseas Investment Insurance was provided to cover only losses due to events constituting political risk such as war or internal disorder. The new and expanded Overseas Investment Insurance insures against loss due to commercial risks, such as bankruptcy linked with FDI, as well as political risks. The new Overseas

Investment Insurance goes a long way toward promoting the establishment of production facilities abroad by small and medium-sized Japanese firms.

In addition, MITI participates in a new type of multinational reinsurance system for promoting corporations in advanced countries to perfect FDI in developing countries. The Multinational Investment Guarantee Agency (MIGA), which was set up in 1988, is an international organization to reinsure losses from exports and overseas investments which governments are not able to cover. This means the formation or organization of a multinational official support system for FDI.

Hybrid of Official Aid and Private Investment

The OECF and the EXIM Bank, as mentioned above, may carry out equity investment to assist in development projects. The Japan International Development Organization (JAIDO) was established in 1989 for the purpose of making equity investments in industrial cooperation-related projects in the manufacturing sector of developing countries. JAIDO is organized as a third-sector corporation invested in by the OECF (one-third equity shares) and 80 private corporations (two-thirds), and intends to reinforce ODA-related projects that contribute mainly to the building of developing countries' infrastructure. The Federation of Economic Organizations in Japan (Keidanren), which promoted the establishment of JAIDO, will set up a new organization (the Japan-China Investment Promoting Organization) in the near future.

The OECF has equity investment with another type of investment corporation, the Japan ASEAN Investment Company (JAIC). JAIC was founded in 1981 with 137 member corporations of the Japan Association of Corporate Executives (Keizai Doyukai) as shareholders, and the JAIC-1 Investment Fund, amounting to ¥7 billion, was established in 1988. As of July 1990, the amount of the five JAIC investment funds (JAIC 1-3 and JAIC P1-2) totalled ¥71.6 billion.

JAIC generally invests its funds, which are procured by the JAIC Investment Funds, as venture capital in unlisted companies in the ASEAN member countries (Indonesia, Malaysia, the Philippines, Singapore, Thailand, and Brunei) to assist their economic development and growth. As of January 1991, it had invested in 50 ASEAN corporations. The investment fund's assets are jointly owned by its members based on the ratio of their initial investment in the fund. The investment fund exists for a duration of 10 years from the date of establishment. Investments are normally made at the face value of the shares of the company. However, in some cases of existing companies, they are made in amounts exceeding the face value.

These new types of investment company act as go-betweens for ODA and private investment and therefore as accelerators of both Japan's FDI and the economic development of Asian countries.

INTERNATIONAL LOGISTICS AND THE TRANSFORMATION OF A NEW ASIAN TRADING SYSTEM

International Multimodal Transportation and Rapidly Increasing Transactions in Asian Waters

Nonvessel Operating Common Carriers and Overseas Activities of Japanese Forwarders

At the end of 1989, the National Diet of Japan established two laws related to physical distribution (the Commercial Law for Cargo Shipping and Commercial Law for Automobile Cargo Shipping). They eradicated old transportation laws and, for the first time in 40 years, recognized the revolution in physical distribution.

International and domestic integrated intermodal transportation, which has advanced with the development of containerized cargo shipping, became the major means of international physical distribution at the beginning of the 1980s. In order for integrated intermodal transportation to be conducted smoothly, it must be a total physical distribution system including all elements that constitute the distribution system: unit-crafting, warehousing, forwarding (harbor and custom-house brokerage), truck transport, shipping, etc. The new law is revolutionary in that it gives a legal foundation to international and domestic integrated intermodal transportation—in other words, the total distribution system—and thereby furthers its progress.

With the use of the total physical distribution system, the barriers between different industries in the distribution system will be eliminated. Shipping and air freight will expand into land transport businesses such as warehousing, forwarding, and trucking. The warehousers and forwarders will themselves seek to control shipping, air freight, and trucking. The term that represents the broken barriers of the distribution system is the unfamiliar nonvessel operating common carriers (NVOCCs). An NVOCC is a "common carrier that does not operate the vessels by which the ocean [and air] transportation is provided, and is a shipper in its relationship with an ocean [and air] common carrier" (according to Section 3 (Definitions) in the "Shipping Act of 1984," USA). These are warehousers, forwarders, or trucking operators who rent space from shipping firms that operate vesseles. These businesses are "common carriers" that do not possess vessels (NVOCCs) and are responsible for international multimodal transport.

According to the "United Nations Convention on International Multimodal Transport of Goods of 1980," international multimodal transport means the carriage of goods by at least two different modes of transport on the basis of a multimodal transport contract. A multimodal transport contract is a contract whereby a multimodal transport operator (including NVOCCs) undertakes, against payment of freight, to perform or to procure the performance of international multimodal transport.

International multimodal transport has been developing in line with containerization. In the period between 1950 and 1970, liner shipping was an advantageous operation with utilization as its last stage—that is, a port-to-port operation. A new era began with containerization, which emerged in the 1970s. Containerization is a system of multimodal transport (door-to-door), in which either marine or air transport plays the role of nucleus while the operation of road transport, forwarding, or warehousing for physical distribution plays a secondary role. This has basically changed the characteristics of the industry related to physical distribution.

The container gave forwarders the opportunity to develop their two basic traditional functions, land arrangements to a port, and port-forwarding operations (including documentation) connected with shipments. With the availability of shipping space in the form of a container, forwarders have become operators of the total physical distribution or international multimodal transport system at the door-to-door level. Today warehousers and trucking operators conduct the same business as NVOCCs.

According to the 1989 survey of the Japan International Freight Forwarders Association (JIFFA), out of the 139 Japanese forwarders covered, 72, or 51.8%, had business bases of some kind in other countries as of the end of 1988. A freight forwarder generally establishes an overseas base in the form of a local subsidiary, a joint venture with local interests, and/or a representative's office.

In the form of overseas facilities, 49 of the 72 Japanese forwarders had local subsidiaries, 15 more than the 34 in 1987. In a regional breakdown, nine local subsidiaries were newly established in the USA, followed by five each in Singapore and Hong Kong, which are both increasing in importance as relay points for physical distribution. The number of forwarders with joint ventures overseas was 27, seven more than in the 1987 survey. The 28 companies had a total of 57 joint ventures. Thus a rather limited number of forwarders had such tie-up arrangements abroad, averaging two per Japanese company. By region 49 of them were concentrated in East Asia (*Shipping and Trade News,* December 12, 1989).

Rapid Development of Asian Container Transactions

Container transactions in Asian waters have increased remarkably recently. According to the *Containerization International Yearbook 1990,* six of the 10 largest container ports in the world are in the western Pacific, including Singapore, Hong Kong, Taiwan, Japan, and South Korea. The rapid development of Asian container transactions has been aided by Asian economic interdependence and by the development of Asian export-oriented trade aimed mainly at North America and Europe.

In the first half of the 1980s the interdependence between North America and Asia contributed to a rapid increase in intra-Pacific trade, but the situation has been changing since 1986. Japan and the Asian NIEs have been weakening their degree of dependence on the other side of the Pacific. In other words, Asian countries have been developing their own markets interdependently.

The same trend is verified through cargo traffic statistics. According

Table 4. Recent Trends in Container Cargo Traffic from Asia to North America, by Geographical Origin (carried by container ships, on a TEU basis).

	1982	1983	1984	1985	1986	1987	1988
Japan							
Growth rate (%)		10.0	29.0	14.5	4.1	− 6.8	− 13.8
Share (%)	(37.7)	(35.5)	(36.7)	(37.2)	(33.6)	(29.4)	(27.8)
NIEs							
Growth rate (%)		26.2	24.3	12.4	21.4	10.2	− 15.3
Share (%)	(46.9)	(50.7)	(50.5)	(50.2)	(52.9)	(54.6)	(50.9)
of which Taiwan							
Growth rate (%)		33.9	24.9	17.7	26.0	8.8	− 20.9
Share (%)	(24.2)	(27.8)	(27.8)	(29.0)	(31.7)	(32.3)	(28.1)
ASEAN							
Growth rate (%)		5.9	11.7	12.8	11.6	17.8	12.3
Share (%)	(12.2)	(11.1)	(9.8)	(9.8)	(9.5)	(10.5)	(12.9)
of which Thailand							
Growth rate (%)		12.9	25.0	29.2	26.9	14.5	24.2
Share (%)	(2.2)	(2.1)	(2.1)	(2.4)	(2.6)	(2.8)	(3.9)
Growth rate of total		16.7	24.5	13.0	15.1	6.7	− 9.0

Source: *Shipping and Trade News*, October 5, 1989 (Special Issue).

to Table 4, which shows the recent trends of container cargo traffic (on a TEU basis) from Asia to North America, this cargo flow registered the first year-to-year decrease in 1988, after increasing for many years. Shinoda (1989) suggested the following individual salient points in the table:

1) Traffic originating in Japan, which continued to increase until 1986, decreased for two straight years in 1987 and 1988.

2) Cargo originating in Taiwan continued to increase in volume in 1987, when it surpassed that from Japan and was greater than the cargo flow from any other Asian country. In 1988, however, even this Taiwanese volume fell off sharply, registering a greater year-to-year decrease rate than that from Japan.

3) Although not indicated in the table, Hong Kong cargo traffic also suffered a steep drop in 1988, resulting in a downturn in the combined cargo volume from all the Asian NIEs that year. The rate of decrease was also greater than that of cargo originating in Japan.

4) On the other hand, cargo flow originating from ASEAN has grown constantly with no exception even in 1988. In that year, when cargo volumes from Japan and the Asian NIEs markedly decreased, that from ASEAN as a whole registered a double-digit growth rate, with particularly high growth registered by traffic from Thailand.

Shinoda broke down cargo traffic to and from Asia into three routes in his prediction of future trends: from Asia to North America (A); from North America to Asia (B); and between different points in Asia (C). In terms of the volume of cargo traffic in 1988, (A) was greater than (B), and (B) was greater than (C). In the growth rate since 1984, however, (B) has been higher than (C), and (C) higher than (A). Thus the share of North America-bound cargo flows in the total is quickly shrinking, mainly due to the appreciation of the yen and Asian NIE currencies and US-Asia trade and investment friction. "If we try to forecast the relative propositions of the three routes in 1993," Shinoda said, "an exact reverse of that in 1988, i.e., (C) greater than (B) and (B) greater than (A), is very likely. Thus the cargo traffic on (C) will quickly expand and the growth of that on (A) will slow down."

According to a survey of Japan's import container-cargo traffic, the share of cargo originating in Asia to the total rose sharply from 35.9% in 1985 to 47.1% in 1989, while that originating in North America decreased to 30.8% from 36.8% in the same period.

The countries and regions of Asia are strengthening their mutually complementary relationships in industrial production, while Japan in particular is absorbing Asian-made products. In this way, the formation of a new Asian trading system reflects the existence and deepening of interdependence of production and consumption in Asian economies.

Overseas Production and Two Types of International Logistics

Manufacturers pursue overseas production in three ways on the basis of two different categories, ownership and nonownership relations. Industrial cooperation without ownership in forms such as licensing, production sharing or cooperative production, production consignment or compensation trade, etc., permits foreign companies to produce Japanese manufacturers' products. Japanese manufacturers can launch overseas production through joint-venture agreements with local partners, who provide valuable knowledge of local customs, markets, and business practices and, at times, technical skills, as well as contributing a portion of equity. Complete ownership of foreign subsidiaries is a third method of obtaining overseas production facilities. This permits maximum control of Japanese corporations' production, quality, and distribution activities in the regional and/or global aspects.

Today, large-scale Japanese corporations, especially those in electronic and electric manufacture, operate transnational production, marketing, and financing activities. Those worldwide functional activities and investments are supervised and coordinated at headquarters, including approval of major investments in plant capacity. In addition, international intracompany product movements are centrally controlled, on a day-by-day or even hourly basis, by a central group, variously termed distribution, transport, or coordination, and therefore systems for coordinated management and planning of logistics on a regional or global level have been developed. Multinational corporations, in other words, pursue intracompany logistics from the viewpoints of global production and marketing.

Small- and medium-scale Japanese businesses have also been establishing overseas production facilities in Asia for the purpose of exporting products to third countries or to Japan, especially in the forms of joint ventures and industrial cooperation without ownership. Therefore, they need an efficient physical distribution system to manage the international flow of products from source to users. Such physical distribution is concerned with the outward movement of products from the seller or producer to the customer or consumer as part of business logistics by distribution-related firms that seek economic rationality in door-to-door delivery (from source to user), damage-proofing, continuity, consolidation, and cost-consciousness.

International logistics are classified into two categories: intracompany logistics basically controlled by a multinational corporation, and business logistics managed by distribution-related corporations such as forwarders, warehousers, and shippers.

The word "logistics" was originally a military term meaning the art of transport, supply, and quartering of troops. It has come to have a broader meaning in industrial-military use. According to the National Council of Physical Distribution Management (USA), logistics is "the integration of two or more activities for the purpose of planning, implementing and controlling the efficient flow of raw materials, in-process inventories, and finished goods from point of origin to point of consumption." International logistics, whether intracompany or business, is the art or method of managing the international flow of materials and products from source to user. The logistic system includes the total flow of materials, from the acquisition of raw materials to delivery of finished products to the ultimate users, and related counterflows of information which both control and record material movement. Technological innovations in telecommunication and transportation have created opportunities for integration in favor of Japanese multinational manufacturers and distribution-related corporations.

The Increasing Asian Orientation of the Japanese Economy

Not only in North America and Europe, but also in the Asian region, there has been a marked increase in moves, centered on ASEAN, toward regional unification and the management of production, physical distribution, and capital. Japanese companies are establishing operational headquarters in Singapore and actively establishing international procurement centers and central distribution centers linking Japan, the Asian NIEs, and ASEAN. In addition, land transportation, warehousing, marine transportation, and other companies engaged in physical distribution and related activities are also building comprehensive physical distribution networks in Asia, centered on Singapore, which are designed to link global networks encompassing Japan, Asia, Europe, and North America. All of these help to form comprehensive international distribution systems, and are designed to make possible the centralized management of multipolar (multinational) production and production processes.

Behind this revolution in Asian distribution is the increasing tendency of the Japanese economy to transcend national borders and to orient itself increasingly toward Asia. Japanese companies invest in the Asian NIEs and ASEAN in order to counter trade friction and rises in currency values. Investment in Asia has increased rapidly as a result of corporate strategies aimed at establishing international production facilities targeting the markets of Europe and North America and reverse imports to Japan.

The transfer of production facilities to other parts of Asia is making Japan's economic structure increasingly borderless. Since 1986 in particular, as investment in ASEAN has become increasingly brisk, Japan's traditional production and trading systems have been undergoing radical changes. (See Table 5, which gives the example of the electronics industry.) The Japanese economy has long been described as being led by the processing trade or by exports. Related industries have been concentrated in major domestic industrial areas, and production processes systematized through interdependent structures embracing domestically based industries. But the appreciation of the yen and trade friction have changed this system. Since the beginning of the 1980s, international production facilities targeted at the North American, European, and Japanese markets have been established in the Asian NIEs and the ASEAN countries, encompassing divisions producing parts and materials. This system has grown increasingly multinational in character. The appreciation of the yen, the comparative advantage of the price of labor and other factors of production, and measures taken by recipient countries to encourage investment have meant that facilities for manufacturing parts, materials, and manufactured goods spread first from Japan to the Asian NIEs and then from the Asian NIEs to ASEAN. Thus production systems have become increasingly Asia oriented.

The energy powering the spread of production and manufacturing processes throughout Asia also exists in the recipient countries. Amid the active efforts by ASEAN countries to attract export-oriented investment, Japanese companies and companies in the Asian NIEs are today dispersing production facilities throughout Asia.

Moves to form networks among Japan, the Asian NIEs, and ASEAN which are based on an international division of labor which provides for mutual complementation in respect of parts and materials, and moves to establish facilities in ASEAN countries for product assembly and manufacture, are inconsistent with the continuity and consistency of manufacturing processes. In other words, if this is a multinational spread based on technological superiority and comparative advantage in the prices of factors of production—in the production of parts and materials and in processing—then the more disjointed and unravelled the production and processing processes become, the more the multipolarization of production processes will accelerate. Production processes spread haphazardly throughout Asia must once again be

Table 5. Production of Electronic Products, by Country and Type of Product.

	A. Consumer electronics															
	TV sets	VCR sets	Radio receivers	Headphone stereo players	Radio sets with tape recorders	Other telecom equipment	Stereophones	CD players	HiFi speaker systems	Car stereos	Electronic ranges	Room fans	Refrigerators	Washing machines	Other household appliances	Total of household appliances
South Korea	1		1	1	2	2	3	1		2					3	8
China	2		1	1	1	1		1	1	1					4	7
Taiwan	6	3	5	1	1	3	4	8	1	2	2	3	3	2	9	19
Hong Kong															2	2
Thailand	7			2	1					1	1	6	7	3	11	16
Singapore	5		3	2	4	3	6	4		5	1			1	10	18
Malaysia	10	4	4	2	3	2	5	2		5		2	3	2	8	26
Philippines	3		1				2					2	2	2	5	5
Indonesia	2		1		1		1					2	2	1	4	4
India		1													4	5
Iran															1	1
Asia	36	6	16	9	13	11	21	16	2	16	4	15	17	11	61	111
Europe	13	21					6	9	1	6	5				5	41
Canada	2															2
U.S.A.	13	5							4	5	4	1	1		16	34
North America	18	5	4		4		4		4	6	4	2	1		21	45
South America	12	5	4	1	6	1	8	3	2	4	4		1	1	1	16
Africa	4	1	4		3	1	1		2	2		2	3		5	5
Australia	3														1	3
New Zealand																
Oceania	3															1
World	86	48	28	16	28	13	48	28	11	34	17	19	22	12	181	221

Source: Denshi (Electronics), Nov. 1989.

Table 5. (continued)

	C. Industrial electronics																
	Line telecommunications equipment	Wireless telecommunications equipment	Automobile telephones	Pocket pagers	Facsimiles	Other carrier telecommunications equipment	Broadcasting equipment	Electronic computers	External memory equipment	Printers	Other electronic computer equipment	Medical electronic equipment	Electronic calculators	Copying machines	Electrical measuring instruments	Other industrial electronic equipment	Industrial electronic machinery and equipment
South Korea	1	1						2		1			1	1	2	3	11
China													3		2	2	7
Taiwan	5	1	1	1									1		2	10	13
Hong Kong	1	1	1			1											3
Thailand	2				1										2	5	10
Singapore	2				1			1								3	7
Malaysia	1								1							3	5
Philippines				1												2	3
Indonesia															1		1
India																1	1
Iran																	
Asia	12	3	2	2	2	1		3	1	1			5	7	9	29	61
Europe			2		3			2		6	1			8	3	9	24
Canada																1	1
U.S.A.	2		4	1	2			6	3	3	1			3	2	21	37
North America	2		5	1	2			6	3	3	1			3	2	24	48
South America					1								1	1	1	6	8
Africa					1												1
Australia	1		1	1			1									1	1
New Zealand															1	1	
Oceania	2		1	1			1									2	2
World	15	3	18	4	9	1	1	11	4	18	2		6	13	15	72	136

Source: Denshi (Electronics), Nov. 1989.

Table 5. (continued)

	B. Electronic parts																		
	Resistors	Capacitors	Condensers	Acoustic parts	Magnetic heads	Small type of motors	Connectors	Switches	Small machine parts	Compound parts	Magnetic tapes	Semiconductor chips	ICs	Cathode-ray tubes for TV	Other parts for household equipment	Other parts for industrial equipment	Other electronic parts	Total of electronic parts and components	Total
South Korea	4	15	15	4	7	5	5	9	3	9		3	6		8	6	9	57	71
China		1	2	2	1	3	2	2	1			2	1	2	2	2	3	17	26
Taiwan	14	14	16	6	6	7	5	12	8	9		4	2		12	3	13	76	102
Hong Kong	1	1	2	1		1		2	1	1					1	3	4	12	16
Thailand	1	4	1			1	1	1		1	1	2	1		4	2	4	19	39
Singapore	3	7	7	3	1	2	1	1	2	5		2	4	1	14	5	6	42	61
Malaysia	4	6	10	1	2	3	4	7	5	2		4	4		14	7	5	49	75
Philippines		2	2	1	2	2		1		3		1						6	10
Indonesia																			5
India						1												1	7
Iran																			1
Asia	27	58	55	18	19	25	18	35	29	30	1	18	18	3	55	28	44	279	413
Europe		1	4	1	1	4	4	5		7	6	3	6	1	13	7	5	46	188
Canada								1						1	1	1	1	3	6
U.S.A.	3	7	4	4	1			4		4	4	4	6	3	6	5	13	53	113
North America	3	2	6	5	1	1		5	1	4	5	5	6	4	9	7	18	68	138
South America	4	5	6	5			1	3	3	2		2			2	1	3	16	34
Africa																			5
Australia																			4
New Zealand																			1
Oceania																			5
World	34	64	71	29	21	38	23	48	24	43	12	28	38	6	79	43	78	489	656

Source: Denshi (Electronics), Nov. 1989.

coordinated into a cohesive system.

Comprehensive physical distribution systems managed by computers have the power to coordinate widely spread production systems. The formation of integrated sea and land (or air and land) transportation and cargo-tracing systems within the framework of trade in Asian home waters is transforming transportation processes into inventory-management systems. It is also the desire of the business community that production systems with an Asia-wide spread be managed in an integrated manner in ways such as this. In this lies the foundation of the revolutionary transformation in Asian distribution.

Penetration of the Borderless Phenomenon

The revolutionary transformation of Asian distribution systems is a phenomenon of the Asianization of the Japanese economy. The assembly industries of Japan, such as those for electrical products and automobiles, were developed in the Tokyo-Yokohama, Nagoya-Tokyo, and Kobe-Osaka industrial belts. A network of related industries that shared the same suppliers for parts and materials was created centered around the assembly manufacturers. This was a vertically integrated industrial structure that acted as a unit from source to finish. The major channels in the regional industrial network—Yokohama, Nagoya, and Kobe—were the major trade ports for importing raw materials and exporting products.

Japanese firms previously designed and manufactured parts in Japan and then exported them; however, recently production abroad, including parts, has increased rapidly. Along with the move of production facilities abroad, the vertically integrated industrial structure as a unit has come apart. An interesting phenomenon is appearing in this borderless economy. In North America and Europe the trend toward local development and production in the consumer area is intensifying. However, in Asia the situation is a little different. It is not structured for production in the consumer area; rather the production sites directed toward Europe and the USA are taking a regional form that includes the Asian NIEs and ASEAN.

The shift in investment from the Asian NIEs to ASEAN is mostly a product of the intent to target its exports for North America, Europe, and Japan. Parts are procured throughout Asia including Japan and the assembly of products is carried out in various countries. In Southeast Asia, a network for the standard division of labor is proceeding not only for finished goods but also for parts production. It is remarkable how production activities in the Asian region are becoming borderless through the international division of labor system that evolved from targeting markets abroad, such as Europe and the USA. The reasons for this are the geographically distant marketplace and the borderless production process that must procure parts from various areas in Asia.

The more the production process and the marketing routes expand geographically, the more firms must deal with production and marketing dilemmas. Previously, business activities such as orders, production, inventory, and supply were centralized in one location and it was possible to keep timely continuity, as exemplified by Toyota's *kanban* (just-in-time) method. With parts production and assembly factories spread across national borders, the timing of parts and products supply begins to affect the running of a business. It is therefore inevitable that the amount of freight in the distribution process (distribution inventory) will increase or that parts and products will accumulate in warehouses in case of the unexpected. Also, fluctuations in exchange rates have a direct impact on the production and sales activities of corporations.

Corporate strategy has also changed with the new wave of borderless business activity (multinationalization). Logistics have necessarily become strategic, including global parts procurement and product collection and delivery, international procurement of facilities, international use of personnel for R&D and maintenance, internationalization of capital procurement, and hedging of exchange rate risks. It is only natural for corporations that have established production sites in several areas in the Asian region to place operational headquarters (OHQs) or integration centers in Singapore or Hong Kong and to be involved in international procurement office (IPO) or central distribution center (CDC) functions as well as capital procurement of exchange risk management functions.

Logistics for Action: Sony International Singapore

Regional OHQs and CDCs

With Asia becoming the international production focal point targeted at the entire world market, Singapore has become an active focal point of logistics. A symbol of this is OHQs (an OHQ is equivalent to a district general office). OHQ is the status given by the Singapore Economic Development Board (EDB) in Singapore to corporations in that country which manage affiliated companies from countries in the surrounding region. To companies with this status, preferential tax rates are granted for 10 years. Management can deal with planning, procurement, technical assistance, marketing and sales promotion, training/personnel, finance/accounting and capitalization, and investment advice as well as various types of service businesses and international aid activities within corporations. Since its start in February 1988 through June 1989, 22 companies have attained OHQ status and Japanese companies such as Sony, Fujikura Densen, and Omron are included on the list. Matsushita Electric Industrial Co. and Hitachi received the status in February 1989 and March 1990 respectively.

Sony has factories for audio, TV, and video products and parts, two each in Taiwan, Korea, and Thailand, three in Malaysia, and one in Singapore. In 1990 a new semiconductor factory in Thailand and two factories in Malaysia went into operation, one for floppy disks and the other for videos. The OHQ for Matsushita Electric Industrial Co., Asia Matsushita Electronics Singapore (AMS), manages 22 group factories and trading companies in the Southeast Asian region. The OHQ for Fujikura Densen Ltd., Fujikura International Management Singapore (FIMS), controls 15 affiliated companies in the NIEs including Korea and the ASEAN region. Whether they have received EDB OHQ status or not, the majority of Japanese corporations are interested in using Singapore as an overall base for distribution and money management functions such as settlement of accounts.

Sony International of Singapore (SONIS) is Sony's general headquarters for the Southeast Asian region, and Sony's Southeast Asian factories and affiliated companies are connected by a communications network (Fig. 7). This communications network cannot be considered without the specialized distribution warehouses built by Mitsui-Soko Co. In order to develop an integrated international distribution business a specialized workplace is needed. Containerized freight must be packaged according to the destination of the end user and placed in a single container. It is also an important job to divide the contents of the opened containers according to the factory destination. This workplace is called the distribution warehouse. Numerous parts from different countries are received by factories and used together as a unit. So that factories can receive the parts for each assembled unit as a complete set, "kit assemblies" of related parts are also undertaken.

The distribution warehouse for Sony in Singapore is the CDC, which procures parts from around the world to be used by factories in the Southeast Asian region. The CDC also collects products manufactured within its control area for delivery worldwide. The CDC function is similar to the "heart" of the distribution system by connecting the "arterial system" that provides parts to various Asian factories with the "veins" that collect the manufactured products or semi-finished goods.

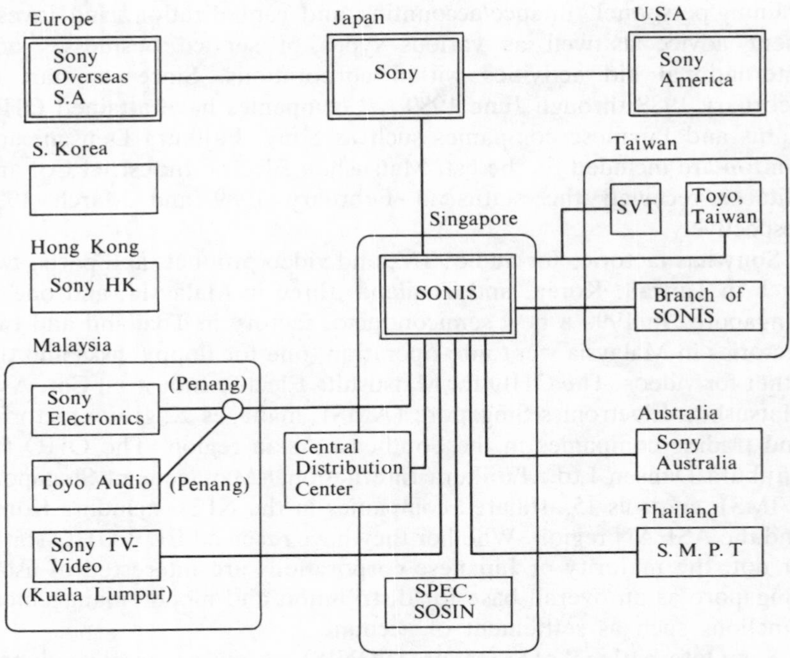

Fig. 7. Sony's integrated information network
Source: Graph from *Nikkei Computer,* May 22, 1989, modified based on interviews with Sony officials.

SONIS is the IPO that directs and manages the CDC through its Asia information communications network, an information (nervous) system. It supervises and adjusts the flow of parts necessary to active production in the region and the flow of manufactured products (veins). This new activity of Sony in Southeast Asia is part of the global logistic network that extends throughout the world to Japan, North America, Europe, and Southeast Asia. Starting in 1991, Sony will introduce into its structure a worldwide general information communications system. Through this system, the headquarters will be connected on-line with its 39 domestic companies, nine US companies, 18 European companies, and five Southeast Asian companies as well as important cooperating firms. Production and sales planning, which was previously drawn up in monthly units will change to weekly planning. After two years this plan is expected to reduce by half the required inventory and will cut the time from receipt of orders to delivery by two-thirds.

Domestic and overseas subsidiaries (sales companies) will place orders for videos, TVs, and radio/cassette players based on estimated demand with the personnel in charge of each division at the Sony Tokyo headquarters. Each division will draw up production plans for the coming week based on those orders. After orders are received, the details of the plans will be communicated to production factories, cooperating firms, and parts manufacturers scattered throughout the world. Goods will then be delivered one week later.

If radio/cassette players are to be produced in a Malaysian factory (a local company), for example, SONIS will receive the parts sent from parts manufacturers and affiliated companies in various areas, and through IPO the parts will be sent to the factory. When the Malaysian factory has completed assembly of the semi-manufactured products or products according to the plan, IPO will deliver them to SONIS. The radio/cassette players will be shipped through SONIS to subsidiary firms throughout the world.

SONIS, the general headquarters for Southeast Asia in Singapore, functions as a strategic unit for Sony's global logistics. Factories in the ASEAN countries and Asian NIEs are the focal points of production targeting the world, but the parts and materials must be procured from Asia including Japan and other areas throughout the world. The various types of products which are made in the Asian region must be distributed throughout the world at the direction of headquarters. Sony's global plans for production and sales are drawn up weekly in various division offices in Tokyo. SONIS, as a strategic support unit based at the Asian production site, oversees the district distribution system that involves parts procurement and product sales.

The basic concepts of distribution management are the symbolized by the just-in-time and point-of-sale (POS) information control systems as well as the zero inventory system for internationally based production and sales. This concept is being put into practice by the IPO functions of SONIS—a subsidiary of SONIS, Sony Logistics Singapore, actually manages the CDC for the Asian region—and the company's global information communications network. Like Sony, other major electronics manufactures such as Matsushita Electric are considering global logistics that integrate production, sales, and distribution. They are planning information communications networks that stretch across the globe to connect Japan, North America, Europe, and Southeast Asia.

Toward "Account Settlement Without Currency Exchange"

A flow of money always accompanies the flow of goods. How are account settlements handled when the exchange rate fluctuates and money flows through the countries which control the exchange? The concept behind exchange rates and account settlements at SONIS is to attempt to create a system of "account settlements without exchange" at the factories in the Asian region. The ASEAN region excluding Singapore is subject to exchange rate control. Exchange losses occur easily because it is not possible to take in foreign capital to hedge against exchange rate risk under the principle of actual demand, which is only valid for the selling and buying currencies seen particularly in actual merchandise trade.

SONIS procures parts and materials needed in factories scattered throughout the Asian region, receives payment for the sale of finished goods, and then settles accounts using the local currency. It is possible to conduct "account settlement without exchange" with SONIS as its focal point by using local currencies when each of the factories purchases parts and materials from abroad and sells the goods abroad.

SONIS itself has an exchange account for local currencies. Actually, a large part of this exchange can be "married" (canceling out foreign currency debits with foreign currency payments). The portion that cannot be canceled is used as a hedge against risk by using the Singapore futures exchange or international money markets. The SONIS "account settlement without exchange" that deals with factories in the Asian region using local currencies is connected to the CDC in Singapore. SONIS controls exchange risks in order to maintain the Asian IPO functions and the just-in-time and POS strategies developed on an international scale.

Business Logistics in ASEAN: The Case of Mitsui-Soko

Leading corporations that are expanding into the Asian region normally process information and manage account settlements at their Japanese headquarters even if production is carried out locally. The local site of Mitsui-Soko manages distribution of items by integrating the task from the level of customer orders and production through shipment and delivery (Fig. 8). In 1989, Mitsui Singapore International (MSI) completed a second distribution center simultaneously with the distribution warehouse built for exclusive use by Sony, for manufacturers who were extending their businesses into Southeast Asia. This warehouse is connected with local companies in Bangkok and Kuala Lumpur by computer, and it will be connected by a computer system with bonded warehouses which was completed in early 1990 in Johor Bahru and Penang, Malaysia. This system will be the foundation of a bonded truck and container shipping service in both directions between Singapore and Malaysia.

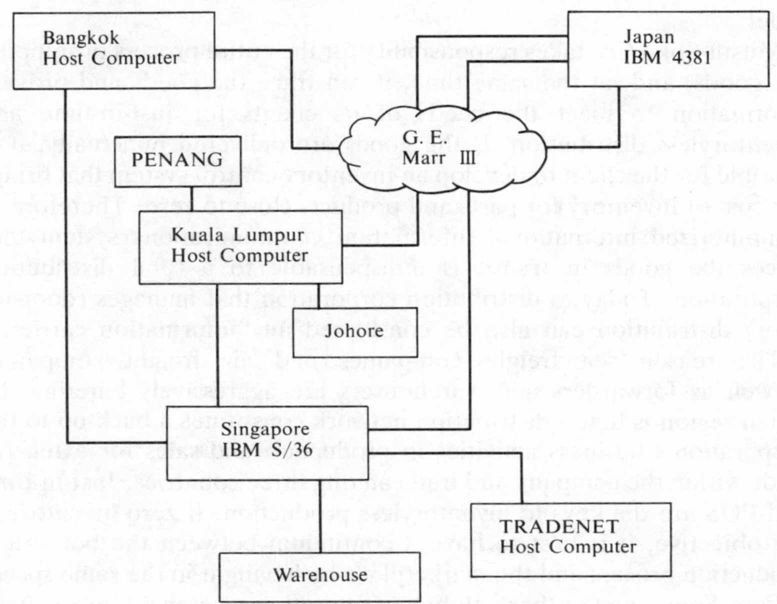

Fig. 8. The Asian network of Mitsui-Soko Co., Inc.
Source: Mitsui Soko Co.

These warehouses not only function as leased space but are distribution (processing) warehouses that also do such things as sorting and locating goods and making up kit assemblies. The distribution warehouses in Singapore and the bonded warehouses in Malaysia and Thailand constitute a group managed by computer.

Mitsui-Soko Co. is an integrated distribution corporation that manages the entire freight shipping process. Let us suppose a Japanese corporation (shipper) in Penang wishes to ship parts or products via Singapore to a third location, for example, Dallas, Texas. In this case, Mitsui-Soko Co. will truck the cargo collected in Penang to bonded warehouses along the border of Johor Bahru. (In Johor Bahru it is possible to pass goods through Singapore customs while they are still in the bonded warehouse, which may also reduce transit time to Singapore.) In Singapore, the goods that arrive at the distribution (bonded) warehouses are loaded, as an NVOCC, into container vessels destined for Los Angeles. Space is purchased at a discount on regular container vessels. In Los Angeles, after custom procedures have been completed, the container freight is transferred to cross-continental railways. Finally, it is delivered by truck to the customer who placed the order.

Mitsui-Soko Co. takes responsibility for the entire process of shipping the goods, and, at the same time, it can trace the goods and provide information to meet the needs of its clients for just-in-time and inventoryless distribution. If the goods are delivered punctually, it is possible for the client to develop an inventory control system that brings the cost of inventory for parts and products close to zero. Therefore, a computerized international information communications system that traces the goods in transit is indispensable to a total distribution corporation. Today, a distribution corporation that manages (door-to-door) distribution can also be considered an "information carrier."

The reason sea freight companies and air freight companies as well as forwarders and warehousers are aggressively entering the Asian region is that a distribution network constitutes a back-up to the corporation's business activities in production and sales for extensive trade within the company and trade among three countries. Just-in-time and POS are the keys to inventoryless production. If zero inventory is the objective, it is best to have a continuum between the borderless production process and the marketplace by having it in the same space.

For Sony and other global corporations, global information communications systems create a stream of parts and products between the various parts of the world rather than an "inventory reservoir." With a global distribution network, the flow of goods is managed at all times, and an attempt is being made to establish inventoryless production systems on an international scale by speeding up the process. There is a trade-off in cost, however. The global corporations integrate production, marketing, and distribution through international information and communications networks, yet the actual distribution business is conducted more often by specialists. It is not easy for small and medium-scale companies to create an information network at their own expense.

Distribution business corporations are creating total distribution systems—in other words, integrated distribution networks within the Asian region interconnected by computers that are in turn directly connected to Japan, North America, and Europe. The total distribution project, as business logistics aimed at the foreign market, is attempting to create this distribution system on an Asian and international scale and is motivated by the need to resolve the contradictions in "time and space" brought about by the borderless economy.

When the economy becomes borderless, a company's production or production process expands multinationally. On the other hand, inventoryless systems such as just-in-time and POS demand a continuity of time in the production process and unification of the time between production and marketing. With the Asian and global integrated distribution systems constructed by global corporations and the distribution industry, multinational corporations are creating "timeless space." The creation of world- and/or regionwide "timeless space" is becoming an important segment of the multinational corporations' strategies to establish and govern world- and/or regionwide production processes.

CONCLUSIONS: REGIONWIDE PRODUCTION NETWORKS VERSUS NATIONAL ECONOMIES

In the rapid process of industrialization in developing Asian economies, Japan has made a strong commitment in terms of both trade and investment to Asian NIEs, the ASEAN countries, and China. A firm's borderless or multinational production network is often defined on the basis of "ownership," especially majority ownership. Ownership is one important criterion for estimating international intracompany production organization. The general preference for ownership as a measure of production networks comes partly from its ease of perception, i.e., visibility.

There are, however, tight but invisible (without ownership) production ties between Japanese firms and local Asian ones, especially when the former dominates the supply of materials, parts or semifinished products, and/or machinery and equipment. Capital goods shipped from advanced economies to developing ones usually embody comparatively advantageous technologies. As long as they exclusively possess technological advantages, Japanese firms can build up international intracompany production networks without ownership in relation to local Asian firms. The export of capital goods to local firms without ownership has a stronger potential for establishing subcontracting ties between Japanese and local firms than FDI with majority ownership. In the transfer of technology or transplantation of part of the production processes from Japan to developing Asian countries, Japanese firms aggressively pursue the acquisition of majority ownership of their overseas (local) production facilities. In other words, FDI with majority ownership may be a crucial strategy for a private company to keep local firms from becoming competitive on their home ground.

As well, there seems to be a contradiction between Japan's FDI-promoting systems tied in with official or quasiofficial aid and Japanese multinational corporations' world- or regionwide integrated production, and therefore physical distribution, systems.

The former, FDI-promoting systems related to aid drive Japan to transplant its existing industries to other Asian countries, supporting their economic and social infrastructures. As a consequence of a flood of FDI from Japan (and Asian NIEs), Asia is forming several nationwide and/or subregional industrial areas. In the circumstances of multipolarization of the Asian industrial structure each developing country is naturally encouraged to build up its own national economy and to improve its bargaining position vis-à-vis developed countries.

In contrast, the Japanese multinational corporations' borderless integrated production systems basically tend to reject the host country's nationalism or a foreign government's national economic independence policies, since they could prevent multinationals from integrating borderless production or distribution networks.

The establishment of a national economy opposes the formation of a private company's borderless networks. However, this contradiction is harmonized by the outward economic policies of developing Asian countries, especially aggressive acceptance of export-oriented investment. Furthermore, both Japan's mature economy and other Asian export-oriented economies encourage nationalism to coexist with regionalism in Asia. The more mature and sophisticated the Japanese economy becomes, the more other developing Asian countries can establish bases for industrialization, which is another problem, outside the scope of the present paper.

References

Economic Planning Agency (EPA). 1990. *Economic Survey of Japan 1988-89*. Tokyo: EPA.

Export-Import Bank of Japan. 1989. *The Export-Import Bank of Japan: Role and Function*. Tokyo: Ex-Im Bank.

Ministry of International Trade and Industry (MITI). 1990. *Nichibei Kozomon-daikyogi Saishuhokoku* (Final Report on Japan-U.S. Structural Impediments Initiative). Tokyo: MITI.

Overseas Economic Cooperation Fund (OECF). 1990. *Annual Report 1990*. Tokyo: OECF.

Shinoda, M. 1989. "Why Do Cargo Flows in Asia Deserve Note?" 40th Anniversary Supplement of *Shipping and Trade News,* October.

Swoboda, A. 1968. "Vehicle Currencies and Foreign Exchange Markets: The Case of the Dollar." In R. Z. Aliber (ed.), *International Market for Foreign Exchange*. New York.

Appendix: Japan's International Private Industrial Cooperation (January-December 1989, based on JETRO survey).

A. Joint Development and Technology Transfer

Country & Region	Manufacture																					
	High-technology																					
	Semiconductors and ICs	Computers	Biotechnology & Chemicals	Telecommunications equipment	New materials	Robots	Others	Subtotal	Electronics	Machinery	Automobiles	Iron & Nonferrous metals	Chemicals	Textiles	Food	Others	Total	Finance	Construction & Real estate	Telecommunications & Information	Others	Total
U.S.A.	48	80	16	7	10	1	59	221	18	86	28	12	48	12	29	25	479	34	46	61	176	796
Canada				1			1	2	2	6		2	2	1	4	1	20	3	4	1	15	43
Latin America										2	7	2			1		12		1		6	19
Europe	6	20	4	5	7		23	65	12	91	33	8	42	43	16	46	356	21	15	19	125	536
EC	6	20	4	5	7		23	65	12	89	33	8	40	42	16	45	350	21	14	19	124	528
Oceania		2	1				1	4		2	3	1	4			2	16	1	8	1	8	34
Australia		2					1	3		2	3	1	3			2	14	1	6	1	7	29
New Zealand			1					1					1				2		1			3
Asia	5	22	1	5	3	4	13	53	56	92	33	18	25	32	25	35	369	22	20	12	77	500
China		4	1	1	1		2	9	17	29	9	7	10	11	7	11	110	9	5	4	15	143
Taiwan	2	5			1			8	5	9	3	1	1	3	4	7	41	1	1		10	53
Hong Kong										2		1		3		3	9	5	2	3	5	24
S. Korea	2	7				4	9	22	29	35	9	3	9	3	3	6	119	7		1	29	156
ASEAN	1	5		2				8	3	6	8	4	2	7	9	7	54		9	4	17	84
Indonesia		1		1				2	2	2	3	1		3		2	15		4	1	8	28
Thailand		1		1				2		2	3	1	2	3	4	5	22		1		5	28
Philippines	2							2				2		1	1		6		1		1	8
Singapore	1	1						2		2					2		6		1	3	3	13
Malaysia									1		2				2		5		2			7
Others		1		2	1		2	6	2	11	4	2	3	5	7	1	36		3		1	40
Middle East & Africa		1						1		1	3	1	2		1	1	10		3		1	14
U.S.S.R. & East Europe		1	1					2		3	3				1		9				7	16
Total	59	126	23	18	20	5	97	348	88	283	110	44	123	88	77	110	1,271	81	97	94	415	1,958

B. Joint Ventures (Minority Ownership)

Country & Region	Manufacture																				
	High-technology																				
	Semiconductors and ICs	Computers	Biotechnology & Chemicals	Telecommunications equipment	New materials	Robots	Others	Subtotal	Electronics	Machinery	Automobiles	Iron & Nonferrous metals	Chemicals	Textiles	Food	Others	Total	Finance	Construction & Real estate	Telecommunications & Information	Others	Total
U.S.A.	10	16	6	3	15		11	61	13	20	65	16	30	4	11	18	238	15	33	14	88	388
Canada	2							2		1	6	2			1	8	20	1	1	1	4	27
Latin America		1			1			2	2	2				2	1	4	13	1				14
Europe	3	4	2	1	4		14	28	13	14	16	5	22	5	6	8	117	28	8	6	59	218
EC	3	4	2	1	4		14	28	13	14	16	5	22	5	6	8	117	28	8	6	58	217
Oceania		1		1	1		1	4		1	5	3	1	2	4	6	27	2	6		13	48
Australia				1	1		1	3		1	5	3	1	2	4	4	23		6		12	41
New Zealand		1						1			1					1	3	1			1	5
Asia	7	18	2	2	7		12	48	53	85	65	28	55	30	32	89	485	20	24		117	646
China	1	8	1	1			7	18	11	12	3	4	8	10	13	23	102	11	8		33	154
Taiwan	1	1	1		4			7	9	15	14	5	6		4	11	71		4		33	108
Hong Kong		1						1	4	1			2	1	1	3	13	4	3		10	30
S. Korea	2	1			1		5	9	10	24	14	4	13	3	4	8	89	2			6	97
ASEAN	3	7		1	2			13	15	31	31	15	26	16	10	41	198	3	9		35	245
Indonesia		1						1	5	9	2	2	4	1	5	30		4		6	40	
Thailand		3		1				4	12	19	17	9	14	9	8	27	119		5		18	142
Philippines	1	3						4		1	1	1		1	1	1	1	2			1	13
Singapore	1							1	1	3		2	4			1	12				5	17
Malaysia	1				2			3	1	3	4	1	6	2		7	27	1			5	33
Others									4	2	3					3	12					12
Middle East & Africa										1	1					1	3	3				6
U.S.S.R. & East Europe											1				3	3	7					7
Total	22	40	10	7	28		38	145	81	124	160	54	108	43	58	137	910	70	72	21	281	1,354

C. Direct Investment (Majority Ownership)

Country & Region	Manufacture																					Total
	High-technology																					
	Semiconductors and ICs	Computers	Biotechnology & Chemicals	Telecommunications equipment	New materials	Robots	Others	Subtotal	Electronics	Machinery	Automobiles	Iron & Nonferrous metals	Chemicals	Textiles	Food	Others	Total	Finance	Construction & Real estate	Telecommunications & Information	Others	
U.S.A.	44	56	4	13	10	1	41	169	49	108	138	25	61	5	32	56	642	30	109	28	366	1,226
Canada	1							1		2	5				1	3	12	4	5		11	32
Latin America		1		2			3	6	10	10	8		2	3	2	6	47	4	1		15	67
Europe	10	11	3	6	6		16	52	45	47	28	2	25	6	7	9	221	88	24	4	233	570
EC	10	11	3	6	6		16	52	45	47	28	2	25	6	7	9	221	88	24	4	232	569
Oceania		1		1			1	3		1	3	2			4	4	17	2	30		21	76
Australia		1		1			1	3		1	2	2			4	4	16	2	23		19	60
New Zealand											1						1		4		2	7
Asia	29	17		11	3	1	21	82	112	82	31	10	39	20	14	57	447	34	17	5	155	658
China	1	2		1			1	5	6	11	3			2	1	6	34		1		15	50
Taiwan	4	3		1	1		3	12	14	13	4	2	5	1	1	6	58		1	1	11	71
Hong Kong	1			1			2	4	5	6	1	1	2	9	3	6	37	21	5	2	34	99
S. Korea	4	1					3	8	4	2				1	1	4	20	4	1		14	39
ASEAN	19	11		8	2	1	12	53	83	50	21	7	32	6	8	35	295	9	8	2	80	394
Indonesia									1	4			1	2		2	10	1	1	1	7	20
Thai	5	6		2	1		4	18	29	24	13	4	12	1	4	16	121	2	1		25	149
Philippines		2		3				5	1				4				10				4	14
Singapore	7	2		2	1	1	5	18	23	15	4	1	13		4	9	87	5	4	1	37	134
Malaysia	7	1		1			3	12	29	7	4	2	2	3		8	57	1	2		7	77
Others											2			1			3		1		1	5
Middle East & Africa														1			1	3			8	12
U.S.S.R. & East Europe															1		1					1
Total	84	86	7	13	19	2	87	313	216	250	213	39	127	35	61	135	1,389	215	186	37	809	2,636

2 Industrial and Trade Structures of Asian Newly Industrialized Economies

Masaharu Hanazaki

The Japan Development Bank

INTRODUCTION

In the late 1970s South Korea, Taiwan, Singapore, and Hong Kong—the newly industrialized economies (NIEs)—began attracting global attention. While the advanced countries had trouble dealing with the aftereffects of the oil crises, chronic stagflation, and the trade imbalances characteristic of the period, the Asian NIEs maintained their high growth based on aggressive export drives. The new economies were thus rapidly catching up with their advanced counterparts.

In the 1980s, the pace of their growth slackened a bit, but the so-called Four Dragons continued to grow. Through their processing trade, the NIEs have exerted a strong impact on the advanced countries. With ever-tightening economic relations between the Asian NIEs and Japan, more and more Japanese companies have set up shop in these regions. Not only garments, sundries, and other light industry goods, but also television sets, tape recorders, and other electrical appliances have increasingly found their way into the Japanese market. Japanese interest in the Asian NIEs is growing rapidly. Meanwhile, it is a fact that with trade imbalances facing them, some developed countries—including the USA—are voicing concern and even protectionist sentiments in connection with the growing new economies.

This paper attempts to analyze the increasingly influential NIEs in Asia, with the emphasis on the industrial and trade structures that sustain their growth. These topics will be addressed in comparison with the economies of major developed countries.

ASIAN NIES IN THE WORLD

Comparing the Asian NIEs with key developed countries in recent years economic performance reveals interesting indicators. The average annual real economic growth rate between 1980 and 1988 was 8.9% for South Korea, 7.5% for Taiwan, 6.6% for Singapore, and 7.1% for Hong Kong. These figures far surpass the corresponding indicators of major developed countries, with 4.1% for Japan, 2.9% for the USA, and 1.7% for Germany. The growth rate for all Asian NIEs (weighted average) was 8.0% for the same period. This vigorous growth was reflected in the low unemployment rate, with 2.4% in 1987 for the Asian NIEs (weighted average). The NIEs' unemployment situation was better than Japan's 2.9% not to mention the other advanced countries who suffer chronically high unemployment rates. But the rate of increase in the GNP (GDP) deflator—a representative inflation indicator—was 4.7% for all Asian NIEs (between 1980 and 1987), the same as the USA, and higher than Japan's 1.5% and Germany's 3.0%.

The indicators of economic scale are as follows. The nominal GNP (converted to US dollars at average exchange rates[1]) for all the Asian NIEs in 1988 was about US$350 billion, far lower than that of the USA ($4.85 trillion) or Japan ($2.84 trillion). Of the NIEs, South Korea and Taiwan predominated, with $155 billion and $117 billion, respectively, for the same year. The two economies account for about three-quarters of the entire output of the Asian NIEs.

The nominal GNP per capita for the Asian NIEs was about $5,000 in 1988, lagging far behind Japan, the USA, and Germany. Because these three countries are among the highest in terms of per capita GNP, the NIEs—for all their galloping growth—have yet to fulfill some differentials with the advanced countries in economic prowess and living standards.[2] It should be noted, moreover, that there are considerable discrepancies in per capita GNP among the NIEs. Hong Kong has $9,500 and Singapore $9,000—already equaling several OECD member countries such as Ireland and Spain.

Overall, it is a fact that there are gaps between the Asian NIEs and the developed countries on a GNP (GDP)-based economic scale. Nevertheless, the new economies keep impacting the world economy significantly because of the vast scope of their trade. The total volume of the Asian NIEs' exports in 1988 amounted to $224 billion, about 85% of what Japan exported during the same period ($265 billion). Total imports by the NIEs came to $209 billion, already exceeding those of Japan ($187 billion).

Trends in Economic Growth Rates

A long-term review of the changes in economic growth rates for the advanced countries and other major economies reveals a trend of continuous high growth among the Asian NIEs since the 1960s (Table 1). In the 1960s, when external and domestic conditions for growth were fairly well provided for in many countries, the real economic growth rate was 4.9% for the world economy (4.9% for advanced countries [OECD members] and 5.0% for developing countries).[3] During that decade, the Asian NIEs achieved a growth rate of 9.0%, second only to Japan's (10.5%). This occurred in the middle of Japan's postwar high economic growth.

Table 1. Trends of Economic Regions' Real Economic Growth Rates (Annual Average Growth Rates, %).

	1960-1970	1970-1980	1980-1988	1986	1987	1988
Advanced countries (OECD members)	4.9	3.4	2.9	2.6	3.5	4.4
USA	3.8	2.8	3.1	2.8	3.7	4.4
Japan	10.5	4.6	4.1	2.5	4.5	5.7
EC	4.8	2.9	2.1	2.6	2.7	3.7
Developing countries	5.0	5.6	3.3	4.0	3.8	4.1
Southeast Asia	4.5	5.4	7.3	6.8	8.0	9.0
NIEs[1]	9.0	9.1	8.0	10.7	11.8	9.0
South Korea	9.5	8.4	8.9	11.7	11.1	11.0
Taiwan	9.6	9.7	7.5	10.6	12.4	6.8
Singapore	9.2	9.1	6.6	1.8	8.8	11.1
Hong Kong	6.5[2]	9.4	7.1	11.9	13.8	7.4
Middle East	8.0	6.1	0.9	− 0.6	− 0.8	3.8
Western Hemisphere	5.7	5.9	1.2	4.0	2.9	0.3
Africa	5.0	3.8	1.2	2.3	1.1	2.3
World Total[3]	4.9	3.9	3.0	3.0	3.5	4.3

Notes: 1. For the Asian NIEs, the figures are weighted averages in terms of nominal GDP.
2. Figure for 1966-1970.
3. Communist bloc excluded.

Sources: *International Financial Statistics, World Economic Outlook*, IMF.
Economic Outlook, OECD.
Official statistics of the countries and regions listed.

In the 1970s, the oil crises, drastic changes in the international financial system, bouts of inflation, and recession on a global scale cut deeply into the growth rates of OECD member countries (3.4% in the

1970s compared with 4.9% in the 1960s). Despite the adverse circumstances, the Asian NIEs maintained their pace, with a growth rate of 9.1%, comparable to their growth in the 1960s. It is interesting to note that these economies have one thing in common with Japan and some other advanced countries: they have few natural resources.

In the 1980s, the OECD member countries were confronted with structural problems that were difficult to solve: slow adjustments in their labor markets, current account imbalances, growing financial difficulties, shrinking frontiers of technological progress, and aging populations. The result was a still lower average growth rate (2.9% for 1980-1988). By contrast, the Asian NIEs remained active, continuing their high economic growth (8.0% on average for 1980-1988).

Long-term Trends in Industrial Structure

According to Ricardo and to the Heckscher-Ohlin theorem, the trade structure of a country in relation to its trade partners overseas is determined by the relative volumes of its endowments of capital, labor, and production technology. Because this factor—input in a broad sense and the output therefrom—makes up a distinct industrial structure connecting a nation's industries, the nation's trade structure tends largely to be determined by its industrial structure. The Asian NIEs are small in geographical area and are not blessed with natural resources. To develop economically, these regions had no choice but to promote trade by industrializing their economies. The NIEs' efforts translate into large shares of exports and imports for their scale of economy. A very close connection exists between industrial and trade structures in these economies. The following sections provide an overview comparing the Asian NIEs with their advanced counterparts in industrial and trade structures. Viewed in this manner, the course followed by the NIEs in economic development may become clear.

The four Asian economic regions are first compared with the USA, Japan, and Germany. The appraisal includes nominal GDP and employment by industry (primary, secondary, and tertiary) between 1970 and 1987 (Figs. 1 and 2). Appreciable differences in industrial structure are observed not only between the developing and the developed economies, but also among the NIEs themselves.

Compared to the share of primary industry in GDP, Singapore and Hong Kong had very low percentages—equal to or lower than those of the developed countries. South Korea and Taiwan, on the other hand, saw their primary industry gradually lose its share, which nevertheless remained higher than those of the developed countries. There are

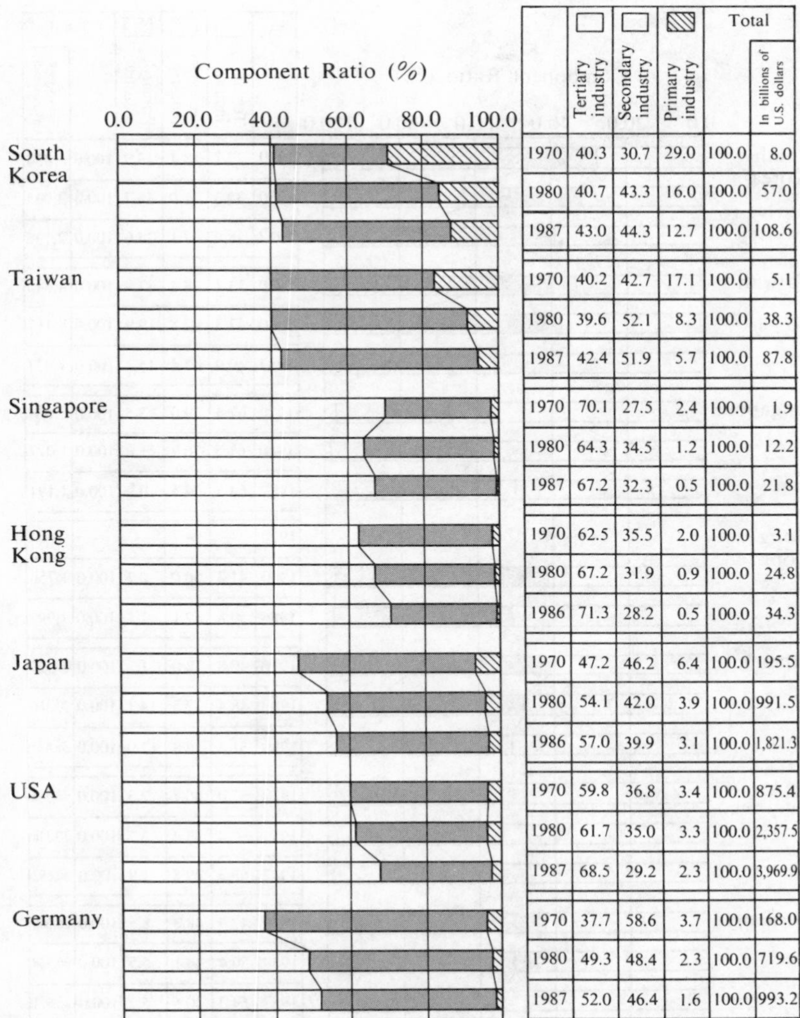

	Year	Tertiary industry	Secondary industry	Primary industry	Total	In billions of U.S. dollars
South Korea	1970	40.3	30.7	29.0	100.0	8.0
	1980	40.7	43.3	16.0	100.0	57.0
	1987	43.0	44.3	12.7	100.0	108.6
Taiwan	1970	40.2	42.7	17.1	100.0	5.1
	1980	39.6	52.1	8.3	100.0	38.3
	1987	42.4	51.9	5.7	100.0	87.8
Singapore	1970	70.1	27.5	2.4	100.0	1.9
	1980	64.3	34.5	1.2	100.0	12.2
	1987	67.2	32.3	0.5	100.0	21.8
Hong Kong	1970	62.5	35.5	2.0	100.0	3.1
	1980	67.2	31.9	0.9	100.0	24.8
	1986	71.3	28.2	0.5	100.0	34.3
Japan	1970	47.2	46.2	6.4	100.0	195.5
	1980	54.1	42.0	3.9	100.0	991.5
	1986	57.0	39.9	3.1	100.0	1,821.3
USA	1970	59.8	36.8	3.4	100.0	875.4
	1980	61.7	35.0	3.3	100.0	2,357.5
	1987	68.5	29.2	2.3	100.0	3,969.9
Germany	1970	37.7	58.6	3.7	100.0	168.0
	1980	49.3	48.4	2.3	100.0	719.6
	1987	52.0	46.4	1.6	100.0	993.2

Fig. 1. Trends of GDP Component Ratios by Industry (%)

Note: Primary industry consists of agriculture, forestry, and fisheries; secondary industry is made up of mining, manufacturing, and construction; and tertiary industry includes all operations excluding those of primary and secondary industries.

Sources: Official statistics of the countries and regions listed.

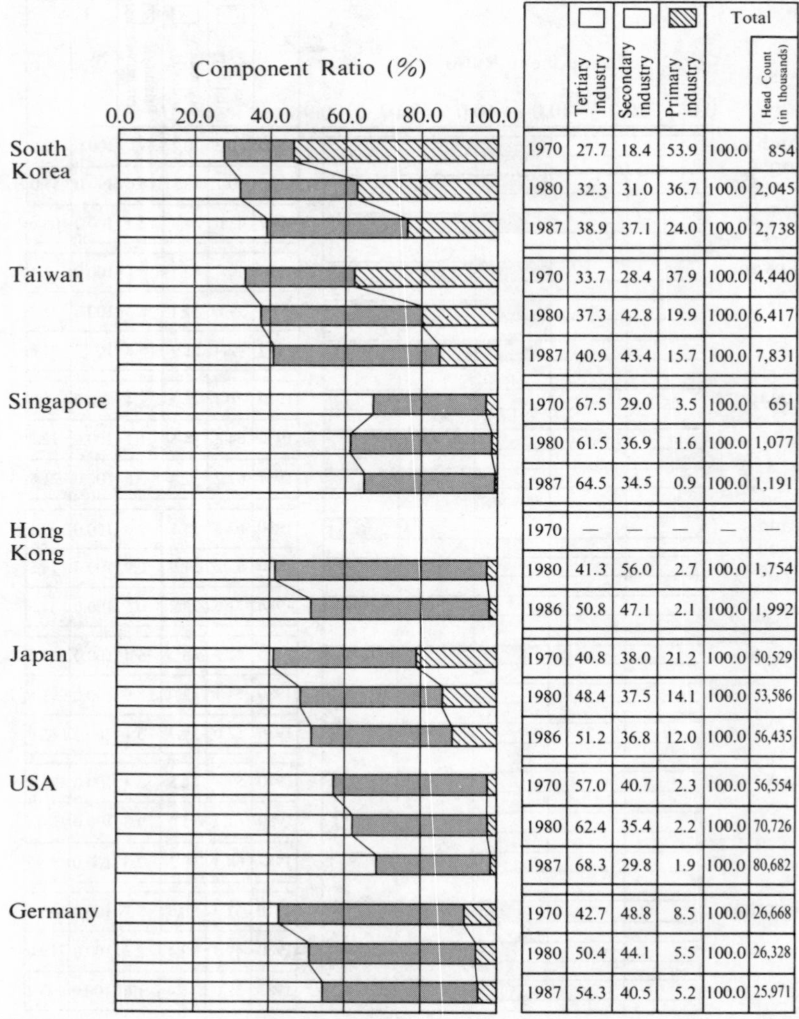

	Year	Tertiary industry	Secondary industry	Primary industry	Total	Head Count (in thousands)
South Korea	1970	27.7	18.4	53.9	100.0	854
	1980	32.3	31.0	36.7	100.0	2,045
	1987	38.9	37.1	24.0	100.0	2,738
Taiwan	1970	33.7	28.4	37.9	100.0	4,440
	1980	37.3	42.8	19.9	100.0	6,417
	1987	40.9	43.4	15.7	100.0	7,831
Singapore	1970	67.5	29.0	3.5	100.0	651
	1980	61.5	36.9	1.6	100.0	1,077
	1987	64.5	34.5	0.9	100.0	1,191
Hong Kong	1970	—	—	—	—	—
	1980	41.3	56.0	2.7	100.0	1,754
	1986	50.8	47.1	2.1	100.0	1,992
Japan	1970	40.8	38.0	21.2	100.0	50,529
	1980	48.4	37.5	14.1	100.0	53,586
	1986	51.2	36.8	12.0	100.0	56,435
USA	1970	57.0	40.7	2.3	100.0	56,554
	1980	62.4	35.4	2.2	100.0	70,726
	1987	68.3	29.8	1.9	100.0	80,682
Germany	1970	42.7	48.8	8.5	100.0	26,668
	1980	50.4	44.1	5.5	100.0	26,328
	1987	54.3	40.5	5.2	100.0	25,971

Fig. 2. Trends of Component Ratios of Employment Distribution by Industry (%)

Note: Primary industry consists of agriculture, forestry, and fisheries; secondary industry is made up of mining, manufacturing, and construction; and tertiary industry includes all operations excluding those of primary and secondary industries.

Sources: Official statistics of the countries and regions listed.

reasons for this disparity. On the one hand, reliance on their transit trade ports allowed Singapore and Hong Kong to prosper over many years as commerce-oriented city-states, with a traditionally minimal emphasis on their agricultural sectors. South Korea and Taiwan, on the other hand, still retained their agricultural traditions even as they pushed ahead with their recent industrialization. In South Korea and Taiwan, the share of primary industry in overall GDP composition was far lower than the percentage of the workers engaged in the same industry. The situation is similar to that of Japan, suggesting the low level of labor productivity often found in the agricultural sector of a geographically narrow nation.

Regarding the trends of secondary and tertiary industries, again there were differences between South Korea and Taiwan on the one hand, and Singapore and Hong Kong on the other. In 1970, South Korea and Taiwan found their secondary industries situated lower in component ratio than their tertiary industries with the exception of Taiwan in GDP terms. Since then, rapid industrialization in the two regions pushed their secondary industries to a level equalling or exceeding their tertiary industries. Meanwhile, Singapore and Hong Kong saw their tertiary industries engross about two-thirds of the entire picture (except for Hong Kong in employment terms)—a share far surpassing that of their secondary industries. Singapore's and Hong Kong's large share of tertiary industry may be a reflection of the economic foundation of city-states long dependent on trade and commerce, rather than as a manifestation of the long-standing development of service-oriented economies. The two regions developed in recent years into major international financial centers. This is another factor important for its contribution to boosting the tertiary industry of these regions.

As evident from the situations in the USA, Japan, and Germany, the developed countries tended for their tertiary industries to increase their share at the expense of their secondary industries.[4] During its so-called high-growth period from 1955 up to the first oil crisis, Japan kept its secondary industries constant in component ratio and sometimes even increased that ratio in intermittent phases. The oil crisis, however, plunged the nation into a low-growth period. Since then, the decline of Japan's secondary industries and the growth of its tertiary industries have persisted.

It is very interesting to see what kinds of trends in industrial structure South Korea and Taiwan—two economies with large secondary industry shares—will follow from now on. Dependence on secondary industries, especially manufacturing, for their high growth may present South Korea and Taiwan with only limited chances of success in either their domestic or overseas markets. Their domestic markets are still limited in scope, and the growing trade friction with their trade partners will likely deprive the two economies of their rapid economic growth-related dependence on external demand.

Their high growth has improved both South Korea's and Taiwan's living standards. The distribution of consumer goods among the public became almost as widespread as in developed countries. Given these favorable factors, the two economic regions might from now on realign their industrial structures and position their tertiary industries in the mainstream. Possible measures include pushing ahead with increasing the expenditures for services, and improving the local financial and capital markets that lagged behind their developed-nation counterparts.

GLOBAL TRADE FLOW AROUND THE ASIAN NIES

In terms of economic scales such as GDP, Asian NIEs still lag behind the major developed countries. But these regions are becoming major players in world trade, as pointed out in the first section. This section analyzes the trade structure of the Asian NIEs in more detail. The purpose is to clarify the characteristics of the regions' export-led economic growth.

Figure 3 depicts the flow of trade among major developed countries and economic regions, with the Asian NIEs conceptually placed at the center. The area of each of the circles—indicating Japan, the USA, the Asian NIEs, and Western Europe—represents the absolute values of exports and imports in ordinal numbers for the countries or regions. The width of each interconnecting band showing the flow of trade among the countries and regions corresponds to the value of trade for each route. As seen in Fig. 3, Western Europe greatly surpassed Japan, the USA, and the Asian NIEs in trade volume. This is because Europe's so-called intratrade was very active. For the 12 EC member countries that conduct approximately 85% of all Western European trade, the trade with Western European countries amounted to 70% of all EC exports and imports. As is well known, Japan exported far more to the USA than did the USA to Japan. Between 1980 and 1987, Japan's imports increased annually by a mere 0.9%, with the USA increasing its exports at 1.6% per year while allowing its imports to grow without restraint. As a result, the trade imbalance between the two countries snowballed.

The trade amount of the Asian NIEs in 1987 reached $177.9 billion for exports and $156.5 billion for imports (intratrade included). The regions' exports amounted to 70% of those for the USA and their imports to 80% of the comparable figures for Japan. The import values

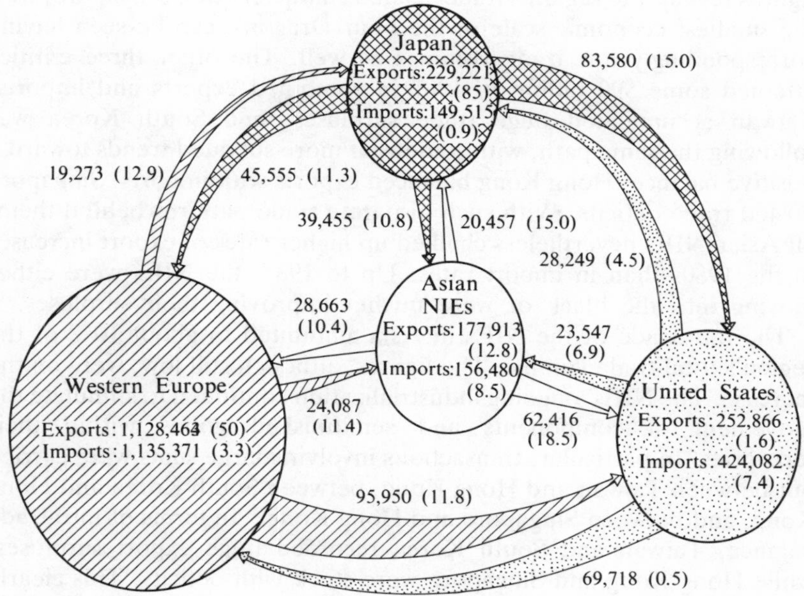

Fig. 3. Global Trade Flow around the Asian NIEs

Notes: 1. Values (in $ million) are based on 1987 data. The numbers in parentheses are the rates of average annual growth between 1980 and 1987.
2. The values of exports and imports of the Asian NIEs and Western Europe include intratrade.
3. The total export values for the countries and regions listed are caluculated on an FOB basis (in FAS terms for the USA). The total import values are on a CIF basis.
4. The data on trade flow between the countries and regions listed is in principle based on the export statistics of the exporting countries and regions involved.

Sources: *Direction of Trade Statistics Yearbook*, IMF; and official statistics of the countries and regions listed.

already exceeded those of Japan. Looking at the flow of trade, one can see the Asian NIEs conducting brisk transactions with the world economic regions where external transactions are most active—Japan, the USA, and Western Europe. In this respect, the Asian NIEs have firmly established their status as key regions for global trade.

In terms of the bilateral trade balance between the Asian NIEs and their trading partners, a considerable imbalance can be seen. The NIEs maintained a somewhat favorable balance with Western Europe, accumulated large surpluses with the USA, and posted huge deficits with Japan.

A comparison of the four NIEs in terms of 1987 import and export figures reveals the region's trade-related characteristics. Singapore, with the smallest economic scale of the Four Dragons, can be seen having correspondingly low trade volumes as well. The other three entities attained some $90 billion in 1987 in combined exports and imports. Taiwan accumulated huge trade surpluses, and South Korea was following the same path, with somewhat more subdued trends toward a positive balance. Hong Kong balanced exports with imports. Singapore posted trade deficits. With such disparate trade patterns behind them, all Asian NIEs nevertheless chalked up higher rates of export increases in the 1980s than in import rates. Up to 1987, the NIEs were either moving into the black or were further improving their surpluses.

The intratrade of the NIEs in Asia amounted to about 10% of the region's total trade volume. The figures, although still low, were on the increase. The NIEs' ongoing industrialization continued to stimulate the movement of components and semifinished goods within their territories. In particular, transactions involving large sums were carried out between Taiwan and Hong Kong, between South Korea and Hong Kong, and between Singapore and Hong Kong.[5] In terms of intratrade balance, Taiwan and South Korea recorded huge export surpluses, while Hong Kong and Singapore were stuck with deficits. This clearly reflects the different ways in which these economic regions operate. On the one hand, Taiwan and South Korea were improving their industrial foundations and expanding their supporting industries. On the other hand, Hong Kong and Singapore, because of their narrow geographical areas, depended more on their industrialized neighbors for components and semifinished goods.

Asian NIEs' Trade by Trading Partner and by Commodity

One of the most conspicuous characteristics of Asian NIEs' trade in the 1980s was the dramatic increase in exports to the USA. Already in 1980, exports from the four Asian NIEs to the USA alone were $19.0 billion, about a quarter of the region's entire exports. The rate of increase in US-bound exports remained much higher than to any other trading partner. In 1987, the NIEs' combined exports to the USA reached $62.4 billion, 35% of the region's total for the year. The NIEs' exports to Japan remained at about 10% of their total export volume. The surging yen in the past few years strengthened the Asian NIEs' relative competitiveness in trade. This was a major factor that boosted the NIEs' exports to Japan (11.5% in 1987).

Intraregional exports between the Asian NIEs remained at about 10% of the NIEs' total exports throughout the 1980s (9.6% in 1987). In

1980, the NIEs' exports to Western Europe amounted to 18.7% of the economies' total exports, a substantially high percentage. In the last few years, however, a shift in trade toward the USA created a pothole in the NIEs' exports to Western Europe (16.1% in 1987).

In terms of the Asian NIEs' imports, the USA's share dropped (from 17.6% in 1980 to 14.1% in 1987), while the percentage of imports from Western Europe rose (from 11.8% in 1980 to 14.1% in 1987). The trend was the reverse of the case for exports. The Asian NIEs' highest percentage of imports came from Japan, a source that provides as a single nation more components and other industrial supplies to the NIEs than any other country in the world. The more the Asian NIEs industrialized, the more they had to depend for supplies on external sources, especially upon Japan. In 1987, the NIEs' imports from Japan amounted to 26.4% of their total imports. Meanwhile, intraregional imports from other NIEs also rose, reflecting the active trading of components and semifinished goods within the region (9.5% in 1987).

The Asian NIEs' trade may now be broken down individually and collectively according to major products. Figures 4 and 5 classify by commodity the exports and imports of the Asian NIEs and major developed countries. These classifications are based on the United Nations' Standard International Trade Classification (SITC). Of the exports by such industrially advanced countries as Japan, the USA, and Germany, machinery (a category comprising general and electrical machinery as well as transport equipment) was most prominent. Japan in the 1980s registered particularly rapid rises in its export of such representative electronic products as computers, semiconductors, and VCRs. Automobile exports, already high in percentage with respect to Japan's total exports, climbed further in dollar terms during the same period. Under these conditions, Japan's machinery exports continued to increase. In 1988, the machinery category constituted nearly 70% of the country's total exports.

By commodity, the Asian NIEs all increased their shares of machinery exports. Singapore, a technology-oriented city-state bent on inviting high-tech investments from abroad, particularly increased its share of electrical machinery exports (from 16.2% in 1980 to 34.3% in 1987). Singapore's machinery exports reached 48% of its total exports in 1988, about the same level as that of the developed countries. South Korea's percentage of machinery exports in 1970 was 7.3%, lower than any other Asian NIE. Since then the share shot up, reaching 39% in 1988. The sharp advance was attributable to growing Korean exports of such electronic products as color televisions, VCRs, and computers, as well as to rapid rises in motor vehicle exports to North America.

South Korea

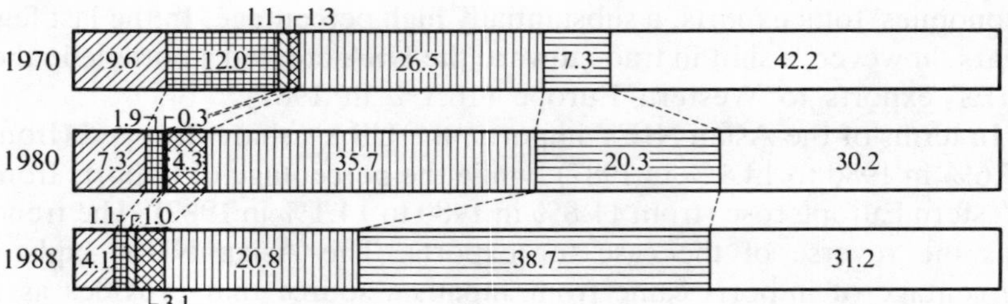

Taiwan

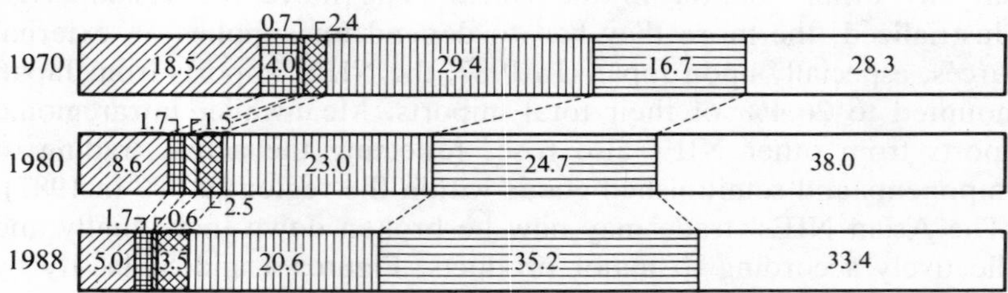

Singapore

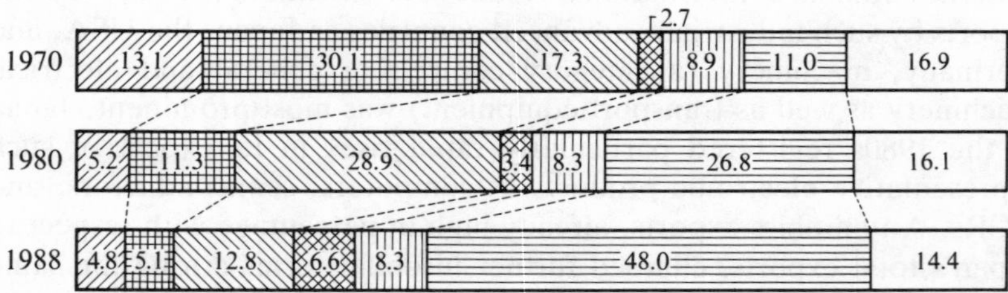

Hong Kong

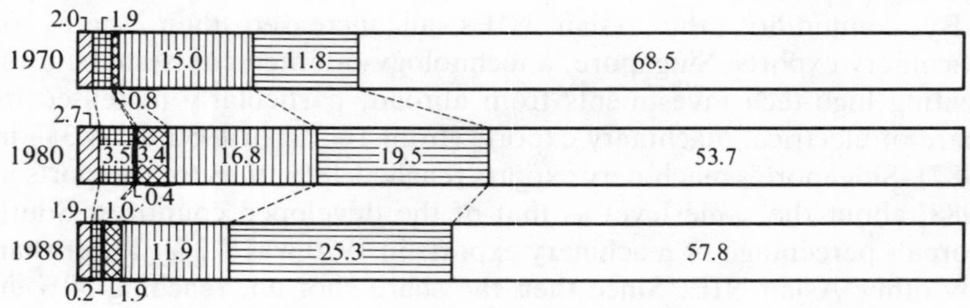

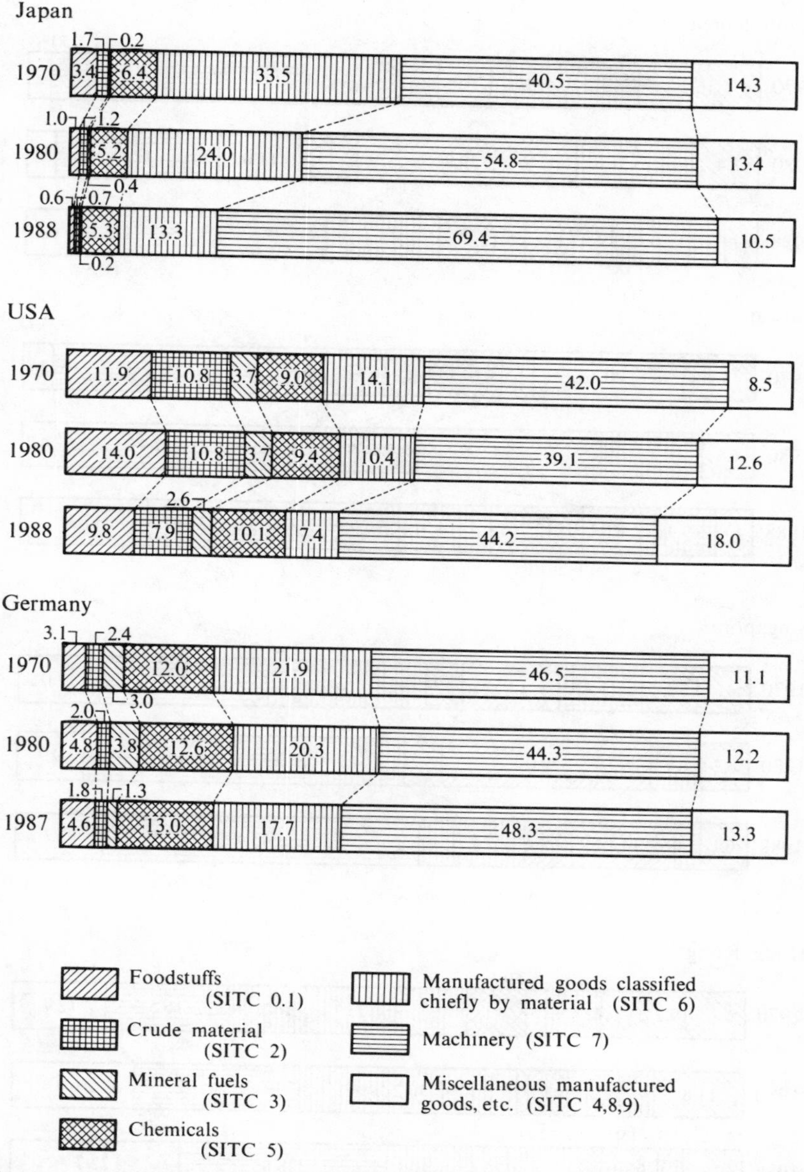

Fig. 4. Compositions of Asian NIEs' and Major Developed Countries' Exports by Commodity (%)

Sources: Official statistics of the countries listed.

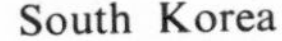

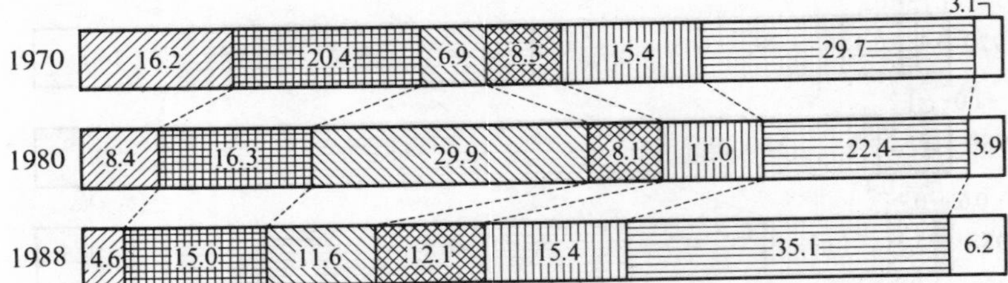

Taiwan

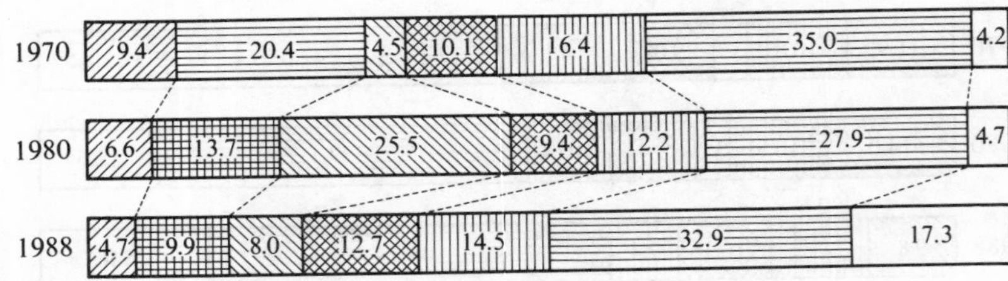

Singapore

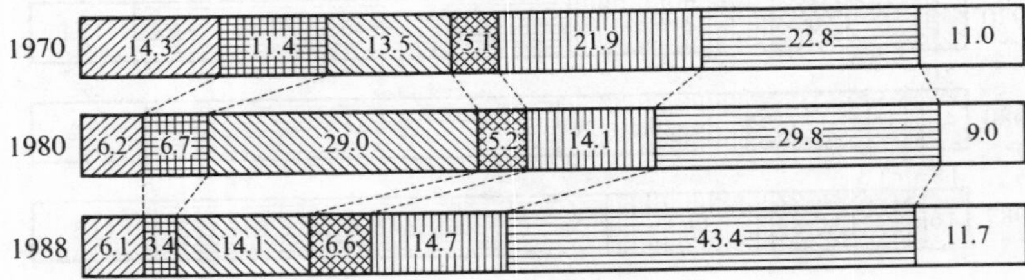

Hong Kong

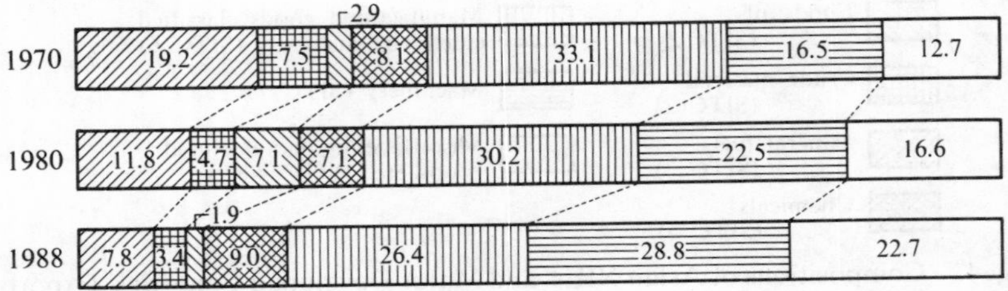

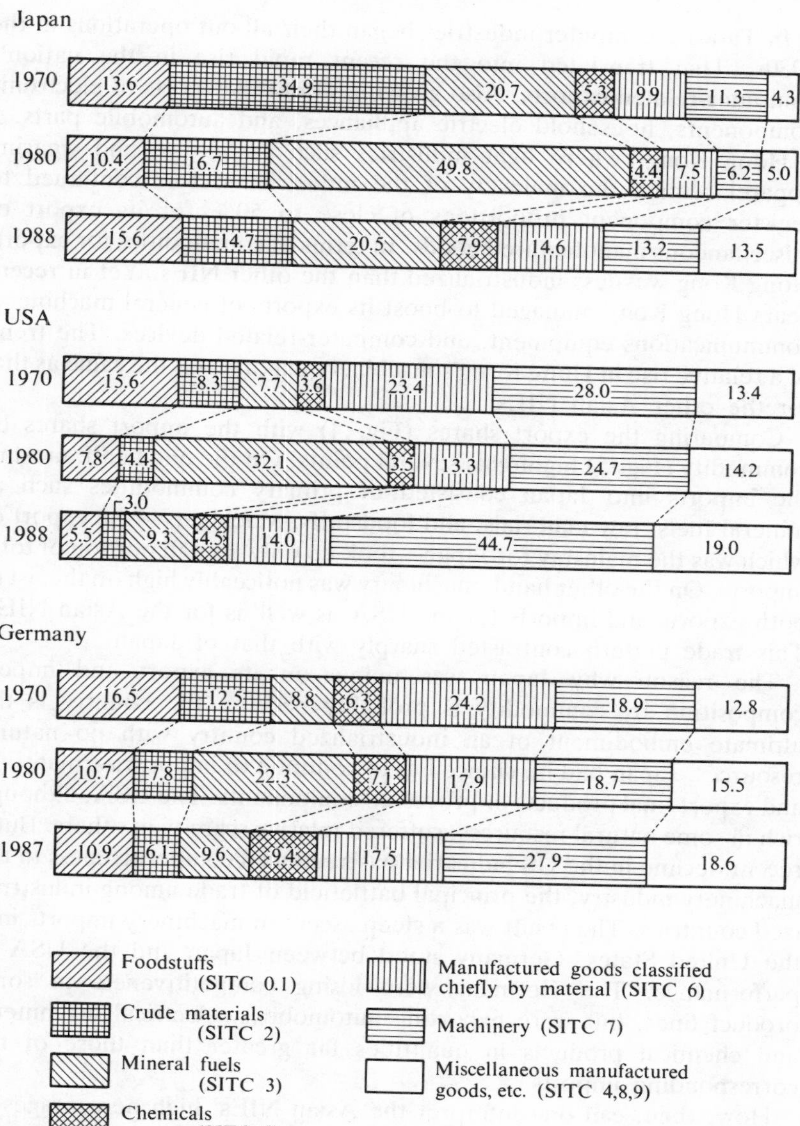

Fig. 5. **Compositions of Asian NIEs' and Major Developed Countries' Imports by Commodity (%)**

Sources: Official statistics of the countries listed.

In Taiwan, computer industries began their all-out operations in the 1980s. That translated into the recent rapid rise in the nation's computer-related exports. Also growing were the exports of electronic components, household electric appliances, and automobile parts.

Hong Kong, where light industries such as textiles and wearing apparel remain the mainstay of the industrial sector, continued to register component proportions of close to 50% for its export of miscellaneous manufactured goods. In terms of commodities for export, Hong Kong was less industrialized than the other NIEs. Yet in recent years Hong Kong managed to boost its exports of general machinery, communications equipment, and computer-related devices. The trend of a relative rise in Hong Kong's machinery exports was the same as that for the other Asian NIEs.

Comparing the export shares (Fig. 4) with the import shares by commodity (Fig. 5) highlights several points. On the one hand, most of the imports into Japan consisted of primary commodities such as mineral fuels, raw materials, and foodstuffs. Machinery—the export of which was the mainstay for Japan—took up only a small portion of total imports. On the other hand, machinery was noticeably high on the list of both exports and imports for the USA as well as for the Asian NIEs. This trade pattern contrasted sharply with that of Japan.

The reason why Japan was unique in its export and import composition by commodity is probably because the country is the ultimate embodiment of an industrialized country with no natural resources. Japan had no choice but to continue to import raw materials and export final products or processed components. The USA, although rich in some natural resources, suffered relative scarcity in others. But a recent decline in the US industrial basis reduced competitiveness in the machinery industry, the principal battlefield of trade among industrialized countries. The result was a steep ascent in machinery imports into the United States. Germany stood between Japan and the USA in performance. The Germans were losing competitiveness in some product lines, but were exporting automobiles, electrical machinery, and chemical products in quantities far greater than those of the corresponding imports.

How, then, can one interpret the Asian NIEs' high percentages in both machinery exports and imports? It only took some 20 years for these regions to industrialize and make their presence felt in the world economy. As mentioned earlier, it was also true that because of their limited economic scale and population, the individual NIEs still maintained considerable gaps with developed countries. Under such constraints, the NIEs tended to see the scope of their industrial structure limited relative to their production scale of finished goods.

It was and is quite a different story with Japan. In Japan, the manufacturers of final goods are situated atop a huge, pyramid-like, flexible hierarchy supported by contractors, subcontractors, component manufacturers, and other entities ready to perform all kinds of subordinate tasks for their parent companies. Thus, the scope of Japan's industrial structure was and is enormous. For their part, the Asian NIEs had no such extensive production set-up. This was probably the reason for the Asian NIEs' dependence upon overseas sources for components and semifinished goods.

To determine whether the above hypothesis can bear scrutiny, let us use South Korea's machinery component industry as an example (Table 2). South Korea's machinery industry, with its primary emphasis on electrical machinery and transportation equipment, firmly established itself as the country's leading industry. The industry contributed immensely to boosting South Korea's trade surpluses. Despite that, as far as the components were concerned, all segments of the industry except those for the production of electronic components chalked up persistent import surpluses.

More specifically, between 1982 and 1986, the output of exportable components increased by as much as 25% per annum. But the domestic production of components was unable to keep up with demand in either quantity or quality. To remedy the shortages, component imports rose at an average annual rate of 22%. The proportion of excess imports to the total volume of domestically produced parts was more than 30% in 1982, but then diminished gradually until 1985. In 1986, expanding business reduced the availability of components, pushing up the level of component imports by $2 billion over the previous year. The excess imports to domestic production ratio of components was expected to rise again.

Prosperous Coexistence with the Developed Countries

The foregoing sections shed light on the way in which the Asian NIEs rapidly grew and accumulated trade surpluses, as well as what was behind their phenomenal growth. It was also pointed out that the NIEs' growing trade surpluses formed a sharp contrast to the USA's ballooning trade deficits.

One of the best ways to reduce the trade imbalance among the Asian NIEs, the USA, and Japan may be to reaffirm the principle of self-rule and establish a framework of economic policy coordination emphasizing structural readjustments. The rapidly ballooning US trade deficits can

Table 2. Trends of South Korea's Component Exports and Imports ($ million, %).

		1982	1983	1984	1985	1986	Average rate of growth between 1982 and 1986
General-purpose parts for machinery	Exports	69	66	87	94	139	19.1
	Imports	234	263	308	289	434	16.7
	Balance	− 165	− 197	− 221	− 195	− 295	—
	(Balance/output) × 100	− 35.1	− 34.1	− 35.7	− 27.9	—	—
General machinery parts	Exports	112	268	204	142	247	21.9
	Imports	370	453	458	517	771	20.1
	Balance	− 258	− 185	− 254	− 375	− 524	—
	(Balance/output) × 100	− 95.5	− 61.3	− 82.7	− 103.6	—	—
Electrical machinery parts	Exports	163	215	302	279	260	12.4
	Imports	325	431	568	547	908	29.3
	Balance	− 162	− 216	− 266	− 268	− 648	—
	(Balance/output) × 100	− 41.1	− 42.1	− 50.2	− 46.1	—	—
Electronic parts	Exports	1,079	1,446	2,129	1,998	2,989	29.0
	Imports	1,231	1,695	2,097	1,985	3,140	26.4
	Balance	− 152	− 249	32	13	− 151	—
	(Balance/output) × 100	− 8.4	− 10.3	0.9	0.4	—	—
Transport equipment parts	Exports	153	162	199	247	298	18.1
	Imports	627	699	850	862	834	7.4
	Balance	− 474	− 537	− 651	− 615	− 536	—
	(Balance/output) × 100	− 47.6	− 41.2	− 40.4	− 37.0	—	—
Precision machine parts	Exports	63	82	103	75	107	4.5
	Imports	123	167	205	166	277	22.5
	Balance	− 60	− 85	− 102	− 91	− 170	—
	(Balance/output) × 100	− 63.8	− 69.1	− 54.5	− 53.5	—	—
Total of parts	Exports	1,639	2,239	3,024	3,826	4,040	25.3
	Imports	2,910	3,459	4,486	4,366	6,364	21.6
	Balance	− 1,271	− 1,220	− 1,462	− 540	− 2,324	—
	(Balance/output) × 100	− 31.5	− 23.3	− 21.5	− 7.9	—	—
Final products (for reference)	Exports	6,299	7,898	9,773	9,887	9,933	12.1
	Imports	4,001	5,048	6,475	7,480	5,995	10.6
	Balance	2,298	2,850	3,298	2,407	3,938	—
	(Balance/output) × 100	20.0	21.0	19.8	13.8	—	—

Source: Component Industries of the Republic of Korea, Industrial Research Bureau, Republic of Korea.

be attributed mainly to a severely enervated US industry brought on by the dollar's misalignment during the early years of the Reagan administration. US industry has yet to recover fully from the far-reaching effects of the dollar's misalignment. What the USA might be called on to do is to have a thorough understanding of the current situation and have its companies make sustained efforts to innovate, develop new products, and invest in rationalizing measures under long-term managerial views. This would allow US industry to catch up where it has been left behind.

As far as trade balance is concerned, Taiwan and South Korea may be separated from Singapore and Hong Kong. Taiwan and South Korea have each accumulated considerable volumes of trade surplus, whereas Singapore and Hong Kong have yet to get rid of their structural tendency to pile up trade deficits. Of course, as has already been pointed out, both Singapore and Hong Kong also registered considerable trade surpluses with the USA. In principle, trade balance is much more meaningful—and should be given that much more attention—when considered on a multilateral basis rather than on a bilateral level. In that sense, Singapore and Hong Kong should not be singled out and penalized for the surpluses they accumulated from trade with the USA. Moreover, Hong Kong and Singapore are each city-states based on free trade. Their markets are much more open to imports than those of most developed countries. In this connection, Singapore and Hong Kong have few serious problems to address from an international point of view. Domestically, however, these economies seem to have three major structural problems that will need mid- and long-term adjustments.

First of all, both Singapore and Hong Kong let their domestic industries depend on the USA for as much as a quarter of their total export volume. Although their dependence on the USA for export markets is not as heavy as that of Taiwan or South Korea, a lopsided dependence on a single nation makes Singapore and Hong Kong quite vulnerable to business cycles or other economic fluctuations of their biggest trading partner. The fewer the number of its export outlets, the more risks an exporting country must take. To avoid putting so many eggs in one basket, Singapore and Hong Kong might wish to diversify their export destinations. With their dependence on the USA reduced, the two economies may be able to let their exporting industries grow more steadily.

A second problem common to Singapore and Hong Kong is the serious shortage of labor in recent years. In particular, the absolute number of available workers is so small compared with the scale of these economies that labor shortages may become the chief culprit preventing the economies from expanding in 1989. On a mid- to long-term basis, poor availability of labor can discourage foreign-affiliated firms from setting up shop in these regions. The proper authorities of Singapore and Hong Kong might wish to take drastic measures to provide a viable work force, including inviting labor from abroad. At the same time, corporations may be called on to push ahead with their efforts to rationalize their operations and invest more in labor-saving measures. These actions will finally enhance capital-labor ratios, and will diminish the bottleneck of labor shortage for the two economies.

A third problem confronting Singapore and Hong Kong is the underdeveloped state of their component manufacturing operations. This problem stems from the very nature of the two regions' economic structure: a city-state economy that must make do with the small amounts of capital and labor it possesses. It will take time to improve this situation. A mid-term option would be to invite foreign-affiliated component manufacturers into the territories. With the supporting industry beefed up this way, Singapore and Hong Kong can improve their production efficiency, stabilize their industrial performance, reinforce their international competitiveness, and help reduce their trade deficits. These measures constitute a yardstick according to which the two regions' industries might wish to operate.

One common denominator for South Korea and Taiwan is their overwhelming dependence on the USA for exports, about 40% of their total exports. For the two regions, the success in exports to US markets has vindicated the soundness of their export strategy that set the USA as their primary target. For its part, US industry has become so weakened that the USA now has to depend on the Asian NIEs for significant quantities of products. Clearly, if South Korea and Taiwan adhere to their US-oriented export policies, not only economic but also political friction will intensify across the Pacific. Assuming that US industry will gradually recover from its current doldrums, one could expect little substantial increase in South Korea's and Taiwan's exports to the USA.

Under such circumstances, South Korea and Taiwan might wish to reduce their dependence gradually on the USA for exports and actively diversify their export outlets into other areas. Candidate destinations may include East Asia—including Japan, the EC countries, Oceania, and other developed or developing regions where the market potential is high. In 1988, Taiwan's exports to Japan were growing even as its exports to the USA were receding. This is one more step in the right direction from a long-term point of view. South Korea is also curbing drastically its exports to US markets while boosting its exports to Japan at a rate higher than that of Taiwan. The Koreans' effort to diversify their export markets is beginning to bear fruit, although not as clearly as in the case of Taiwan.

South Korea and Taiwan might be called on to keep up their effort at domestic market liberalization even as they diversify their export possibilities. It is a fact that South Korea and Taiwan are opening their markets wider than ever before. Possible targets for the two economies from now on might include more product lines to be scratched off their import restriction list, tariff reductions, and simplified customs procedures. These measures will provide the two export-driven economies with a free trade framework that will ensure and enhance their status in the world community.

Fiscal and monetary policies may be devised and implemented in a way that will minimize such economically disturbing factors as inflation and unequal distribution of income, while ensuring stable growth of domestic demand, the basis for economic growth. Foreign-exchange markets should be run so that exchange rates reflect the actual demand-supply conditions in the marketplace as much as possible.

In terms of overall economic performance, the Asian NIEs grew rapidly in recent years and increased their international competitiveness. Their manufacturing sector, however, still has some catching up to do with Japan whose extensive scope of supporting industries, high production efficiency, and accumulated technical expertise are on a par with the world's highest standards. In the 1980s, external conditions, such as exchange rates, worked more or less favorably for the Asian NIEs, turning them into viable competitors of Japan. Today, with so much attention focused on what the NIEs will do next, the prospects for their continued prosperity may not be as bright or assured as they used to be. The regions could face growing external obstacles to their export operations.

To deal with the increasingly severe situation surrounding them, the Asian NIEs must have their industries pursue energy- and labor-saving measures and other rationalizing efforts, introduce state-of-the-art equipment, and expand research and development facilities. All these efforts will serve to enhance overall corporate prowess. As far as product lines are concerned, the NIEs might wish to add higher value and sophistication to what they produce from now on. This will allow the NIEs to retain their customers by setting themselves apart from those closing in behind them—ASEAN and other developing economies.

There is a possibility that the measures proposed above might cause substantial internal friction within the Asian NIEs, when and if implemented. The fact remains, however, that these regions benefited enormously from trade and other transactions with—and capital inflow from—many foreign countries before achieving today's prosperity. To maintain their growth from now on, it is indispensable for the NIEs to maintain close, harmonious economic relationships with the USA, Japan, and other developed countries as well as the developing economies in their neighborhood. In that sense, the Asian NIEs might take measures to minimize short-term internal discomfort that will arise from the understandably unpopular structural readjustments, and then pursue the changes head-on. Such a forward-looking posture cannot fail to draw international praise and appreciation, which in turn will further advance the status of the NIEs in the world community. With their enhanced standing, the Asian NIEs may well serve as an effective go-between between developed and developing countries whose interests often conflict over economic issues.

In East Asia, Japan still enjoys overwhelming superiority in terms of economic scale, standard of living, industrial competitiveness, and technological expertise. With these reserves and achievements in its arsenal, Japan is being called upon to contribute much more to the world community. Already, fairly close economic ties exist between Japan and the Asian NIEs. More and more Japanese firms are setting up shop in these regions and transferring their technology to local personnel. The trend is expected to continue. Imports to Japan from the NIEs have been increasing in recent years. But given its huge market potential, Japan still has vast room for imports. Because the Asian NIEs are having difficulty in boosting their exports to the USA, Japan offers these regions a very attractive market. On the one hand, Japan should properly devise and implement its fiscal and monetary policies to enable domestic demand to grow at a stable pace. On the other hand, Japan should gradually cede to the Asian NIEs its markets where Japanese goods have lost comparative advantage to the NIEs' products.

At present, developed countries are trying to reinforce their domestic industries through various means. Notable examples of their efforts include the US-Canada Free Trade Agreement, and the European Common Market in the near future. But the East Asian region, especially Japan and the Asian NIEs, could suffer considerably from such economic blocs that may be formed from now on in more and more areas throughout the world. The trend could ultimately hamper the growth and stability of the global economy. Avoiding such an eventuality requires Japan to keep building and to preserve East Asian countries' trust. With support from these economies, Japan should be able to increase its influence in the world economic community as the leader of the East Asian economic sphere with a view to establishing a global free-trade framework.

Notes

1. For comparisons of economic scale or living standards in terms of dollar-converted GNP, it would be better to use exchange rates of purchasing power parity (PPP). With no data available, however, on the PPP exchange rates of the Asian NIEs, these figures were calculated in dollars using actual exchange rates.

2. The average price levels in the Asian NIEs are probably lower than those in the advanced countries. Therefore, if calculated in terms of PPP exchange rates, the differential between the two groups will likely turn out to be smaller.

3. Classifying the 24 OECD members as developed countries and the others as developing is but an expedient method for ranking nations in terms of economic performance. The IMF and the World Bank call the OECD members—minus Greece, Portugal, and Turkey—developed countries.

4. This apparent trend does not necessarily underline the tendency of an economy to become service oriented. Refer to Blades (1987) for corroborative reviews of the service orientation of the developed economies.

5. One reason for the burgeoning trade between Taiwan and Hong Kong and between South Korea and Hong Kong is the increasing indirect trade between China and South Korea and between China and Taiwan being conducted by way of Hong Kong. Formal diplomatic relations have not yet been established between China and South Korea and between China and Taiwan.

References

Blades, D. 1987. Goods and services in OECD countries. *OECD Economic Studies,* No. 8/Spring.

Economist Intelligence Unit. 1988. *China, Japan and the Asian NICs—Economic Structure and Analysis.*

Japan External Trade Organization (JETRO). *The World and Japan's Direct Overseas Investment.* Issued annually (in Japanese).

JETRO. *The World and Japan's Trade.* Issued annually (in Japanese).

Kikuchi, Shuichiro. 1988. International division of labor in the machine industries among Japan, Asia's NICs and the ASEAN countries. Research Report No. 120, Economic and Industrial Research Department of the Japan Development Bank (in Japanese).

Korea Development Bank. 1984. *Industry in Korea.*

OECD. 1979. *The Impact of the Newly Industrialising Countries.*

OECD. 1987. *The Newly Industrialising Countries—Challenge and Opportunity for OECD Industries.*

OECD. 1987. *Recent Trends in International Direct Investment.*

Schive, C. 1988. Foreign investment and technology transfer in Taiwan: Past experience and future potential. *Industry of Free China.* Executive Yuan,

Republic of China, August 25.
World Bank. *World Development Report*. Issued annually.
World Economic Information Services. *ARC Report*. One per country (in Japanese).

3 Japanese FDI and the Forming of Networks in the Asia-Pacific Region: Experience in Malaysia and Its Implications*

Takeshi Aoki

Institute for International Trade and Investment

Malaysia's annual economic growth rate was 8.9% in 1988 and 8.8% in 1989, and was expected to be 9.4% in 1990; the 1990 growth rate was the highest of the preceding 12 years. Observing this good performance, leading local economic magazines and economists have reported that Malaysia is ready to face the 1990s with confidence. On the strength of its economic momentum since 1988, Malaysia is aspiring to join the ranks of the newly industrializing economies (NIEs) by 1995 or at the latest by the end of the century. In addition, the country ambitiously plans to double per capita income through the 1990s.

The most important factor in the Malaysian economy's strength in the latter half of the 1980s was a notable inflow of foreign capital. This not only accelerated economic growth, expanded the export of manufactured goods, and created jobs, but also rationalized the industrial structure. Foreign capital is also in the ongoing process of forming networks between industries, which may be the most remarkable change in the Malaysian economy.

By focusing on such newly formed networks, this paper examines the possibility of Malaysia's becoming an NIE, and the implications of forming domestic and international networks on economic development in the Asia-Pacific region.

*This paper summarizes the key points made in Takeshi Aoki, *Malaysia Keizai Nyumon* [Economic Development in Malaysia] (Nihon Hyoronsha, 1990), and Takeshi Aoki, *Asia Keizai no Seijuku* [Maturing Asian Economies] (Keiso Shobo, 1991).

BOOMING INTERNAL AND EXTERNAL DEMAND

The recent good performance of the Malaysian economy can be attributed to both domestic and external demand, which have meshed to reinforce each other. Table 1 shows the country's economic growth rate by GDP component. Among domestic components, private investment in particular has assumed a leading role, along with exports. The annual growth rate in the level of private investment was 22% in 1988, 31% in 1989, and 25.4% in 1990; that of public investment, which was 33.5% in 1989, was expected to have dropped to 10.1% in 1990. Private consumption, with a 56% share in total GNP, has also shown three consecutive years of double-digit growth rates, of 16.1% in 1988, 15.9% in 1989.

Table 1. Annual Changes in GDP Expenditure by Component (%).

	Consumption		Investment		Exports	Imports	GDP	Manufactured
	Private	Public	Private	Public				products
1980	12.7	25.1	17.9	38.1	3.2	20.5	7.4	9.2
1981	5.1	13.3	4.1	41.5	−0.8	5.6	6.9	4.7
1982	3.3	8.7	− 2.3	20.7	10.7	13.8	5.9	5.8
1983	3.2	4.6	8.8	7.2	12.3	9.0	6.3	7.9
1984	6.5	−4.9	7.5	− 1.6	13.8	6.5	7.8	12.3
1985	0.5	−0.9	− 8.6	−10.4	0.4	−9.8	−1.0	−3.8
1986	−10.0	1.3	−16.6	−20.4	11.8	−6.5	1.2	7.5
1987	2.1	1.5	6.2	−17.0	14.6	8.5	5.4	13.4
1988	16.1	4.9	22.0	5.0	11.8	24.5	8.9	17.6
1989	14.3	7.6	31.0	33.5	18.2	30.2	8.8	12.0
1990	10.5	5.9	25.4	10.1	15.4	19.6	9.4	15.8

Note: 1978 year price.
Source: Economic Report and *Annual Report.*

Exports also exhibited double-digit growth over the five years from 1986 to 1990. This was due to the rapid increase in exports of manufactured goods, supported by the recovery of prices for primary commodities. Production of manufactured goods for export has diversified, as indicated by the fact that the share of manufactured goods exports in total exports surpassed that of the five biggest primary commodities (rubber, logs, palm oil, natural gas, and oil) in 1988, reached 54.7% in 1989, and was projected to reach 60% in 1990.

The robust business climate has promoted the expansion of production and restructuring of the economy. In particular, the manufacturing sector experienced positive growth in 1986 after a negative growth rate in 1985, and since then has registered double-digit growth rates. Reflecting this, the percentage share of the manufacturing sector in the GNP rose to 22.5% in 1987, surpassing the 21.8% share of agriculture for the first time since independence in 1957. The share of manufacturing increased to 25.6% in 1989 and was forecast to reach 27% in 1990.

INFLOW OF FOREIGN CAPITAL

In addition to the high domestic and external demand, foreign capital has notably helped to support the robust performance of the Malaysian economy. In 1988, foreign capital inflow to Malaysia totalled M$2 billion in 572 projects, 2.7-fold and 2.4-fold increases, respectively, over the previous year (Table 2). In 1989, despite a slower inflow, the amount and number of projects were M$3.4 billion and 679, respectively. In 1990, the amount of foreign capital inflow had totalled M$6.2 billion. This surge in capital inflow can be attributed to the relaxation of restrictions on foreign capital investment announced by Prime Minister Mahathir Mohamad in October 1986.

In the five years 1986-1990, the aggregate inflow of foreign capital amounted to M$12.9 billion, which composed a substantial 78% of cumulative foreign investment from 1957 to 1990. Of the domestic investment approved by the Malaysian Industrial Development Authority (MIDA), the share of foreign capital was nearly one-third of the total in the period 1987-1989. Japan is the biggest foreign investor in Malaysia, with a 25% share in 1988, 31.1% in 1989, and 28.5% in 1990. (The latter figure is second to Taiwan's 37.8%.)

This rapid capital inflow from Japan was driven by the sharp appreciation of the yen. Japan's surplus capital and desire to shift production overseas has created a favorable situation for Malaysia, which is earnestly seeking economic development through industrialization. Malaysia is now hoping for as much Japanese investment as possible.

BECOMING A NEWLY INDUSTRIALIZED ECONOMY

Malaysia is trying to diversify and make more sophisticated the structure of its production and exports using foreign capital as a lever. The country expects that capital inflow from abroad will continue for the next several years, which will promote further industrial restructuring. In this way, Malaysia is hoping to maintain an annual economic growth rate of 7% through the 1990s.

If this high growth rate and restructuring continue, Malaysia believes that it will become an NIE during the 1990s. Riding its current

Table 2. Foreign Direct Investment in Malaysia (approved).

Year	Amount (M$ millions)	Increase rate(%)	Japan's share(%)
1980	247.7	—	14.4
1984	275.4	− 7.1	24.4
1985	324.9	18.0	25.1
1986	524.5	61.4	11.1
1987	750.0	43.0	30.8
1988	2010.5	168.0	27.9
1989	3401.1	69.2	31.3
1990	6227.9	83.1	28.5

Source: MIDA data.

momentum, the Malaysian Institute of Economic Research proposed the Double Income Plan (DIP) at the National Outlook Conference in November 1988. According to DIP, the annual economic growth rate in the 1990s will be 9.77%, taking into account a population growth rate of 2.6% per annum. Per capita income should reach M$10,600 (US$4,000) by the end of the century, up from M$6,150 (US$2,269) in 1990.

PROBLEMS AND SHORTAGES

In spite of the rosy prospects for the future of the Malaysian economy, there are still serious problems to be solved. These include shortages of skilled laborers and technology, burdensome regulations, and an inadequate industrial structure.

The shortfall of skilled workers at present is calculated at more than 15,000, and can only become worse as the Malaysian economy expands. When developed economies like those in Japan and Western Europe were at the critical take-off stage, skilled workers in the manufacturing sector accounted for between 6 and 8% of the total labor force. In Malaysia today, the corresponding figure is only 2.4%, too small in both percentage terms and absolute numbers.

The number of people engaged in R & D is even more inadequate: about 0.3 in 10,000, or a little over 500 in absolute numbers. In the developed countries, the average number of R & D workers per 10,000 population is between 30 and 40.

Lack of indigenous technology is another serious problem. It is no exaggeration to say that there is almost no technology originally developed by local firms. Almost all technologies used have been imported from abroad, a situation that was severely criticized by UNIDO in its 1985 Industrial Master Plan, along with the lack of indigenous mastery of industrial technology.

The modern industries in Malaysia that require high-level technology are either foreign-owned or joint ventures involving foreign equity capital or technical collaboration, and therefore have direct access to foreign technology through their partners. The resulting complacency has hindered the formulation of a comprehensive policy for developing indigenous industrial technology in Malaysia, and the institutional mechanisms and R & D necessary to foster such activities remain inadequate. The total financial resources allocated to R & D in Malaysia are estimated at around 0.5 or 0.6% of GDP, compared with 1% in the Republic of Korea and 2 to 3% in the advanced industrial countries. For the manufacturing sector the gap is even wider, because the majority of this 0.5 to 0.6% is spent on the primary sector while other countries spend most of their budgets on industrial research for the manufacturing sector.

The shortage of high-level technical manpower in Malaysia is singled out for special mention as a problem by the UNIDO report. Technology, together with entrepreneurship, is the indispensable backbone of industrialization. In the beginning, technology is imported, and modified and improved to suit local conditions and markets. But Malaysia currently lacks the engineers and technicians who are able to absorb and adapt foreign technology to local products and methods of production, in the process known to economists as technology transfer.

A third problem, of regulations, is one that is specific to Malaysia. The New Economic Policy, launched in 1971, had the aim of equalizing the per-capita incomes of the nation's Malay and Chinese ethnic groups by restructuring a social and economic system in which most Malays were engaged in agriculture and the Chinese minority lived in the cities and worked in the industrial sector. To that end, under the New Economic Policy, the government has established a number of public enterprises which give priority in hiring, training, and promotion to ethnic Malays. At present 90% of Malaysia's 1110 public enterprises are operating in the red and supported by the government. The resulting dominance of nonmarket forces in the economy has led to inefficiency and a weakening of initiative in the private sector. It is said in Malaysia that the NEP has subtracted 1 or 2% from the annual growth rate.

The fourth problem, the vulnerability of supporting industries, is symbolized by the lack of linkages among the sectors of the economy for the supply of intermediate goods. Demand for intermediate goods in one sector tends to be filled by imports instead of by domestically produced goods from another sector of the economy.

The situation began to change dramatically in the late 1980s, however, with the inflow of Japanese investment capital. Japanese manufacturers have contributed to the Malaysian economy not only by creating new job opportunities but also by making linkages among sectors, cultivating human resources, transferring technologies, and spurring the relaxation of regulations.

FORMING NETWORKS

The ongoing restructuring of production and exports has already resulted in almost all of the production of the electronics and electrical equipment industry—99.2%, of which 87% is exported by foreign-owned firms operating in Free Trade Zones (FTZs). The situation is similar for the textile industry, ranked second after electronics and electrical equipment, which exports 92.4% of total production of foreign firms in FTZs. The FTZ system was set up to invite local and foreign firms in specified areas to produce, assemble, and export, using parts and materials imported from abroad. Incentives offered include exemption from import duties on imported capital goods, freedom to remit investment income, and others. At present there are 12 FTZs in Malaysia.

Foreign-owned firms operating in FTZs originally procured almost all their parts and materials from abroad. The ratio of local content in the electronics and electrical equipment industry was only 2%, and in the textile industry only 0.5%. Although FTZ firms contributed to the Malaysian economy in terms of expanded production, exports, and job creation, they had almost no linkage with local firms in terms of procurement. FTZs were sometimes referred to as "export enclaves" or "tenant industries." From the standpoint of the input-output structure, firms in FTZs were independent, which means that they did not procure materials from other firms.

This situation changed rapidly in the latter half of the 1980s, when more foreign-owned firms established operations in Malaysia. Linkages and networks between FTZ and local firms dealing in intermediate goods were formed, with foreign firms acting as hubs of production for local firms. Networks in this case are defined first as the means to ensure more local composition of parts and materials procurement (input-output structure) and second as a means to restructure the international division of labor through foreign trade. The greater the intermediate output and input and demand, the closer the interdependence of the industries involved and the stronger the inducement for higher production.

Balanced national economies have a large proportion of goods and services circulating within the system, which makes continuing increases in per capita income more easily achieved. Malaysia's policymakers strongly desire an intensive input-output structure. The most important contributor to networks that could make this possible is Japan, which has increasingly shifted its production bases to Malaysia since the yen appreciation in 1985.

During the three years from 1987 to 1990, the present author witnessed the process of Japanese firms forming networks in Malaysia, from the most primitive stage of shifting production factories while importing all materials necessary to assemble and export goods to diversifying to involve local firms in procurement. In the course of that process, managerial resources are transferred to local firms and local staff. The most important factor, however, is not simply forming networks or transferring know-how, but depending on local procurement. It is local procurement that induces more local production and strengthens the interdependence of industries through dealing in intermediate goods.

The Malaysian government is trying to foster small- and medium-sized enterprises that can act as core or support industries to create liaisons among industries. The enterprises that have contributed to this most effectively are affiliates of Japanese firms that have shifted their production facilities and established factories in Malaysia. Table 3 shows the changes in the percentage growth rate of local procurement by Japanese affiliates with production facilities in Malaysia between September 1985 and October 1987, during which period the yen appreciated from ¥299 to ¥144 per US$1.00. The data in Table 3 are based on responses to a questionnaire composed by the Japan External Trade Organization (JETRO) Centre, Kuala Lumpur; 60% of respondents reported increasing their share of local procurements, while eight companies procured 100% more locally than previously. Analysis of data after 1988 indicates that Japanese affiliates have continued to increase their rate of local procurement.

The ratio of local procurement by Japanese affiliate firms in Malaysia increased by 77% in 1988 compared to the respective previous year, and by 60% in 1989 (Table 4). The percentage share of locally procured parts and materials in the total production value of Japanese affiliates in Malaysia was 19.7% in 1987, 21.9% in 1988, and 23.7% in 1989, indicating a progressive increase. Electronics and electrical equipment alone accounted for nearly 80% of total local procurement in all industries. In both electronics and electrical equipment the share of locally procured parts and material is approximately 90%, as well as in the transport equipment industry. General machinery and petroleum product manufacturers began local purchasing in 1989.

Table 3. Changes in Local Procurement by Industry.

	Food	Textile	Wood & pulp	Petroleum & chemicals	Iron & non-ferrous metals	Machinery	Electronics & electrical	Transport equipment	Other	Total
Sharp increase (above 100%)			1				6		1	8
Increase	1	2	2	4	1	2	12	3	3	30
No change	1	6	4	1	5		5		5	27
Decrease									1	1
No. of enterprises	2	8	7	5	6	2	23	3	10	66

Note: Comparison between 1985 and 1987, October

Source: Questionnaires by JETRO Kuala Lumpur Centre, 1987.

Table 4. Local Procurement and Production of Japanese Affiliates.

	Production						Local procurement						Ratio of local procurement in production (%)			No. of responses
	(M$ millions)			Composition (%)			(M$ millions)			Composition (%)						
	1987	1988	1989	1987	1988	1989	1987	1988	1989	1987	1988	1989	1987	1988	1989	
Food and agricultural and marine product processing	5	158	175	0.1	2.8	2.1	0	134	156	0.0	10.8	7.8	0	84.8	89.1	3
Textiles and textile products	307	375	486	8.6	6.7	5.8	12	14	21	1.7	1.1	1.0	3.9	3.7	4.3	3
Wood, pulp, and paper	92	103	126	2.6	1.8	1.5	7	11	20	1.0	0.9	1.0	7.6	10.7	15.9	4
Chemical and pharmaceutical products	116	222	277	3.3	3.9	3.3	24	28	14	3.4	2.2	0.7	20.7	12.6	5.1	13
Petroleum products	—	—	—	—	—	—	—	0	3	—	0	0.2	—	—	0	1
Ceramics	8	11	24	0.2	0.2	0.3	0	0	0	0	0		0	0	0	2
Iron, steel, and nonferrous metals	536	793	968	15.0	14.1	11.6	21	26	35	3.0	2.1	1.7	3.9	3.3	3.6	11
Metal products	40	84	113	1.1	1.5	1.4	6	7	16	0.9	0.6	0.8	15	8.3	14.2	5
General machinery	1	7	12	0.0	0.1	0.1	0	1	2	0.0	0.1	0.1	0	14.3	16.7	1
Electronics and electrical equipment	1835	2982	4671	51.5	52.9	55.8	546	901	1519	78.0	72.8	76.6	29.8	30.2	32.5	35
Transport equipment	370	621	1129	10.4	11.0	13.5	42	64	133	6.0	5.1	6.7	11.4	10.3	11.8	4
Precision equipment	—	—	—	—	—	—	—	—	—	—	—	—	—	—	—	—
Other sectors of the manufacturing industry	254	292	384	7.1	5.2	4.6	42	50	62	6.0	4.0	3.1	16.5	17.1	16.1	13
Total	3562	5637	8365	100	100	100	700	1236	1981	100	100	100	19.7	21.9	23.7	95

Note: Questionnaires by JETRO Kuala Lumpur Centre, March 1990.

Table 5. Local Procurement by Japanese Affiliates by Source (M$ millions).

	Japanese			Local companies			European/US			Asian NIEs			ASEAN		
	1987	1988	1989	1987	1988	1989	1987	1988	1989	1987	1988	1989	1987	1988	1989
Food and agricultural and marine product processing			0.5	0.1	134	155									
Textiles and textile products	5	7	12	1	1	2	5	5	6	1	1	1			
Wood, pulp, and paper				7	11	20			0.4						
Chemical and pharmaceutical products				24	27.8	13.6									
Petroleum products						3									
Ceramics															
Iron, steel, and nonferrous metals	0.1	0.1	0.5	19	23	31	2	3	3						
Metal products	3	2	3	3	5	13			0.1					0.1	0.2
General machinery				0.2	1	2									
Electronics and electrical equipment	102	143	362	247	448	676	116	265	333	25	16	42	56	29	106
Transport equipment	31	38	78	8	20	38	3	6	17						
Precision equipment															
Other sectors of the manufacturing industry	2	2	1	20	24	31	20	24	30						
Total	143.1	192.1	457	329.3	694.8	984.6	146	303	389.5	26	17	43	56	29.1	106.2

Not all locally procured parts and materials are supplied by purely local companies. Purchase sources can be broken down into purely local companies, Japanese affiliates, and European or US sources (Table 5). Nearly half of all local procurement comes from purely local companies; together with that from Japanese affiliates, they accounted for more than 70% of the total in 1988 and 82.9% in 1989. The joint share of European and US affiliates was around 20%, slightly less than that of Japanese firms. The share of local procurement is largest in the electronics and electrical equipment industry at 70%, followed by the chemical and pharmaceutical industry until 1987, when the food processing industry gained second place.

In resource-based industries, Japanese affiliates procure very little material from other Japanese affiliates; instead wood, petroleum, and ceramics, for example, are procured from purely local firms. Japanese affiliates in Malaysia also purchase parts and materials from Asian NIEs and ASEAN affiliate firms in Malaysia (Table 4), especially materials destined for the electronics and electrical equipment industries.

Table 6 shows the number of source companies broken down into local, Japanese, European/US, ASEAN, and Asian NIE affiliates. The number of supplying subcontractors was 1,297 in 1987, 1,915 in 1988, and 2,688 in 1989. Since there are approximately 20,000 subcontractors in Malaysia, the share of local firms doing business with Japanese affiliates is around 13%, although this number is an overestimate since one subcontractor may supply several Japanese affiliates.

Excluding the petroleum and precision instrument industries, the number of subcontracting firms has increased markedly, with shares of 30.5% in 1987, 38.3% in 1988, and 45.2% in 1989. Sharp increases are especially notable for Japanese and Asian NIE affiliates. As well as in the electronics and electrical equipment industries, resource-based industries have a relatively high share of local subcontractor supply.

Materials and components that cannot be procured locally are supplied by import. Imports by industry and country are shown in Table 7. Aggregate imports from Japan, Asian NIEs, and the ASEAN nations had shares of 56.7% in 1987, 70.2% in 1988, and 56.7% in 1989. The sharp increase in 1988 is attributed to a surging demand for intermediate products to catch up quickly with competitors. Japan's share in the aggregates was 69.4% in 1987, 76.6% in 1988, and 66.8% in 1989. Singapore, the second largest foreign supplier, had 26.3%, 20.7%, and 27.8% shares in the three years. Taiwan also increased its import share to 2.4% in 1989, up from 1.5% in 1987.

Most imports (around 80%) from Japan come from the parent companies of Malaysia-based affiliates, and are destined for the

Table 6. Number of Subcontractors by Sector.

	Total			Japanese affiliates			USA & Europe			Local			ASEAN			Asian NIEs		
	1987	1988	1989	1987	1988	1989	1987	1988	1989	1987	1988	1989	1987	1988	1989	1987	1988	1989
Food and agricultural and marine product processing	20	75	62											50	30			
Textiles and textile products	248	255	264	46	47	48	33	33	36	164	170	175	4	4	4	1	1	1
Wood, pulp, and paper	95	95	109						1	5	5	8						
Chemical and pharmaceutical products	67	49	94	2	2	2	2	2	4	55	65	78						
Petroleum products			2									2						
Ceramics		35	167									12						
Iron, steel, and nonferrous metals	136	157	191	3	5	7	7	8	15	29	37	46	2	2	3	2	1	1
Metal products	31	78	121	3	9	14	5	5	10	20	48	71	5	10	20	2	5	5
General machinery	3	10	25							3	10	25						
Electronics and electrical equipment	400	733	1214	78	163	406	11	17	25	299	433	675	12	16	21	10	108	93
Transport equipment	86	94	106	22	23	25	5	5	6	43	47	53						
Precision equipment																		
Other sectors of the manufacturing industry	211	304	433	11	13	18	10	19	26	185	207	271	4	4	4	1	1	1
Total	1297	1915	2688	165	262	520	73	89	123	803	1022	1416	27	86	82	16	116	101

Table 7. Imports of Japanese Affiliates by Industry.

	Imports from Japan (M$ millions)			From parent companies (M$ millions)			% ratio from parent company			Asian NIEs and Thailand (M$ millions)			Singapore (M$ millions)		
	1987	1988	1989	1987	1988	1989	1987	1988	1989	1987	1988	1989	1987	1988	1989
Food and agricultural and marine product processing	1	10	12	1	9	11	100	90	91.7	0.3		0.5	0.3		0.5
Textiles and textile products	43	59	72	19	26	34	44.2	44.1	47.2	14	29	30.2	8	13	24
Wood, pulp, and paper			0.1						0	0.1	0.2	0.1			
Chemical and pharmaceutical products	329	1292	625	313	1268	568	95.1	98.1	90.9	281.7	436.8	586	281	436	585
Petroleum products			4.2								2.6			2.6	
Ceramics		0.5	8		0.5	8		100	100						
Iron, steel, and nonferrous metals	190	270	343	131	240	31.8	68.9	88.8	92.7	25	39	61	1	4	7
Metal products	13	29	35	10	19.7	20	76.9	67.9	57.1	4	6.1	9	3	5	9
General machinery	0.8	6	10	0.8	6	10	100	100	100						
Electronics and electrical equipment	698	1070	1518	588	865	1257	84.2	80.8	82.8	299	407	864	251	359	679
Transport equipment	125	270	499	46	92	155	36.8	34.1	31.1						
Precision equipment											0.6	1.8			0.2
Other sectors of the manufacturing industry	75	79	143	70	69	116	93.3	87.4	81.1	0.6	2.2	5.4	0.4	1	2
Total	1414.8	303.3	3131.3	1178.8	2595.2	2497	83.3	85.6	79.8	624.7	923.7	1558	536.7	820.6	1306.7

electronics, electrical equipment, and pharmaceutical industries. Of imports from Thailand, Taiwan, and Hong Kong, 99% are electronics and electrical equipment, while those from Singapore are electronics and electrical equipment, chemicals, and pharmaceuticals. The number one import category from Korea is iron, steel, and nonferrous metals.

Table 8 indicates local sales by industry. As seen in the table, the average percentage of local sales is about 40% of production value. Percentages are relatively high in such industries as transport equipment (the highest), followed by chemicals and pharmaceuticals, electronics and electrical equipment, and iron, steel, and nonferrous metals. These three sectors accounted for 78.4% of total sales. The share of transport equipment has continued to increase, and in 1989 it accounted for one-third of local sales by Japanese affiliates. Textiles has also seen an increase in the share of local sales.

Japanese affiliates are doing business in both buying and selling, and in the process are creating networks among enterprises through trading goods and services. More precisely, the Japanese affiliates are creating forward and backward linkages, as formulated by Hirschman, through local procurement and local sales.

Malaysia has been trying to create linkages among industries by developing its automobile industry, which is typical of an assembling industry. But these local efforts have not until now been completely successful in building linkages. It is not an exaggeration to say that Japanese affiliates are performing this function, through local procurement and sales.

The export structure of foreign-affiliated firms can be summarized as follows (Table 9). 1) The rate of increase in the proportion of products exported was 66% in 1988 and 43% in 1989, higher than the rate in Malaysia as a whole. 2) The average export ratio of production is about 60%. 3) Electronics and electrical equipment occupy 78% of total exports, followed by textiles and textile products, of which the share has decreased recently. 4) In terms of destination, Japan is the biggest client, purchasing 23.4% of exports in 1987, 24.6% in 1988, and 20.5% in 1989. The second-biggest customer is Singapore, which purchases around 15% of Malaysia's exports currently.

Since Japanese affiliates in Malaysia function on both sides of the supply-and-demand coin, this has contributed to the forming of networks by trading goods and services, and to the spillover effect of economic dynamics by transferring managerial resources and know-how. Network patterns can be categorized into five types (as illustrated in the figure appended to this chapter) in terms of the degree of local procurement, the most important factor in network formation.

Table 8. Domestic Sales of Japanese Affiliates in Malaysia.

	Domestic sales (M$ millions)			Composition (%)			Ratio of domestic sales to production value (%)		
	1987	1988	1989	1987	1988	1989	1987	1988	1989
Food and agricultural and marine product processing	5	13	16	0.3	0.6	0.5	0	8.2	9.1
Textiles and textile products	68	84	227	4.7	3.9	6.7	22.1	22.4	46.7
Wood, pulp, and paper	31	33	38	2.1	1.5	1.1	33.7	32	30.2
Chemical and pharmaceutical products	80	176	217	5.5	8.2	6.4	69	79.3	78.3
Petroleum products	—	—	—	—	—	—	—	—	—
Ceramics	3	4	5	0.2	0.2	0.1	37.5	36.4	20.8
Iron, steel, and nonferrous metals	384	533	724	26.6	25	21.5	71.8	67.2	74.8
Metal products	15	19	31	1.0	0.9	0.9	37.5	22.6	27.4
General machinery	1	7	12	0.1	0.3	0.4	0	0	0
Electronics and electrical equipment	373	518	788	25.7	24.3	23.4	20.3	17.4	16.9
Transport equipment	370	620	1128	25.5	29.0	33.5	—	100.0	100.0
Precision equipment	—	—	—	—	—	—	—	—	—
Other sectors of the manufacturing industry	121	139	183	8.3	65	5.4	47.6	47.6	47.7
Total	1450	2136	3370	100.0	100.0	100.0	40.7	37.9	40.3

Table 9. Export Structure of Japanese Affiliates by Industry.

	Sales to overseas markets (M$ millions)			Composition (%)			Export ratio (%)			Japan			USA			Singapore		
	1987	1988	1989	1987	1988	1989	1987	1988	1989	1987	1988	1989	1987	1988	1989	1987	1988	1989
Food and agricultural and marine product processing	0	145	159	0	4.1	3.2	0	91.8	90.9								31	36
Textiles and textile products	239	291	259	11.3	8.3	5.1	77.9	77.6	53.3	51	92	144	12	8	6	2	2	2
Wood, pulp, and paper	61	70	88	2.9	2.0	1.8	66.3	68.0	69.8	36	40	47				11	15	18
Chemical and pharmaceutical products	36	46	60	1.7	1.3	1.2	31.0	20.7	21.7	21	20	26	1	1	2	3	9	12
Petroleum products	—	—	—	—	—	—	—	—	—									
Ceramics	5	7	19	0.2	0.2	0.4	62.5	63.6	79.2					1	10	2		3
Iron, steel, and nonferrous metals	151	260	244	7.1	7.4	4.9	28.2	32.8	25.2	133	208	187		3	2	14	22	43
Metal products	25	65	82	1.2	1.9	1.6	62.5	77.4	72.6			0.2		5	9	25	51	54
General machinery	0	0	0	0	0	0	0	0	0							12		
Electronics and electrical equipment	1462	2464	3883	69.2	70.4	77.7	79.7	82.6	83.1	239	490	592	41	142	271	222	417	540
Transport equipment	0	1	1	0	0	0	0	0	0	0.4	0.4	0.2						
Precision equipment	—	—	—	—	—	—	—	—	—									
Other sectors of the manufacturing industry	133	153	201	6.3	4.4	4	52.4	52.4	52.3	14	12	26	34	6	48	26	34	34
Total	2112	3501	4995	100	100	100	59.3	62.1	59.7	494.4	862.4	1022.4	88	166	348	317	581	742

Pattern 1: This is the simplest, most primitive network. The Japanese parent company shifts its production facilities to Malaysia and imports all the necessary materials and components from Japan, and subsequently exports all the products overseas. Japanese affiliates that have already secured overseas markets in Europe and North America try to export to Japan as an additional market.

Pattern 2: This is the same basic network type as in Pattern 1, except that a company from a third country joins a Japanese affiliate and supplies parts and components instead of importing from Japan, with the aim of lowering costs of production due to yen appreciation. Pattern 2 sometimes precedes Pattern 1.

In Pattern 2, however, the import of essential material from Japan continues, and local procurement means purchasing parts and components from another Japanese affiliate with an established business. Even in the case of third-country purchases, the parts and components are procured from Japanese affiliates in the third country.

Pattern 3: In Pattern 3, both local firms and other Japanese affiliates supply Japanese affiliates in Malaysia. But even with sales success, new clients must be found, and local companies must learn to supply new products to strict specifications. In some instances, the Japanese affiliate gives technical advice and assistance to local firms to help them meet new specifications. Although this form of technology transfer is intentional, unintentional transfer also occurs. Once a local firm has succeeded in selling parts or components to a Japanese affiliate, more orders come in from other companies. When the orders are too voluminous to be filled by a single producer, the local firm must make subcontracting agreements with other local firms, thus effectively transferring technology and know-how.

Pattern 4: This is a subcontracting network. Local firms and Japanese affiliates deliver products to multiple purchasers, including other Japanese-affiliated firms and foreign companies. In the machinery industry in Japan, the average company is served by 8.2 subcontracting firms. In Malaysia, where there are fewer large companies, subcontractors supply rivals that compete on world markets. This is accepted by the parent companies as long as parts and components meet specifications and are of good quality. This situation favors local firms and multinational corporations rather than Japanese affiliates.

Pattern 5: Patterns 4 and 5 are the most commonly practiced. In pattern 5, a core Japanese affiliate procures parts and components from other Japanese affiliates of conglomerates in Japan, if necessary also procuring from Japanese affiliates not under the umbrella of a parent company. This pattern is sometimes called a "convoy."

Table 10. Distribution of Subcontractors by Industry.

	Fewer than 5	6-10	11-15	16-20	21-25	26-30	31-35	More than 36	Total
Food and agricultural and marine product processing									
Textiles and textile products	1								1
Wood, pulp, and paper									
Chemical and pharmaceutical products	1								1
Petroleum products									
Ceramics									
Iron, steel, and nonferrous metals		1							1
Metal products	4	1							5
General machinery			1						1
Electronics and electrical equipment	11	1	1	1				2	16
Transport equipment		1	1	1	1	1			5
Precision equipment	4			1					5
Other sectors of the manufacturing industry	8	1							9
Total	29	5	3	3	1	1		2	44

Source: JETRO Kuala Lumpur Centre, October 1989.

Affiliates of Asian NIEs also form networks. As is the case for Japanese-affiliated firms, the core industry is electronics and electrical equipment. As shown in Table 6, the number of Asian NIE affiliates acting as subcontractors to Japanese affiliates has sharply increased, from 16 in 1987 to 116 in 1988.

Table 10 summarizes the results of a 1989 JETRO Kuala Lumpur Centre questionnaire survey of 129 firms. Of the 129, 44 (34.1%) reported having subcontractors; the average number of subcontractors serving one company was fewer than five in 65.9% of the 44. The majority of survey respondents with subcontractors were nonresource-based firms (42 of 44), of which 16 were in the electronics and electrical equipment industry. The next most numerous respondents were from the transport equipment, precision equipment, and metal products industries, in that order. Among those three, transport equipment firms had the greatest number of subcontractors, reflecting the variety of parts and components required. Fifty-one (89.4%) of Japanese affiliate respondents indicated that they were "satisfied" or "rather satisfied" with their subcontracting relationships.

Thus Japanese affiliates are playing an important role as hubs in the establishment of networks. This is perhaps the most remarkable feature of the third, current wave of foreign direct investment in Malaysia. A recent trend of foreign direct investment, especially of that from Japan, is that there is almost no new investment in integrated circuit (IC) and semiconductor production, while videotape recorders (VTRs) production investment is increasing, another contribution to network formation. Reasons for moving production facilities to Malaysia have been changing too. The survey results given in Table 11 show that the motive for investing in Malaysia of 17 firms was aiming for horizontal international division of labor, and 15 firms were planning to produce finished goods. This is in sharp contrast with US multinationals in Malaysia, which do not form networks in spite of the fact that nearly all are producing ICs and semiconductors.

FORMING INTERNATIONAL NETWORKS

As with domestic networks, the most important factor in the formation of international networks is Asian affiliates of Japanese firms, and the driving force for their formation is the sharp yen appreciation, particularly after 1985. Asian affiliates of Japanese firms now procure material, parts, and components not only from local firms abroad but also from those in third countries.

JETRO Trade Centres in the ASEAN nations have researched the

Table 11(a). Motives for Japanese Direct Investment in Malaysia (response).

	Acquisition of natural resources and/or raw materials	Development of the local market	Providing production facilities for related Japanese affiliates	Horizontal division of labor in the parent corporation			Other	Total
					[Parts & Intermediate goods	Finished goods]		
Food and agricultural and marine product processing	1	1		1	1			3
Textiles and textile products	1	1	1	2	2		2	7
Wood, pulp, and paper	2	1	1	1	1			5
Chemical and pharmaceutical products		6	2	2	1	1		10
Petroleum products		3	1	2		2	1	7
Ceramics	2	6	3	2	1	1	2	15
Iron, steel, and nonferrous metals		3	1	4	1	3	1	9
Metal products				1		1		1
General machinery								
Electronics and electrical equipment		8	13	17	2	15	2	40
Transport equipment		1		5	4	1	1	7
Precision equipment		5	2	3	2	1	1	11
Other sectors of the manufacturing industry	1	9	4	8		8	2	24
Total	7	44	28	48	15	33	12	139

Table 11(b). Motives for Japanese Direct Investment in Thailand (response).

	Acquisition of natural resources and/or raw materials	Development of the local market	Providing production facilities for related Japanese affiliates	Horizontal division of labor in the parent corporation	[Parts & Intermediate goods	Finished goods]	Other	Total
Food and agricultural and marine product processing	1	5	1	2	1	1	1	10
Textiles and textile products		15	4	7	1	6	2	28
Wood, pulp, and paper	2		1	1				4
Chemical and pharmaceutical products	3	16	2	1	1		3	25
Petroleum products		1	1					2
Ceramics		2	1					3
Iron, steel, and nonferrous metals		15	4	2		2		21
Metal products		4	4	2	1	1	3	13
General machinery		1		7	3	4	1	9
Electronics and electrical equipment		12	10	25	4	21	1	48
Transport equipment		13	3	3	2	1	1	20
Precision equipment				5	3	2		5
Other sectors of the manufacturing industry	3	15	11	11	1	10	4	44
Total	9	99	42	66	17	48	16	232

Table 12. Distribution of Factories of Japanese Affiliates.

		Foods	Textiles	Wood & pulp	Petroleum & chemicals	Iron & nonferrous metals	Machinery	Electronics & electrical equipment	Transpor-tation equipment	Other	Total
Singapore	N. America	2			4	5	3	19		7	40
	Europe	1			3	1	1	13		4	23
	Asia	5	2		17	12	11	85	3	22	157
	Korea				2		2	11		3	18
	Taiwan	1	1		1		2	20		7	32
	Hong Kong	1			1	3	1	6		3	15
	Thailand	1	1		3	4	1	9		3	22
	Malaysia	1			2	3	1	16	1	2	26
	Indonesia				3	2	1	6	1	2	15
	Philippines				2			6		1	9
	India				1		1	2			4
	China				1		1	3			5
	Other	1			1		1	6	1	1	11
	No. of firms	7	2		20	15	8	63	3	35	153
Malaysia	N. America		3	1	2	1		13	4	2	26
	Europe		3		2			11	1	1	18
	Asia	2	12	1	12	7	3	58	16	12	124
	Korea		1		1			2	2	2	11
	Taiwan		1		2			14	2	3	23
	Hong Kong		1		1			6		1	9
	Singapore	1	1		2	2	1	12		1	20
	Thailand	1	3		2	3		5	4	1	19
	Indonesia		4	1	3	1	1	4	4	2	20
	Philippines		1		1			5	1	1	9
	India							3	2		5
	China					1	1	4	1	1	8
	Other										
	No. of firms	3	8	8	6	8	3	36	5	11	88

Table 12. (continued)

		Foods	Textiles	Wood & pulp	Petroleum & chemicals	Iron & nonferrous metals	Machinery	Electronics & electrical equipment	Transportation equipment	Other	Total
Thailand	N. America	1	3		2	2	1	7	14	1	31
	Europe	1	2			1		5	8	1	18
	Asia	8	18	3	44	9	7	29	49	12	179
	Korea	1	2		4	2		3	5		17
	Taiwan	1	3		8	2	3	6	12	2	37
	Hong Kong	1	1		2	1		2			7
	Singapore	1			6	1	2	5	2	1	18
	Malaysia	1	3		7			3	10	1	28
	Indonesia	1	8		10	2	1	5	12	2	41
	Philippines	2			5	1	1	3	7		19
	India							2	1	6	8
	China		1		2						3
	Other						2	3	6	2	13
	No. of firms	12	16	5	16	12	7	13	25	11	117
Indonesia	N. America		2		2	2	3	2	8	5	24
	Europe		2				2	1	6	3	14
	Asia		25		35	5	9	17	43	40	174
	Korea		3		6	1	1	1	3	4	19
	Taiwan		6		6		2	4	13	6	37
	Hong Kong		3		2			3		4	12
	Singapore		1		6	1		1		6	15
	Thailand		12		5		4	4	9	11	
	Malaysia		10		5	3	1	2	12	4	37
	Philippines				5		1	2	6	5	19
	India							1	3		4
	China										
	Other		3	1	1				2	1	8
	No. of firms	5	19	4	23	12	8	7	21	10	109

distribution of Asian affiliates of Japanese firms by industry and country through questionnaire surveys. In Malaysia, of 84 respondents, only 28 firms had no affiliates outside Malaysia as of November 1988. The distribution of affiliates outside Malaysia is shown in Table 12, along with that of affiliates in Thailand and Singapore. As can be seen from Table 12, international networks have the following characteristics.

1) Asian affiliates of Japanese firms have concentrated upon establishing factories in the ASEAN nations.

2) Those affiliates with factories in one ASEAN member country usually set up additional factories in other ASEAN countries.

3) By industry, the greatest number of Asian affiliates of Japanese firms are in electronics and electrical equipment, textiles and textile products, transportation equipment, petroleum products and chemicals, and iron and nonferrous metals, in that order.

4) Among Asian affiliates with production facilities in both ASEAN and other countries in Asia, the greatest number are in electronics and electrical equipment, followed by petroleum products and chemicals, transportation equipment, textiles and textile products, and iron and nonferrous metals. The top five industries based outside ASEAN are the same, except that machines and food products occupy fourth and fifth places, respectively.

5) Asian affiliates of Japanese firms with production facilities in ASEAN nations have economic and business relationships. Of 64 respondents to a JETRO survey, 21 (33%) reported having such relationships with other ASEAN businesses. In Singapore, Thailand, and Indonesia, responses were positive among 43%, 25%, and 25% of respondents, respectively. This indicates that network formation is proceeding apace, not only within but also outside ASEAN.

6) The formation and intensification of networks in Asia generally occur among enterprises under the same parent group and/or those in the same industry (so-called horizontal specialization). About two-thirds of firms responding to another JETRO Kuala Lumpur Centre survey reported that the division of labor in the same group will develop rapidly in the near future (Table 11). Thirty-two of 78 firms responding believed that the international division of labor would develop worldwide, 26 answered that it would occur in Asia, and 20 that it would occur in ASEAN members.

In particular, networks are forming rapidly between Singapore, Malaysia, and Thailand, all of which are located in the Malay Peninsula. The latter two aspire to become NIEs by the end of this century. This process might be called the "NIE-ization" of the Malay Peninsula. At the same time, through the formation of networks in and among the three countries on the peninsula, a horizontal division of labor is being developed, driven by the Asian affiliates of Japanese firms. These are the most remarkable changes that have been brought about by Japanese affiliates operating in the Malay Peninsula since the yen appreciation of 1985.

THE "DOUBLE FUNCTION" OF SINGAPORE

Labor-intensive industries have increasingly relocated production bases to ASEAN member nations due to labor shortages, wage increases, and currency appreciation. At the same time, NIEs have been encouraging direct investment from abroad. The main goal of such investment is the manufacturing industry, in which the machinery sector receives the majority share. The main reason for Asian NIEs to encourage investment in the machinery sector is that it is rapidly becoming less competitive. The rate of increase in Japanese machinery imports from Asian NIEs was 32.7% in 1986, 67.1% in 1987, 57.0% in 1988, and 22.3% in 1989, while for ASEAN as a whole, the rates were 25.8%, 30%, 65.3%, and 200.1%, respectively.

Asian NIEs are inviting direct investment in R&D-intensive and technology-intensive industries, such as machinery, in order to recover international competitiveness and make their industrial structures more sophisticated. They are thus relocating labor-intensive and low value-added industries abroad. This phenomenon is referred to as the "double function" of NIEs in relation to direct investment.

Singapore, with its small land mass, small population, and tight labor market, is using the double function intentionally to foster economic growth. In order to prevent the expansion of labor-intensive industries, the Singapore government levies a tax on employers of foreign workers, which it increased from S$170 to S$250 per worker in 1989. It also reduced the allowable percentage of foreign workers in each firm from 50% to 40%.

RESTRUCTURING THE INTERNATIONAL DIVISION OF LABOR IN THE ASIA-PACIFIC AREA

The double function has important implications in the development of the international division of labor in the Asia-Pacific area. Restructuring is mainly occurring in the form of horizontal international division of labor with an increasing ratio of trade in manufacturing. In Asia this type of restructuring is being strengthened by affiliates of Japanese firms which are export-oriented investors. As seen in Tables 13 and 14, Asian

Table 13(a). International Division into Groups (no. of firms): Singapore.

	Horizontal division of labor within the ASEAN region	Horizontal division of labor in all Asia (including Japan)	Worldwide international division of labor	No plans for horizontal division of labor	Total
Food and agricultural and marine product processing	1	2	2	7	12
Textiles and textile products			1	1	2
Wood, pulp, and paper	1			5	6
Chemical and pharmaceutical products	8	6	3	6	23
Petroleum products	1			2	3
Ceramics		1		1	2
Iron, steel, and nonferrous metals	3	3	3	7	16
Metal products	5	3	3	9	20
General machinery	6	3	1	3	13
Electronics and electrical equipment	12	12	29	11	64
Transport equipment	3		2	2	7
Precision equipment	3	1	2	1	7
Other sectors of the manufacturing industry	14	7	8	19	48
Total	57	38	54	74	223

Table 13(b). International Division into Groups (no. of firms): Malaysia.

	Horizontal division of labor within the ASEAN region	Horizontal division of labor in all Asia (including Japan)	Worldwide international division of labor	No plans for horizontal division of labor	Total
Food and agricultural and marine product processing	1		1	1	3
Textiles and textile products	2	2	1	1	6
Wood, pulp, and paper	3				3
Chemical and pharmaceutical products	1	2	2	2	7
Petroleum products					
Ceramics		3	1	2	6
Iron, steel, and nonferrous metals	1	1	2	8	12
Metal products	1	4		4	9
General machinery		1			1
Electronics and electrical equipment	3	7	13	11	34
Transport equipment	5	2	1	3	11
Precision equipment	3		5	1	9
Other sectors of the manufacturing industry		4	6	7	17
Total	20	26	32	40	118

Table 13(c). International Division into Groups (no. of firms): Thailand.

	Horizontal division of labor within the ASEAN region	Horizontal division of labor in all Asia (including Japan)	Worldwide international division of labor	No plans for horizontal division of labor	Total
Food and agricultural and marine product processing	1	5	1	7	14
Textiles and textile products	2	7	3	13	25
Wood, pulp, and paper	1			3	4
Chemical and pharmaceutical products	4	4	2	11	21
Petroleum products	1			1	2
Ceramics		1		2	3
Iron, steel, and nonferrous metals		6	4	7	17
Metal products	1	2	1	8	12
General machinery	1	3	2	3	9
Electronics and electrical equipment	6	15	18	7	46
Transport equipment	8	1	3	5	17
Precision equipment		1	4		5
Other sectors of the manufacturing industry	5	7	6	23	41
Total	30	52	44	90	216

Table 13(d). International Division into Groups (no. of firms): Hong Kong.

	Horizontal division of labor within the ASEAN region	Horizontal division of labor in all Asia (including Japan)	Worldwide international division of labor	No plans for horizontal division of labor	Total
Food and agricultural and marine product processing		3	1	4	8
Textiles and textile products		2	1	1	4
Wood, pulp, and paper		1	1		2
Chemical and pharmaceutical products		1	2	1	4
Petroleum products					
Ceramics				1	1
Iron, steel, and nonferrous metals					
Metal products	2	3		1	6
General machinery					
Electronics and electrical equipment	5	4	5	4	18
Transport equipment					
Precision equipment	2	3	4	2	11
Other sectors of the manufacturing industry		3		1	4
Total	9	20	14	15	58

Table 14(a). Main Export Markets of Asian Affiliates of Japanese firms (no. of firms): Singapore.

	Japan	NIEs	ASEAN	Other Asian countries	USA	EC	Other	Total
Food and agricultural and marine product processing	6	3	3	1	1	1	2	17
Textiles and textile products		1	2	1	1	1		7
Wood, pulp, and paper	1							1
Chemical and pharmaceutical products	8	11	16	8	8	3	3	57
Petroleum products	2		2	1			2	7
Ceramics								
Iron, steel, and nonferrous metals	5	6	9	3	5		1	29
Metal products	7	9	10	1	3	2	1	33
General machinery	7	3	7	5	4	1	2	29
Electronics and electrical equipment	25	25	30	4	38	28	12	162
Transport equipment	1	2	2	1	1	1		8
Precision equipment	6	3	2	1	3	2	1	18
Other sectors of the manufacturing industry	17	15	29	9	12	5	9	96
Total	83	78	112	35	76	44	33	461

Table 14(b). Main Export Markets of Asian Affiliates of Japanese firms (no. of firms): Malaysia.

	Japan	NIEs	ASEAN	Other Asian countries	USA	EC	Other	Total
Food and agricultural and marine product processing	2		2		1		1	6
Textiles and textile products	3	2	2		3	3	4	17
Wood, pulp, and paper	4	2	1					7
Chemical and pharmaceutical products	2	4	3		1		2	12
Petroleum products								
Ceramics	3	2	4	1	1			11
Iron, steel, and nonferrous metals	6	2	9	5	1	1	2	26
Metal products	3	5	4	2	2		3	19
General machinery	1		1		1	1		4
Electronics and electrical equipment	21	11	16	2	14	10	2	76
Transport equipment	11	1	3		1	1	1	18
Precision equipment	3	2	1	3	3	4		16
Other sectors of the manufacturing industry	13	2	7	1	4	5	1	33
Total	72	33	53	14	32	25	16	245

Table 14(c). Main Export Markets of Asian Affiliates of Japanese firms (no. of firms): Thailand.

	Japan	NIEs	ASEAN	Other Asian countries	USA	EC	Other	Total
Food and agricultural and marine product processing	10	4	5	1	4	2	1	27
Textiles and textile products	16	6	9	6	8	9	6	60
Wood, pulp, and paper	4				2	1		7
Chemical and pharmaceutical products	6	8	8	2	2	1	3	30
Petroleum products		1	2					3
Ceramics	2	1	1	1			1	6
Iron, steel, and nonferrous metals	9	6	7	2	3	2	2	31
Metal products	6	2	2	1	4	3	2	20
General machinery	4		4			1	1	10
Electronics and electrical equipment	30	8	17	4	17	13	10	99
Transport equipment	11	4	7	1	3	1	5	32
Precision equipment	4	3	2				2	11
Other sectors of the manufacturing industry	22	5	8	4	12	11	4	66
Total	124	48	72	22	55	44	37	402

affiliates operating in Malaysia, Thailand, and Singapore are developing the horizontal division of labor in the form of intrafirm division throughout all of Asia.

In the case of Malaysia, Japan is the biggest import supplier, mainly of industrial products. The main import item is machinery (more than 60% of all industrial products), although the share of chemical products and other manufactured goods is increasing. A decrease has been seen in the share of semimanufactured goods, from 27.8% in 1980 to 20.1% in 1988. This change in the composition of imports from Japan reflects changes due to restructuring of Malaysian industrial and export structures. Table 15 shows changes in manufactured import shares by item and country. The following trends can be observed from the table. First, the import shares of both Asian NIEs and ASEAN nations are increasing while that of Japan is decreasing, especially in semimanufactured goods. This reflects the fact that Japanese affiliates procure material, parts, and components from other Asian countries, not from Japan.

The most remarkable feature of the export structure to Japan is that an 85% share is held by primary commodities. Since imports from Japan are almost totally of manufactured goods, the trade structure between Malaysia and Japan is a typical vertical international division of labor. Although Japan holds first place in terms of total export share from Malaysia, that share is decreasing, as is Japan's share (third after the USA and Singapore) of manufactured goods exports. The increase in manufactured goods exports to Japan was 38.8% in 1988 compared to the previous year, which can be seen as promoting diversification and sophistication of the Malaysian industrial structure. Japan's share in total manufactured goods exports has increased after a decreasing trend. These changes are due to the expanded imports of manufactured goods from Japan and to export promotion by Japanese affiliates in Malaysia.

Asian affiliates of Japanese firms should further promote local procurement to strengthen networks and to transfer managerial resources, technology, production know-how, and marketing expertise. The increase in local procurement will increase the production of local firms, thus intensifying input-output structures among industries. Communication between the staff of foreign-owned and local firms can also contribute to technology transfer in procurement agreements.

Increased imports and exports in the Asian-Pacific region will promote international competitiveness and the international division of labor, not only in the region but worldwide. In the course of such development, however, some have raised fears that unbalanced

Table 15. Malaysia's Manufactured Goods Trade by Commodity and Country (%).

		Imports					Exports				
		1980	1985	1986	1987	1988	1980	1985	1986	1987	1988
SITC 5	ASEAN	6.7	15.3	16.0	14.5	15.6	59.8	32.5	32.5	36.8	34.7
	Singapore	5.7	11.3	12.3	12.2	12.2	43.1	24.8	21.9	23.4	22.4
	Thailand	0.3	0.9	1.0	0.9	0.9	4.5	1.7	4.9	7.4	7.0
	Indonesia	0.4	2.5	1.9	0.9	0.6	6.5	4.3	3.2	2.6	2.3
	Philippines	0.3	0.6	0.8	0.5	0.6	5.7	1.7	2.3	3.5	3.0
	Asian NIEs	5.3	5.4	5.9	6.0	6.2	8.4	6.1	9.9	13.2	13.5
	Korea	1.3	1.7	1.7	1.7	1.6	0.3	0.4	1.6	3.3	3.8
	Taiwan	2.8	2.1	2.5	2.7	2.9	1.2	1.2	3.7	3.8	5.0
	Japan	17.7	15.6	17.3	17.5	19.9	6.5	12.3	14.1	14.7	17.8
	USA	21.5	20.6	17.2	17.8	15.9	10.8	20.4	14.6	10.6	15.9
	EC	29.0	27.1	27.0	25.6	22.9	2.4	13.6	13.0	13.5	6.6
	World	100.0	100.0	100.0	100.0	100.0	100.0	100.0	100.0	100.0	100.0
SITC 6	ASEAN	8.8	9.8	10.6	11.4	12.1	11.0	15.3	27.2	28.2	31.5
	Singapore	6.6	6.9	6.3	6.6	7.0	9.1	12.7	22.9	23.7	25.2
	Thailand	1.0	1.4	2.0	2.0	1.7	0.4	0.6	0.7	1.1	2.7
	Indonesia	0.6	1.1	2.1	2.9	3.1	0.4	0.5	1.2	1.0	1.2
	Philippines	0.6	0.4	0.2	0.2	0.3	1.0	1.5	2.3	24.0	1.8
	Asian NIEs	15.1	15.8	18.9	17.8	19.2	5.7	5.8	10.2	10.3	11.6
	Korea	5.9	5.9	5.4	5.3	5.6	1.2	1.3	2.1	2.1	2.1
	Taiwan	6.2	6.3	8.6	9.3	9.1	1.0	1.1	3.5	3.1	3.3
	Hong Kong	3.0	3.6	4.9	5.2	4.5	3.5	3.4	4.6	5.1	6.2
	Japan	37.6	34.9	30.8	27.7	27.6	20.4	13.7	13.2	13.8	11.8
	USA	5.5	5.2	6.8	5.8	6.2	12.7	5.6	10.7	11.2	9.1
	EC	11.0	14.6	13.6	14.1	13.5	30.5	46.5	18.4	17.9	18.6
	World	100.0	100.0	100.0	100.0	100.0	100.0	100.0	100.0	100.0	100.0

Table 15. (continued)

		Imports					Exports				
		1980	1985	1986	1987	1988	1980	1985	1986	1987	1988
	ASEAN	8.1	15.0	15.7	15.8	14.1	19.5	21.8	21.4	22.9	25.7
	Singapore	6.0	10.5	12.2	12.4	10.9	16.0	19.7	18.8	19.4	22.5
	Thailand	0.7	0.7	1.4	1.4	1.6	1.1	1.0	1.1	1.3	1.2
	Indonesia	0.0	0.1	0.1	0.1	0.2	0.7	0.4	0.4	0.7	0.8
S	Philippines	1.3	3.7	2.0	1.9	1.4	1.7	0.7	1.0	1.4	1.2
I T	Asian NIEs	3.4	5.1	5.5	7.1	9.0	6.5	4.8	7.0	9.2	9.7
C	Korea	1.0	2.4	2.4	3.0	2.7	0.1	0.8	1.0	1.6	1.4
	Taiwan	1.6	1.8	2.1	2.9	4.7	0.3	0.7	0.7	1.1	1.2
7	Hong Kong	0.8	0.9	1.0	1.2	1.6	6.1	3.3	5.3	6.5	7.1
	Japan	35.1	33.0	27.0	29.8	32.6	4.6	6.7	7.4	5.0	5.8
	USA	25.6	24.0	30.5	30.2	28.3	44.6	44.6	42.5	41.8	38
	EC	21.0	16.3	16.0	13.5	12.3	16.9	17.3	16.8	15.1	15.5
	World	100.0	100.0	100.0	100.0	100.0	100.0	100.0	100.0	100.0	100.0

Note: SITC =U.N. Standard Intenational Trade Classification.

economic development will occur and trade friction will increase. To mitigate such fears, Japan should open its markets more to absorb manufactured goods exports from Asia-Pacific nations.

Appendix: Netwark Patterns

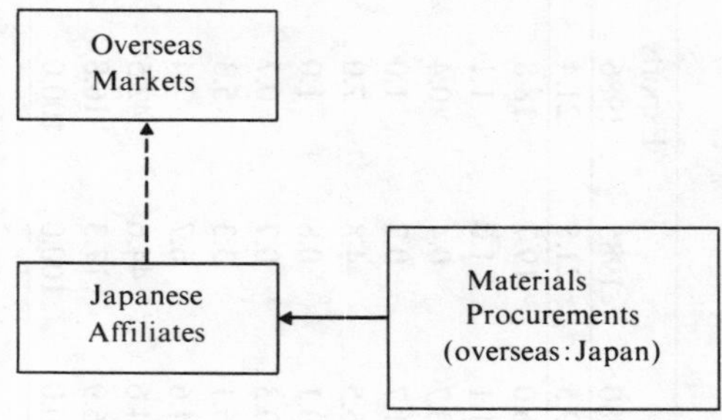

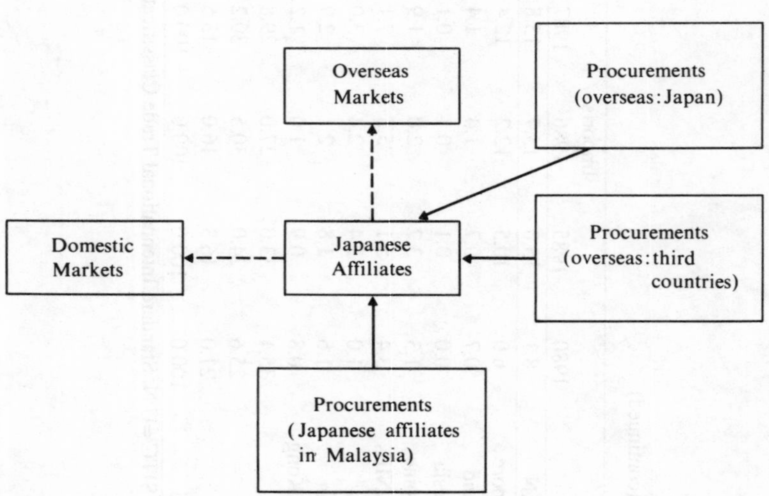

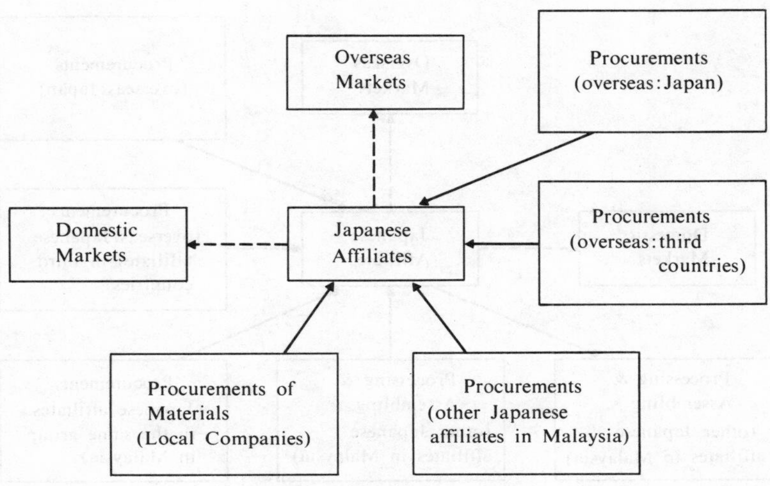
Overseas
Markets
Procurements
(overseas: Japan)
Domestic
Markets
Japanese
Affiliates
Procurements
(overseas: third
countries)
Procurements of
Materials
(Local Companies)
Procurements
(other Japanese
affiliates in Malaysia)

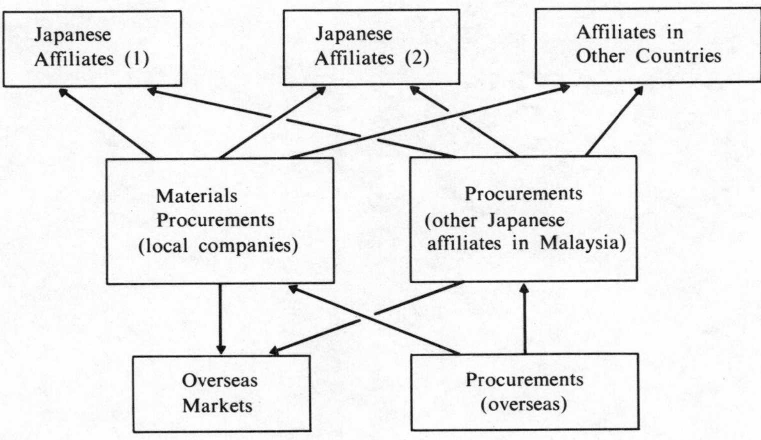
Japanese
Affiliates (1)
Japanese
Affiliates (2)
Affiliates in
Other Countries
Materials
Procurements
(local companies)
Procurements
(other Japanese
affiliates in Malaysia)
Overseas
Markets
Procurements
(overseas)

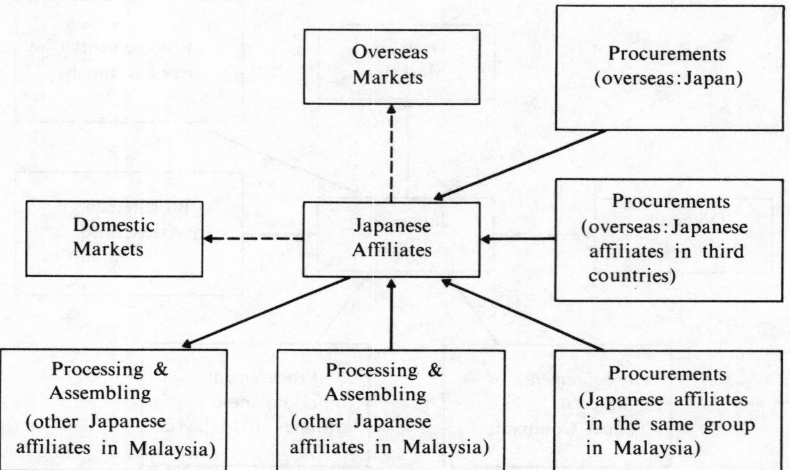
Overseas Markets
Procurements (overseas: Japan)
Domestic Markets
Japanese Affiliates
Procurements (overseas: Japanese affiliates in third countries)
Processing & Assembling (other Japanese affiliates in Malaysia)
Processing & Assembling (other Japanese affiliates in Malaysia)
Procurements (Japanese affiliates in the same group in Malaysia)

4 Technology Transfer from Japan to ASEAN: Trends and Prospects

Soon-Beng Chew*, Rosalind Chew*, Francis K. Chan**

**Nanyang Technological University*
***National University of Singapore*

INTRODUCTION

Japan's emergence as a leading industrial power from the ashes of World War II in just one generation is seen to be intimately linked with its success in adopting and creatively adapting Western technology to its own needs. The spectacular success achieved is a source of hope and inspiration to many, including ASEAN countries. This was reaffirmed by the official "Look East" policy of Malaysia under Prime Minister Mahathir Mohamad.

That Japan has been able to achieve phenomenal economic growth in spite of domestic resource scarcity adds special significance in the current state of international concern and anxiety due to dwindling resource supplies. The key appears to lie in increased industrial efficiency through rapid technological progress. International technological dualism[1] stands as the modern great divide between rich and poor nations. Alleviating mass poverty and deprivation necessitates closing the existing technological gaps. Although this could be achieved through a self-reliant approach, as previously attempted by China at great cost, international transfer of technology appears to be a more effective and efficient method.

As an Asian country that has modernized and industrialized with distinction, Japan seems qualified to serve as a model and potential source of useful technology, particularly for other Asian countries. ASEAN member nations, such as Malaysia and Singapore, certainly think so.[2] The central theme of this paper is to examine to what extent and in what form technology transfer has taken place between Japan and the ASEAN countries, and how the process may be expedited in future.

CURRENT SITUATION AND TRENDS OF TECHNOLOGY TRANSFER

Technology can be simply defined as "the means or capacity to perform a particular activity" (Gruber and Marquis 1969). It can exist either in the form of material capital (embodied in plant, tools, machinery, or other capital equipment items), intellectual capital (knowledge of production, marketing, or financial processes sometimes encoded in specifications, blueprints, patents, etc.), or human capital (specialized skills in management, marketing, finance, and the use and creation of new information and ideas) (Dunning 1982). Since there is no natural unit available to measure the aggregate amount of technology, it is difficult to conceptualize its stock at one point in time or its flow over time and between countries.

There is also no consensus on the concept of technology transfer. The following elements, however, may or may not be included: adoption of an existing technique or technology by a new user (further distinguished between independent firms and subsidiaries); transfer to a different national location (i.e., international technological diffusion); use for a purpose other than the one for which the R&D was undertaken; use in a new way (i.e., with an element of innovation), or use with sufficient absorption of the underlying technological principle to be able to master, adapt, and further develop the imported technology to suit one's own specific needs and conditions. Transfer of technology clearly covers a wide spectrum of activity, from simple importation to operation, repair, and maintenance, mastery of principles, adaptation, and further development (Dunning 1982; Konz 1980).

For the purposes of the present paper, the working definition of international technology transfer is "any transmission of established technology defined above from one country (source) to another (destination) as evidenced by the ability to operate (use in production), repair, and maintain or adapt and further develop to suit one's own conditions." In practice, it is not feasible to observe or verify the higher levels of absorption, although ideally complete absorption and mastery of imported technology by those in the destination are the chief objectives of technology transfer (OECD 1982).[3]

Although difficulties in definition and conceptualization exist in measuring the rate of flow of technology from one country to another, without such attempts at measurement it is difficult to discuss trends over time. The difficulties are compounded by the different modes of technology transfer from abroad. Thus, if technology comes in the form of a "package deal" via foreign direct investment (FDI), it is not possible to isolate the payment for the pure technology element. The practice of transfer pricing to minimize tax payment also distorts the true value of technology transfer, and some means of transfer may escape measurement due to a lack of data.[4] The real inflow of technology in the sense of local absorption is also highly sensitive to the level of local capability in the form of supporting institutions, cultural attitudes, the pool of entrepreneurial talent available, and the level and diffusion of technical education.[5]

Due to the heterogeneity and great variety of methods in which technology is transferred, it is a convention to measure its flow through the different modes of transfer. These include FDI, licensing agreements, technical assistance, joint ventures, technical journals and other literature, and the importation of specialized capital equipment. The following sections focus on FDI and technical assistance, not because they are necessarily the most important or effective modes, but because data on them are readily available.

FOREIGN DIRECT INVESTMENT

Originally the main importance of FDI to the ASEAN nations was as a source of investment finance. As local investment funds became more plentiful, FDI came to be seen as a useful way to secure a set of complementary inputs needed for industrialization still in short supply in the national economy. Those elements bundled together in a convenient package include technological know-how, managerial skills, skilled personnel, and marketing expertise and foreign marketing networks, as well as equity and debt capital. As countries develop and acquire more of those elements, attempts have been made to unbundle the package and to try to secure only those elements still in short supply. This has very often included technological know-how. The ASEAN countries have individually passed through some of those different phases.[6]

It is useful to examine the trends in international FDI before discussing that of Japanese FDI to in ASEAN countries. Table 1 summarizes significant trends in international investment from 1961-1988, and shows that there was an acceleration in the 1960s and 1970s. The average annual rate of increase was 12.6% between 1960-1973 in nominal terms. Despite several erratic swings, since the mid-1970s international investment has been growing at higher levels, with the

Table 1. Net Flow of Private FDI From Advanced to Developing Countries, 1961-1988.

Year	From all advanced countries US$mill.	From the USA US$mill.	From the USA % of advanced total	From Japan US$mill.	From Japan % of advanced total
1961	1833.6	828.0	45.2	98.4	5.4
1962	1495.2	566.0	37.9	68.4	4.6
1963	1603.0	745.0	46.5	76.7	4.8
1964	1571.5	682.0	43.4	39.3	2.5
1965	2468.3	1271.0	51.5	87.4	3.5
1966	2179.3	1110.0	50.9	86.8	4.0
1967	2105.0	1060.0	50.4	66.4	3.2
1968	3151.5	1747.0	55.4	110.3	3.5
1969	2918.6	1363.0	46.7	144.1	4.9
1970	3563.2	1742.0	48.9	261.5	7.3
1971	3874.3	2010.0	51.9	222.4	5.7
1972	4443.1	1976.0	44.5	204.0	4.6
1973	6710.6	2887.0	43.0	1301.1	19.4
1974	7060.1	3788.0	53.7	705.4	10.0
1975	10,493.8	7241.0	69.0	222.7	2.1
1976	7823.9	3119.0	39.9	1084.2	13.9
1977	9498.9	4866.0	51.2	724.4	7.6
1978	11,153.3	5619.0	50.4	1318.3	11.8
1979	12,945.3	7986.0	61.7	690.6	5.3
1980	8896.2	3367.0	37.8	906.0	10.2
1981	15,357.0	6475.0	42.2	2426.0	15.8
1982	10,385.0	5451.0	52.5	364.0	3.5
1983	7791.0	2340.0	30.0	433.0	5.6
1984	10,909.0	4419.0	40.5	1489.0	13.6
1985	6488.0	930.0	14.3	1046.0	16.1
1986	10,968.0	3107.0	28.3	2761.0	25.2
1987	20,895.0	8016.0	38.4	7421.0	35.2
1988		4205.0		8190.0	
Cumulative total:					
1961-1970	22,889.2	11,114.0	48.6	1039.3	4.5
1971-1980	82,899.5	42,859.0	51.7	7379.1	8.9
1981-1987	82,793.0	30,738.0	37.1	15,940.0	19.3

Sources: OECD, *Development Cooperation Review*, various issues, and OECD, Flow of Financial Resources to Developing Countries 1961-1971, 1973. 1961-1980 data reproduced from Chow Siow Yue 1977, Table 1.

peak in 1981 and the nadir in 1985. The increase in international investment was also particularly notable from 1986 to 1987.

Table 2. Japanese Direct Investments in ASEAN Countries.

(US$ million)

Year	1951-69 (1970-87)	1981	1982	1983	1984	1985	1986	1987
Indonesia	148 (9,019)	2434	410	374	374	408	250	545
Malaysia	35 (1,411)	31	83	140	142	79	158	163
Philippines	45 (941)	72	34	65	46	61	21	72
Singapore	24 (3,042)	266	180	322	255	339	302	494
Thailand	78 (1,057)	31	94	72	119	48	124	250
ASEAN total	375 (15,470)	2,834	801	973	906	935	855	1,524
Asia total	584 (26,073)	3,338	1,384	1,847	1,628	1,435	2,327	4,868
World total	2673 (136,658)	8,931	7,703	8,145	10,155	12,217	22,320	33,364
ASEAN as % of Asia	64.2 (59.3)	84.9	57.9	52.7	55.7	65.2	36.7	31.3
ASEAN as % of world	14.0 (11.3)	31.7	10.4	11.9	8.9	7.7	3.8	4.6

Sources: S. Sekiguchi and L.B. Krause. 1980. Direct foreign investment in ASEAN by Japan and the United States. In: Ross Garnaut (ed.). *ASEAN in a Changing Pacific and World Economy*. Japan, Ministry of Finance. *Direct Outward Investment, Declarations and Approvals*; ASEAN Promotion Centre on Trade, Investment and Tourism. 1985. *ASEAN-Japan Statistical Handbook*; ASEAN Promotion Centre on Trade, Investment and Tourism, 1989. *ASEAN-Japan Statistical Pocketbook*.

In the 1980s Japanese FDI caught up with and surpassed that from the USA. This was due to the fact that the USA became a net capital importer, the yen appreciated significantly, and the expanding Japanese trade surplus became a problem. Table 2 shows Japanese FDI in ASEAN countries in comparison with investments in Asia as a whole and the world. Although Japanese international investment has increased, investment in Asia contracted during the period 1970-1987 compared to the period 1951-1969. ASEAN's percentage share of Japanese investment in Asia and worldwide also decreased during the same period. Indonesia and Singapore have continued to be the chief beneficiaries of Japanese investment in ASEAN, with an average share of 55.9% and 14.4%, respectively; they are followed by Malaysia with

10.9%, Thailand with 9.7%, and the Philippines with 7.7% shares.

Table 3: EC and Other Foreign Investment in ASEAN Countries by Country of Origin, 1987.

(US$ million)

	Indonesia[1] (1986)		Malaysia[2]		Philippines[3]		Singapore[4]		Thailand[5]	
	Amt.	%	Amt.	%	Amt.	%	Amt.	%	Amt.	%
EC	92.1	11.1	25.6	8.6	23.4	14.0	114.4	16.6	38.5	21.0
UK	46.1	5.6	10.4	3.5	10.2	6.1	20.1	2.9	12.8	7.0
Germany	16.5	2.0	4.0	1.3	0.7	0.4	42.9	6.2	17.4	9.5
Netherlands	23.3	2.8			8.0	4.8	33.7	4.9	2.9	1.6
USA	153.8	18.6	24.3	8.2	36.0	21.6	258.1	37.5	30.8	16.8
Japan	328.9	39.8	91.6	30.8	28.8	17.3	285.4	41.4	127.1	69.4
Hong Kong	9.6	1.2	11.0	3.7	27.7	16.6			-66.9	-36.5
Other	17.3	2.1	31.1	10.4	3.1	1.9	8.4	1.2	3.9	2.1
Total	826.2	100.0	297.7	100.0	166.6	100.0	687.6	100.0	183.2	100.0

Notes: All figures (except those in Indonesia) were originally in each of the respective country's currency. EC investors in Indonesia include the UK, Netherlands, France, Germany, and Belguim. EC investors in Thailand include the UK, Germany, France, Netherlands, and Italy.

1. Foreign investment projects approved by Investment Coordinating Board.
2. Foreign equity projects approved by Malaysian Industrial Development Authority.
3. Board of Investment approved equity investments under P.D. 1789 as amended and P.D. 218.
4. Investment commitments in manufacturing (excluding petrochemicals).
5. Net inflow of direct investment (equity and loans from parent or related companies including capital funds of foreign commercial banks).

Sources: (Indonesia) *Banka Indonesia Annual Report, 1986/87* (Malaysia, Philippines, and Thailand) Somsal Tambunlertchai and Umphon Panachet. 1990. Foreign direct investment in ASEAN. In: Soon Lee Ying (ed.). *Foreign Direct Investment in ASEAN, 1990,* Tables 8, 9, and 11, pp. 70-73 and 75; (Singapore) *Economic Development Board Annual Report, 1987/88.*

Prior to the influx of foreign investment into ASEAN nations from Japan, the traditional foreign investors were the former colonial powers: the UK in Malaysia and Singapore, the Netherlands in Indonesia, and the USA in the Philippines. As shown in Table 3, by 1987 the Japan had become the leading foreign investor in Indonesia, Malaysia, Singapore, and Thailand and second only to the USA in the Philippines. While the USA and EC countries remain the major foreign investors in ASEAN, Japan has clearly emerged as the largest source of FDI in ASEAN.

The data in Table 4 illustrate another interesting aspect of FDI inflow

Table 4. ASEAN Countries' Private Direct Investment Inflows, 1967-1988.

(US$ million)

Year	Indonesia	Malaysia	Philippines	Singapore	Thailand	ASEAN total
1967	− 10	43	− 9	34	43	101
1968	− 2	30	− 3	26	60	111
1969	32	80	6	38	51	207
1970	83	94	− 29	93	42	283
1971	139	100	− 6	116	39	388
1972	207	114	− 21	191	68	559
1973	15	172	54	389	77	707
1974	− 49	571	4	596	189	1311
1975	476	350	97	611	86	1620
1976	344	381	126	331	105	1287
1977	235	406	209	335	106	1291
1978	279	407	163	739	53	1701
1979	219	647	73	911	50	1900
1980	184	928	40	1454	186	2792
1981	132	1249	170	1653	288	3492
1982	226	1397	15	1296	191	3125
1983	283	1234	103	1063	341	3024
1984	217	763	9	1157	385	2531
1985	334	751	16	875	174	2150
1986	270	510	132	499	274	1685
1987	478	464	336	1136	204	2618
1988	543	650	937	1067	1095	4292
Cumulative total:						
1967-1980	2152	4383	704	5864	1155	14,258
1967-1988	4635	11,401	2422	14,610	4107	37,175

Note: Figures from 1981-1988 were previously in units of SDR.
Sources: IMF, Balance of Payments Yearbook, various issues. 1967-1980 data reproduced from Chia (1977), Table 2.

into ASEAN. Malaysia and Singapore were the most consistent, successful attractions for private direct investment between 1967 and 1988. FDI inflow into the Philippines has been on the rise recently due to the more stable political climate and improved economic performance.

Another interesting trend in international investment apart from growth rates and geographical distribution is the changing sectoral distribution. Investments in developing countries were previously concentrated in resource exploitation and infrastructure. These have declined with the increasing emphasis on investment in manufacturing and service activities. The "push" factor at work in this change is postwar economic nationalism, especially with regard to the ownership and control of natural resources. The "pull" factor is the launching of industrialization programs based often, at least initially, on import substitution. Some countries, starting with the NIEs, began to shift into export-oriented industrialization in the 1970s, away from production for the host-country market toward production for export to the source-country or third-country markets. Cheaper transportation costs as well as host-country incentives also led to more investment in the processing of industrial raw materials in the producing countries. In the service sector, transnational banks have invested abroad to be close to emerging markets in the developing countries.

Table 5. Japanese Direct Investment in ASEAN Countries by Sector, 1986.

(%)

	Indonesia	Malaysia	Philippines	Singapore	Thailand
Agriculture, fisheries	2.3	2.3	4.3	0.1	1.8
Mining	66.5	11.5	43.4	0.1	0.6
Manufacturing	27.2	66.7	40.4	60.2	70.1
Chemical industry	1.5	14.7	7.9	19.2	5.1
Ferrous & nonferrous metals	14.0	12.0	8.9	2.3	5.2
Banking, insurance	2.7	3.8	2.7	11.2	2.8
Other services	3.1	15.6	9.2	28.4	24.7
Total (US$ million)	8763	1283	913	2571	884

Source: Norbert Wagner. 1990. European investment in ASEAN. In: Soon Lee Ying (ed.). Foreign Direct Investment in ASEAN, 1990, Table 6, p. 167.

The sectoral pattern of Japanese investment in ASEAN shown in Table 5 indicates strong country-specific characteristics. In 1986, mining in both Indonesia and the Philippines accounted for 67% and 43%, respectively, of total Japanese investment in the two countries. Malaysia, Singapore, and Thailand, however, had their largest shares of Japanese investment in the manufacturing sector. While manufacturing investment was concentrated in the chemical industry in Malaysia and Singapore, it was concentrated in the textile industry in Thailand. Recently, there has been a new wave of Japanese investment in services in Singapore (39.6%), Thailand (27.5%), and Malaysia (19.4%).

The overall picture of Japanese and total investment in ASEAN appears commendable in terms of growth rates and levels. The contributions of such investments to ASEAN economic development are welcome, but several economists have noted their limited benefits in terms of employment, linkage effects, and foreign exchange earnings (Chew and Thambipillai 1981). Some might have given rise to negative effects such as environmental damage[7] or the potential danger of overdependence on Japan as a supplier and export market since further increases in Japanese investment would lead to even more trade dependence on that country (Djojohadikusumo 1976).[8] From the viewpoint of Malaysia, the critical question is: has Japanese investment been a useful vehicle for transmitting technology to ASEAN countries? In other words, has Japanese investment in ASEAN transferred technology by improving local technical competence (e.g., more or higher skills and training of local personnel), or by increasing local capability to absorb imported technology (e.g., more local R&D)?

Chew and Thambipillai cited a study by Chee and Lee (1979) which found that there is complete technology transfer and even acclimatization of technology in foreign investment in industries that utilize domestic resources but not necessarily in industries that rely on the domestic market and industries that are geared toward the world market.

Many studies have found that foreign firms do not engage in basic research in the host country, whereas they may conduct R&D on product design if the domestic market is substantial. Since this domestic market condition is not met for most products in ASEAN nations, it is not surprising that local R&D is insignificant in ASEAN (Ministry of Science and Technology of Singapore 1979).[9] On the other hand, an early study by Hirono (1969) on Japanese investment in Singapore covering the period up to 1966, when there were 20 manufacturing firms with Japanese affiliation, suggested that such firms tend to do a better job of imparting training to local technicians. The new products and new production processes brought into Singapore were "neither products nor techniques ... startlingly new by Japanese standards." Little effort was expended on improving production techniques through R&D activity. Another complaint often voiced about Japanese-affiliated firms in the ASEAN countries is their tendency to employ a large number of Japanese as compared to, for example, US or European subsidiaries. This is related to the fact that Japanese subsidiaries are reluctant to train local managerial and higher-level technical personnel. Yoshino (1976) argued that the Japanese practice of employing a high proportion of Japanese expatriates is due to the recent origin of Japanese overseas investment, language barriers between Japanese and ASEAN nationals, and the strong hierarchical relationships and tight teamwork characteristic of Japanese management style (Yoshino 1976).

TECHNICAL ASSISTANCE

Japanese overseas technical cooperation started in 1962 with the establishment of the Overseas Technical Cooperation Agency. In 1974 this agency was absorbed by the Japan International Cooperation Agency (JICA) together with the Japan Emigration Service and the Japan Overseas Agricultural Development Foundation. The functions of JICA include:

a) government-sponsored technical cooperation;
b) grant-aid cooperation promotion programs;
c) dispatch of Japan Overseas Cooperation volunteers (JOVCs);
d) the Development Cooperation Program for investment in and financing of development projects;
e) emigration services; and
f) recruitment and training of qualified Japanese experts for technical cooperation.

In 1987 JICA handled 62.8% of the total budget for the Japanese government's technical cooperation programs. Table 6 shows the percentage distribution of the agency's expenditures for 1987 and over the period 1954-1987 by region. The major portion went to Asia, and the biggest share of that to Southeast Asia, followed by Latin America and Africa.

Technical cooperation under JICA covers a wide spectrum, including light and heavy industries, chemical industry, transportation, and construction, as well as agriculture, fisheries, public administration, and management techniques. In 1987, the largest number of trainees came

Table 6. Japanese Technical Cooperation Expenses by Region (percentage distribution).

	1980	1987	1954-1980	1954-1987
Asia	48.8	49.1	52.4	49.6
ASEAN	(36.2)	(30.6)	(34.5)	(33.9)
Middle East	9.7	7.5	10.4	8.8
Africa	14.2	13.8	13.2	12.9
Latin America	21.5	22.1	17.5	22.0
Oceania	1.9	3.1	1.6	2.3
Europe } International organizations	1.9	1.3	1.2	1.4
Other	2.0	3.1	3.7	3.0
Total	100.0	100.0	100.0	100.0

Source: Japan International Cooperation Agency Annual Report, 1981 and 1988.

from Thailand (8.4%), followed closely by Indonesia (8.2%) and Malaysia (7.5%). The largest number of experts dispatched went to Indonesia (12.7%), followed by Thailand (11.4%). ASEAN trainees generally came from the human resources area. Other areas were manufacturing and public health and medicine (Thailand), agriculture and transportation (Indonesia), manufacturing and social infrastructure (Malaysia), agriculture and public administration (the Philippines), and commerce and trade and social infrastructure (Singapore).

Experts were dispatched to the agriculture, transport, and social infrastructure areas for Indonesia, while those in Thailand went to agriculture, human resources, and public health and medicine. The experts for the Philippines were distributed in agriculture, transportation, and public health and medicine. Malaysia had experts in human resources, manufacturing, and forestry. Singapore, which received the fewest trainees and experts, used its experts in human resources, science, culture, and transportation. Thus, the majority of Japanese technical assistance in the ASEAN countries has been in the public sector. The fact that technical cooperation programs have been continuing for a long time, are expanding, and have not generated controversy must indicate that they have generally been successful and appreciated.[10]

OTHER MODES OF TECHNOLOGY TRANSFER

The lack of data and information on other modes of technology transfer prevents any useful discussion of them. Joint ventures and licensing agreements are likely to become more important in the future as ASEAN countries gain local capability and experience enabling them to gain greater local mastery of imported technology. For example, an estimated 30% of the industries in Singapore in 1976 were involved in licensing agreements, 80% of which were know-how agreements (Chow 1977).

IMPLICATIONS OF TRENDS

FDI and technical cooperation are the two main modes of technology transfer not only between Japan and ASEAN but also between other advanced industrial nations and ASEAN. There has been an increasing volume of Japanese technology transfer via FDI and public-sector technical cooperation. While the latter appears satisfactory in nature and scope, ASEAN nations are less satisfied with the former.

There is no doubt that Japanese as well as other sources of foreign investment in ASEAN countries has had a very substantial effect on the industrial structure, on the composition of manufacturing output, and consequently also on trade in manufactured goods in ASEAN. To give just one example, in 1975 about 70% of Singapore's manufactured exports came from enterprises with foreign participation. Wholly foreign-owned firms and joint ventures contributed 84% of total export value. It is doubtful if Singapore's high growth rates in the late 1960s and 1970s could have been achieved without FDI. While the Singapore case may be a special one, most other ASEAN countries have similarly benefited to some extent.

While all this may be conceded, ASEAN countries generally feel that they have reached a stage of industrial development where they could use and absorb more and higher levels of technological know-how and skill, especially in the form of greater local involvement and participation. It is also crucial that they do so at this stage of their economic development to maintain the current growth momentum. For most ASEAN countries, the existing situation and trends will not be sufficient to move them up to the stage of the current NIEs without too long a delay.

A crucial element in trying to accelerate the pace of technology transfer has already been alluded to but not discussed. This is the creation of a conducive domestic environment and capability to absorb, nurture, and further develop transplanted technology. Both the Japanese and Korean experiences have demonstrated the critical role of this domestic preparation for receiving and building on imported technology. There is also no doubt that ASEAN countries need to concentrate more effort than in the past on this.

ASEAN ASPIRATIONS

ASEAN countries, with the exception of Singapore, are basically agrarian, primary commodity-exporting economies heavily dependent on the advanced industrial nations as markets for their resource-based exports and as suppliers of imported capital goods and consumer durables. This colonial type of trade relations exists even more clearly vis-à-vis Japan but is now beginning to undergo dynamic changes as ASEAN countries begin to gain comparative advantage in light manufactures based on labor-intensive, standardized technologies (Economic Society of Singapore 1982).

The major economic and social problems confronting the ASEAN countries are massive urban and rural unemployment and underemployment, unchecked population growth, low productivity, and excessive dependence on primary exports. To solve these interrelated problems, ASEAN countries believe they must industrialize and achieve economic modernization as rapidly as possible in order to assure their people the benefits of modern technology and to break the cycle of poverty and deprivation. In more specific terms, the target is to move away from being mere suppliers of primary commodities and a marketplace for foreign manufactured goods toward an industrial, modern economy. In international economic relations, this will require changing the vertical division of labor between ASEAN countries and advanced industrial nations based on interindustry trade into more horizontal division of labor based on intraindustry trade. It is believed that diversification into manufacturing of increasing sophistication will not only be consistent with the changing international comparative advantage but, by expanding employment and raising overall productivity, improve real living standards and mitigate if not eliminate excessive dependence on a narrow economic base. To achieve this broad set of objectives, the ability to use modern technology is an important contributing factor.

The above remarks apply generally to the ASEAN countries, even in the case of Singapore. However, due to the varying stages of economic and social development and the level and composition of resource endowments among ASEAN countries, the kind of technologies appropriate in each case needs to be further elaborated. For this purpose, it is fortunate that we are able to refer to the country papers presented at the 26th Consultative Committee Meeting of the Colombo Plan held in Nepal in late 1977 with its special topic on "The transfer and adaptation of technology" (Colombo Plan Bureau 1978). Furthermore, five ASEAN country papers (except Brunei) were produced by the respective ASEAN country research teams of the ASEAN-Japan Research Project. Each country paper highlighted its position with respect to the strategy of economic development and objectives of technology transfer (Chng and Hirono 1984). Based on those ASEAN-country papers, the following summarizes their perceptions with respect to technology transfer.

Indonesia

Indonesia recognizes "the need to further their capability in advanced research and science and to adopt advanced technology, at least in selected areas" (Chng and Hirono 1984).[11] The areas specifically mentioned were "geology, geophysics and geochemistry, biology and biochemistry, metallurgy and mineral technology." The purpose of introducing technology changes in Indonesia is "to accelerate the pace of economic progress and development and it is therefore a necessary and urgent case that the government should design and formulate a science and technology policy as part of the national effort in overall development. Suitable policies must be determined on the transfer, expansion, and application of technology for the sake of development consistent with the capacity and internal conditions of the country."

Major weaknesses in scientific research and technology development in Indonesia in the past have been identified as the "fragmentation of research organizations and duplication of activities," and "the lack of qualified research workers." It is hoped that the setting up of the National Centre for Research, Science and Technology in 1975 would improve more effective coordination of research activities.

Several possible priority areas of technical cooperation were identified. In the agricultural sector, these involve Indonesia's rice intensification program, the production, processing, and marketing of tropical fruits and vegetables, the promotion of fresh- and seawater fisheries, and the improvement of tropical pastures to develop livestock farming. Technical cooperation to improve management and exploitation of Indonesia's vast forest resources is high on the priority list.

In industrial areas, five industrial groups (pulp and paper, salt, glass, agricultural implements and machinery, textiles) are listed. In addition, Indonesia favors general technical cooperation to develop small-scale industries and the processing of nondurable (i.e., perishable) agricultural products.

Malaysia

Malaysia strongly stresses the importance of technology transfer as a catalyst for accelerated development of developing countries. It considers the existing rate of technology transfer "not rapid enough to meet the aspirations of the developing countries for more speedy growth," deplores the unfavorable terms and conditions of the transfer, and applauds international efforts "urging the developed countries in creating environments conducive for the inflow of technology into the developing countries of fair and equitable conditions taking into account the specific development requirements of these recipient countries" (Chng and Hirono 1984). The Malaysian country paper went on to discuss the necessity of establishing a new set of international norms to bring about a more equitable sharing of the benefits from the transfer of technology and the need to evolve a national policy framework to exercise discrimination to ensure the appropriateness of imported technologies and to consider the question of absorption and adaptation of those technologies. But it did not go into any detail regarding possible priority areas to be emphasized for technical cooperation.

The Philippines

Based on a study by the Board of Investment in the early 1970s on licensing agreements, it was felt that "strict government policies are needed to strengthen the position of the country in three important aspects of technology: the cost of the technology; the need for and the appropriateness of the technology; and the restrictive provisions inherent in contracts covering technology transfer." In addition, "the diffusion of technologies to the rural areas is a process fraught with" such additional problems as "a dearth in the expertise needed to support technology transfer activities," risk aversion, "problem of tapping appropriate financial markets needed for the option/adaption of new technologies," etc.

In discussing the new pattern of technology transfer, the country paper identified the main element that should be in the national technology policy, namely, the question of appropriateness "to the needs of the country's environment insofar as economic, social and other aspects are concerned." The policy objectives should include "strengthening the bargaining power and acquiring the ability to obtain the best terms and conditions and to link imported technology with the development of local needs," increasing "the capacity to apply technology both imported and indigenous," increasing "demand for indigenous technology," and creating "the ability to involve technologies directly relevant to development objectives."

In terms of possible priority areas of technical cooperation, the Philippines sees potential benefits from the establishment of a central regional body for ASEAN "that will oversee, supervise, monitor and coordinate a network of technological information systems" possibly "in the pattern of Technonet Asia, or an International Development Research Centre" Other ideas include the setting up of "centres of knowledge on appropriate technologies," "a technological assessment project," and "a scientific and technological resource inventory survey." With regard to areas for R&D cooperation, the following broad areas were identified:

a) agricultural production;
b) fisheries development;
c) industrial development and waste utilization;
d) small- and medium-scale industries development;
e) technical manpower planning; and

f) self-help technology for the rural population aimed at maximizing self-sufficiency as far as food, clothing, shelter, and basic community needs are concerned.

Singapore

The Singapore country paper stated that it was not a policy paper but "an attempt to present a number of options vis-à-vis the main theme of the draft outline paper, which is that technical cooperation between developing countries could lead to a more effective and efficient transfer of technology." It confined itself to the problems of technology transfer through technical cooperation among developing countries.[12]

The paper stated that the most important modes of technology transfer to Singapore appear to be:

a) direct foreign investment, including joint ventures;
b) technical assistance programs, training of students, technical, and professional staff, and employment of external "experts";
c) licensing and commercial know-how contracts;
d) import of machinery and equipment;
e) exposure of technical personnel to specialized processes through technical cooperation programmes; and
f) access to sources or centers of published technical information.

It went on to predict that "Joint ventures will become increasingly significant in Singapore's economy and the Government is actively encouraging joint ventures not only in manufacturing but also in shipping, banking, and other service industries."

Concerning the host of possible problems relating to conventional modes of technology transfer, it commented "appropriate technology can be identified, R&D infrastructures can be built up, information centres can be established; administrative weaknesses can be strengthened—measures which can all be undertaken by developing countries." However, it maintained that "the case for more effective technical cooperation programmes among developing countries as vehicles for technology transfer is still valid and should be actively encouraged for the following advantages:

a) in many cases, similarities in cultural background, resulting in better understanding of each other's styles and modus operandi;
b) lower cost of expertise in using "experts" from developing countries;
c) transfer of technology can often be a two-way process;
d) appropriate technology levels [are] easily ascertained and transferred at suitable levels; and

e) [there are] better understanding and awareness of each other's constraints, and limitations."

The paper also saw merit in effecting technical cooperation through "the creation of twinning arrangements between technical institutions (on a bilateral basis) or through networking (on a multilateral basis)" in order to tap "each other's strength and resources for mutual benefit." It suggested the following options for Colombo Plan members:

a) establish a fund to serve as seed money to enable technical institutions from developing countries to liaise and assist one another;
b) establish a network of industrial research institutes to permit informal interaction between key personnel and to identify technical programmes for cooperation.

It considered it "premature to discuss areas for technical cooperation in research and development."

Pang (1976), however, called "for an upgrading of the technological sophistication of the industrial sector and the development of a brain services centre." According to Pang (1976), priority areas were firms manufacturing engines and turbines, assembly parts and components, optical instruments, and other industries that provide forward and backward linkages to big companies. The key element in the strategy is seen to be the creation of a pool of experienced, trained manpower to absorb foreign technology and the capability to generate new knowledge.

Singapore has always adopted a liberal, open-door attitude toward foreign investors. This meant "no restriction on the nationality of business ownership and employment of qualified personnel, no import duty on parts and materials, and no control on the repatriation of profits and capital" (Economic Development Board 1987). Occasionally the government will modify the details of Singapore's economic policies to suit the needs of the country but it strives to maintain a fundamental policy pertaining to a conducive business environment. In 1988, Singapore had about 3400 subsidiaries and joint ventures of which more than 600 were multinational companies with large manufacturing operations.

In addition to success in attracting foreign investors to invest in Singapore, the recent move to encourage multinationals to use the republic as their regional corporate headquarters is an aspect of the government's effort to promote the development of services as another engine of growth—the other being the manufacturing sector. Some of the companies that have already been awarded operational headquarters (OHQ) status now enjoy financial incentives, including a concessionary 10% tax on management fees, interest, and royalty income. From 1986 to 1989 OHQ status companies included companies from the USA, UK, Singapore, Canada, Japan, Australia, New Zealand, Germany, and France (Economic Development Board various years; Teo 1989; Boey 1988; *Business Times* 1989; Chia 1989; Morais 1989).

Being the first Japanese company to be awarded OHQ status, Sony has set an example for other Japanese firms to follow. Fujikura and Omron are two more companies that have since joined the OHQ "club." Other Japanese enterprises interested in the scheme include Asahi Singapore, Kajima Corporation, and Mitsuboshi Belting Singapore (34). Among those who are setting up regional headquarters in Singapore are Mitsui Toatsu Chemicals (Kagda 1988), Yokogawa Electric Corporation (*Straits Times* July 25 1988), Fujitsu (Tsang 1989), and Matsushita, the largest Japanese investor in Singapore to data (Economic Development Board 1988). These companies' effort to upgrade and expand their operations in Singapore positively reflect investor confidence in the republic and the success of the government in developing Singapore into a total business center.

Thailand

The Thai country paper highlighted "the need for introduction and application of technology that can be meaningfully adapted in the indigenous context" and focused on the question of selection and choice of appropriate type of technology. Imported technologies must be adapted to take into account the "social, economic, political, and geographical pattern of one's environment with a view to satisfying the needs and demands of each developing country."

The main modes of existing technology transfer were identified as:

a) imported capital and intermediate goods which range from machinery, equipment, commodities, blueprints, process formulae, and other kinds of proprietary patents, also encompassing ready-made imported merchandise from foreign-based factories or the factories themselves equipped with foreign technicians and technical know-how; and
b) imported technology in the form of technical assistance (experts, equipment and training courses).

The national body to coordinate the work of agencies responsible for the transfer of technology was set up in 1976 in the form of a small division within the National Economic and Social Development Board which works in conjunction with an interdepartmental Committee on

Development of Industrial Technology established a year later. Among the internal shortcomings were high unemployment at the technical and vocational level (40% of graduates in 1974), underutilization of irrigation capacity, low level of expenditure on R&D (0.2% of GNP), and the lack of research on indigenous technology.

A national plan for the application and development of science and technology was formulated as an integral part of the Fourth National Economic and Social Development Plan to serve as general guidelines. The chief objective of generating and using science and technology was stated to be to "narrow down the income gap between the rich and the poor and at the same time accelerate national economic progress." The need for institutional mechanisms at the national and regional levels to facilitate information clearing and promote and coordinate activities was stressed. A list of existing research areas in science and technology projects was provided but no possible priority areas were identified.

FUTURE PROSPECTS

It is clear from the above that not all ASEAN countries in the mid-1970s had a comprehensive national plan for science and technology. This is probably still true for most today. This should be remedied because it is a well-documented fact that the market for technology is subject to serious distortions in favor of suppliers. Government intervention of one form or another is desirable especially to redress the weak bargaining power of the recipient countries. Government initiative is also required to provide a receptive and supportive domestic environment to absorb, diffuse, and adapt imported technologies. Okita and Tamura (1975) reflected on the useful lessons of the Japanese experience:

> The process of the transfer of technology is analogous to the transplantation of a living plant. In order to sustain transplanted technology, it is necessary to provide a receptive environment in the form of a sound industrial base including adequate supply of energy, raw materials, capital and skilled labour, and the existence of related industries.
>
> If the available resources of a country are limited, the first preliminary step for a successful transfer of technology will be to select a certain area of industry where limitations are minimal or can be easily rectified and concentrate all the efforts to provide an adequate environment for that industry.

One should include an appropriate price structure "at least headed in the right direction" as an important element in a receptive domestic environment (Hughes 1975).

A useful framework to discuss and to evaluate the prospects for transfer of technology to ASEAN either from Japanese or other international sources is a systems analysis framework. Thinking of technology transfer as a continuing process, the purpose of the exercise is to identify the weak links in the chain. The main elements of the system are:

a) what is actually transferred (i.e., the technologies);
b) the mode of transfer;
c) the absorptive capabilities of the recipient enterprise/country;
d) the capabilities and motivation of the supplier enterprise/country; and
e) the technology gap between the supplier and recipient (Asian Productivity Organization 1976).

Under (a), one should ask whether the technologies to be transferred are useful and appropriate, in other words, whether the supplier has the kind of technologies the recipient requires. Under (b), one should ask whether the appropriate modes and the logistics required by each mode have been adopted and effectively utilized. Point (c) has already been discussed and should be considered a critical link for successful transfer. Under (d), one should pose the question whether, in addition to having the appropriate technologies for transfer, the supplier is willing and able to effect the transfer. In the case of proprietary type technology, the incentive to impart and the proper inducement or compensation to be made for transfer lie at the heart of the problem. Finally, the technology gap or the differences in the levels of technical competence of the two parties involved will determine the time and resources needed to effect transfer.

The task of evaluating all these factors in the ASEAN/Japanese context is clearly a daunting one and would require much more expert, country-specific information than is available to us. We therefore conclude with some general comments.

On point (a), there should be a consensus that Japan does have the types of technology that ASEAN countries can usefully absorb. On point (c), one would have to consider the different levels existing in each ASEAN country. In addition to the average national level, one must also allow for possible variation in specific sectors. As a result of past effort and investments in physical and social infrastructure, the level should be rising rapidly in all ASEAN countries. However, much more could be done to upgrade the domestic absorptive capability.

The remaining links (b), (d), and (e) are even more difficult to assess. ASEAN countries' dissatisfaction with the existing modes based on FDI and to some extent on joint ventures has already been indicated. ASEAN countries clearly welcome a wider range of choices in the mode of technology transfer, especially in the private sector. The issue is linked to the capabilities and motivation of the suppliers of technology. At the same time, the modes actually adopted may be influenced by the extent of the technology gap between each ASEAN country and Japan. It would seem therefore that ASEAN countries would do well to improve link (c) as this would greatly strengthen their bargaining position and allow them to select the modes more conducive to achieving a smoother transfer. Technical assistance and cooperation to speed up the upgrading process should be accorded high priority.

According to Singapore's former Prime Minister Lee Kuan Yew, the future of ASEAN lies not in growing bigger but in upgrading the economies of member countries to produce higher value-added, information and knowledge-based goods and services. Through a successful export-oriented strategy, Singapore is earlier down the road to economic development than the other ASEAN countries. Becoming the overseas headquarters of multinationals, Singapore can help accelerate regional growth by encouraging multinationals to extend their investments into neighboring economies.

As proposed by Singapore's Prime Minister Goh Chok Tong, the "triangle of growth within ASEAN" concept encompasses the linkages between Singapore and two of its closest neighbors, Indonesia and Malaysia. Instead of individually competing for capital, the three areas can combine their comparative advantages to enhance their attractiveness. Both Batam (Indonesia) and Johor (Malaysia) "could contribute land, gas, water and labour for industrial development, while Singapore could provide management expertise" (Henson 1990). Such economic cooperation would boost bilateral relations. Batam Industrial Park, a joint venture between Singaporean and Indonesian companies, has already been constructed. In addition, Japan's Sumitomo Electric Industries became the first multinational to set up a garment factory at the park, thus incorporating the concept of the Batam-Johor-Singapore growth triangle (Henson 1990).

Notes

1. With about 98% of research and development expenditures originating in the advanced countries of Europe, the USA, and Japan, the already wide technological gap is likely to grow wider in the future unless developing countries redouble their efforts to

close it. See Singer (1970).

2. Policy makers in Singapore felt that it was feasible to achieve 8-10% real growth rates in the 1980s on the basis of a 6-8% growth rate in labor productivity, presumably via enhanced efforts to absorb and utilize new technologies through human capital investment, greater mechanization, automation, and computerization.

3. According to OECD (1982), "... transfer of technology covers two separate situations: the transfer of industrial capacities, and the transfer of capabilities to master, adapt and further develop imported technology."

4. Suppliers of equipment and material, buyers of output, and experience acquired by personnel through previous overseas employment were found to be more important than licensing and technical assistance as sources of process technology in a survey of 112 exporting Korean firms. Concerning sources of information for product innovation, buyers of output and overseas travel by staff were cited as the two main sources. See Westphal, Rhee, and Parsell (1981).

5. The importance of creating a receptive domestic environment for effective absorption of imported technology is shown by the Japanese and Korean experience. For a short account of the Japanese experience, see Okita and Tamura (1975).

6. In Korea, it was found that the different phases or modes of technology transfer occur simultaneously. Thus, FDI or licensing are not important in industries such as plywood, textiles, and apparel which use technologies that can be characterized as mature. FDI is important for acquiring the latest technology as well as market access in the case of electronics and certain chemicals because the technology involved is changing rapidly worldwide. On the other hand, licensing is used in acquiring modern shipbuilding technology. See Westphal, Rhee, and Parsell (1981).

7. One documented complaint of this nature is reported in Morris (1975).

8. For a discussion of the related issue of the comparative appropriateness of Japanese-style investment to conditions of developing countries such as trade-creating complementarity, less capital-intensiveness, etc., see Kojima (1977).

9. The total R&D expenditure incurred in both the public and private sectors in Singapore in 1978 was S$37.2 million, or a mere 0.23% of GDP. See Ministry of Science and Technology of Singapore (1978).

10. For a more detailed discussion of one ASEAN nation, see Loh (1975).

11. This and subsequent quotations come from the respective ASEAN country papers in Chng and Hirono (1984) unless otherwise stated.

12. The exact title of the special topic chosen for discussion is identified in the introduction as "Problems relating to the transfer and adaptation of technology to and among member countries of the Colombo Plan region with special reference to technical cooperation among developing countries."

References

Asian Productivity Organization. 1976. *International Transfer of Technology*. Tokyo: Asian Productivity Organization.

Boey, Kit Yin. 1988. Fujikura subsidiary awarded OHQ status. *Business Times* (Singapore): August 30.

Chee, Peng Lim and Poh Ping Lee. 1979. The role of Japanese direct investment in Malaysia. In: Chew, Soon Beng and Pushpa Thambipillai (eds.), *Japan and Southeast Asia. Occasional Paper 60*. Singapore: Institute of Southeast Asian Studies.

Chew, Soon Beng and Pushpa Thambipillai. 1981. Japan and Southeast Asia. In: Pohl, Manfred (ed.), *Japan 1980/81, Politics and Economics*. Tokyo: Maruzen Asia, pp. 151-194.

Chia, William. 1989. Molex Inc. awarded OHQ status in Singapore. *Business*

Times (Singapore), March 28.
Chng, M.K. and R. Hirono (eds.), 1984. *ASEAN-Japan Industrial Co-operation: An Overview*. Singapore: Institute of Southeast Asian Studies.
Chow, Lai Fong. 1977. *Issues in Technology Transfer with Particular Reference to Patents, Technology Licensing and Technical Cooperation—The Singapore Experience*. Singapore: University of Singapore Press.
Djojohadikusumo, Sumitro. 1976. Resources, Southeast Asia and Japan. In: *Japan-Indonesia Relations in the Context of Regionalism in Asia*. Jakarta: Centre for Strategic and International Studies, pp. 111-137.
Dunning, J.H. 1982. Towards a taxonomy of technology transfer and possible impacts on OECD countries. In: OECD (ed.), *North/South Technology Transfer: The Adjustments Ahead*. Paris: OECD.
Economic Society of Singapore (eds.), 1982. ASEAN external economic relations. In: *Proceedings of 5th Conference of Federation of ASEAN Economics Association*. Singapore: Chopmen.
Economic Development Board of Singapore. 1987. Are you missing out on something? Trade and Industry Minister urges Italian and German business leaders to look closer at merits of investing in Singapore. *Singapore Investment News,* May/June, p. 1.
Economic Development Board of Singapore. *Annual Reports,* various years.
Economic Development Board of Singapore. 1988. Singapore picked for more Asia-Pacific manufacturing and service activities. *Investment News,* October, p. 6.
Gruber, William H. and Donald G. Marquis. 1969. Research on the human factor in the transfer of technology. In: Gruber, W.H. and D.G. Marquis (eds.), *Factors in Transfer of Technology*. Cambridge, Mass.: MIT Press.
Henson, Bertha. 1990. Chok Tong gives Johore government a concept paper. *Straits Times,* May 24.
Hirono, Ryokichi. 1969. Japanese investment. In: Hughes, H. and P.S. You (eds.), *Foreign Investment and Industrialization in Singapore*. Canberra: Australian National University Press.
Hughes, Helen. 1975. Comments on Logorreta's paper. In: Kojima, K. and M.S. Wionczek (eds.), *Transfer of Technology Transfer in Pacific Economic Development*. Tokyo: Japanese Economic Research Centre.
Kagda, Shoeb. 1988. Japanese chemical firm to open regional HQ in Singapore. *Business Times* (Singapore), April 21, p. 18.
Kojima, Kiyoshi. 1977. *Japan and a New World Economic Order*. London: Croom Helm.
Konz, Leo E. 1980. *The International Transfer of Commercial Technology*. New York: Arno Press.
Loh, Wei Leng. 1975. Transfer of technology via technical assistance to Malaysia. 1971-74. In: Fredericks, Leo (ed.). *The New International Economic Order and UNCTAD IV: The Implication for Malaysia*. Kuala Lumpur: Malaysian Economic Association.
Ministry of Science and Technology of Singapore. 1979. Survey of R&D activities in Singapore, 1978. Unpublished report.
Morais, Walton. 1989. Thomson Consumer gets OHQ status for regional HQs. *Business Times* (Singapore), December 6, p. 2.
Morris, C. 1975. The economic dimension of national interest: Japan's influence in Southeast Asia. Claremont: Ph.D. thesis.

OECD. 1982. *North/South Technology Transfer: The Adjustments Ahead*. Paris: OECD.

Okita, Saburo and Shuji Tamura. 1975. Transfer of technology and Japanese experience. In: Kojima, K. and Wionczek, M.S. (eds.), *Technology Transfer in Pacific Economic Development*. Tokyo: Japanese Economic Research Centre.

Pang, Eng Fong. 1976. UNCTAD technology transfer proposals and their implications for Singapore. In: Pang, E.F. and Kit Boey Chow (eds.), *The New Economic Order, UNCTAD and Singapore*. Singapore: Singapore Economic Society and Economic Research Centre.

Singer, Hans. 1970. Dualism revisited: A new approach to the problems of dual society in developing countries. *Journal of Development Studies,* vol. VII (1), October.

Straits Times. 1988. Japanese computer control systems maker seeks OHQ status. *Straits Times,* July 25, p. 14.

Teo, Anna. 1989. EDB aims to grant six OHQ awards a year. *Business Times* (Singapore), January 16, p. 20.

Tsang, Jeffrey. 1989. Fujitsu makes Singapore regional HQ. *Business Times* (Singapore), December 8, p. 3.

Westphal, Larry E., Yung W. Rhee, and Garry Parsell. 1981. Korean industrial competence: Where it came from. *World Bank Staff Working Paper* No. 469, July.

Yoshino, M.Y. 1976. *Japan's Multinational Enterprises*. Cambridge, Mass.: Harvard University Press.

5 Japanese Technology and the New International Division of Knowledge in Asia

Tessa Morris-Suzuki

Australian National University

INTRODUCTION

Like ripples spreading outward on a pond, Asia's industrial revolution continually expands its boundaries. First it was the East Asian "little dragons," South Korea, Taiwan, and Hong Kong, which appeared to be following Japan along the path of industrial growth. Now the nations of ASEAN, above all Singapore, Malaysia, and Thailand, have come to be regarded as "third-generation Japans," rapidly moving into those labor-intensive branches of industry which the more advanced Asian economies are abandoning (Tsuneishi 1990).

Just as the newly industrializing Asian economies are commonly seen as pursuing a path of development first charted by Japan, so it is equally common to suggest that there are particularly useful lessons that they can learn from Japan's experience of absorbing and adapting industrial technology. Japan, it is argued, "shares the same Asian culture," and hence has encountered similar problems in its confrontation with Western industrial technology (Toba 1981). As a famous (or notorious) borrower of foreign technology, Japan is also presented as a particularly appropriate model for contemporary industrializing nations, which likewise rely heavily on imported techniques. In the words of the prominent US scholar of technology Nathan Rosenberg, "the conditions which are necessary for the transfer of technology are not the same as the conditions which give birth to new technologies.... Of course, Japan provides the classic example of rapid industrialization based on the transfer of technology. Thus, Japan's experience not only has a profound importance in its own right. It also has major policy implications for developing nations" (Rosenberg 1987).

In this paper I reassess that approach to economic development in East and Southeast Asia. The notion of deriving lessons from Japan for contemporary industrializing nations is based on an implicit vision of "industrialization" as a linear process in which nations (some starting earlier and others later) pass through a series of successive stages to reach a common goal. As far as technology is concerned, the path of progress is seen as being one where nations gradually move from being imitators and importers of technology to being adaptors and eventually innovators in their own right. The argument that I shall put forward here is that this is too simple a vision of the course of "technological progress." A closer look at Japan's economic development suggests the need for a more complex analysis of changes in technological capacity. From the perspective of this analysis it will become evident that processes of development in contemporary Asian industrializing countries are very different from those that occurred in Japan itself, and are leading to a quite different pattern of technological dynamism: a pattern that might be described as "the new international division of knowledge."

FROM IMPORT TO INNOVATION: THE TRADITIONAL MODEL OF TECHNOLOGICAL CHANGE IN JAPAN

The popular image of Japanese development suggests that Japan began as a borrower and imitator of foreign technology, and has only recently begun to emerge as an innovator in its own right. Some scholars have presented this image in extreme terms. The economist Arghiri Emmanuel, for example, argues that Japan succeeded technologically because it "imitated, copied, plagiarised and pirated ... energetically and up to the limits of legality" (Emmanuel 1982).

A more widely held perspective, however, depicts Japan as a borrower, but as one who successfully modified and adapted foreign techniques to its own needs. As Anders Diehl puts it, "The Japanese had to build up a solid industrial base from the destruction of the Second World War. The nation rallied around a common objective to reach the standard of living, whatever that is, of the western industrialised countries. The best policy to reach this objective was to learn from these countries and do what they had done, improving what could be improved" (Diehl 1984). It is only in the past decade or so, according to Diehl, that Japan has had to confront the problem of shifting from being a modifier of imported ideas to being a creator of original inventions.

From this point of view, the chief lesson of Japan's experience for today's industrializing countries is seen as being that the successful import of technology can, in time, provide the basis for the formation of a strong independent technological capacity. The economist and former Japanese Foreign Minister Okita Saburo, for example, suggests that the contemporary developing nations should seek to imitate Japan's success in choosing and adapting foreign techniques to meet domestic needs (Okita 1980). By a strategy of careful selection, and by "depacking" technology into component parts that could readily be absorbed by local technicians, Japan (according to Okita) ensured that imported techniques were widely adopted throughout industry: "In order to avoid creating foreign enclaves by importing plants and equipment, it is sometimes desirable to 'depack' technology. This will enable the imported technology to spread widely into the national economy. The development of small industry is an essential factor for sound industrialization. Japanese industry's current strength depends very much on the numerous small enterprises which work as subcontractors for large companies or compete independently in the marketplace" (Okita 1989). The implication is that other industrializing nations, by following a similar strategy, can ensure that imported technology "trickles down" to local small firms, and can thus upgrade their whole industrial structure, as Japan has done, to a point where they too may rival contemporary Japan's technological might.

AN ALTERNATIVE VERSION OF THE JAPANESE MODEL

The image of Japan's technological development outlined above certainly has some validity. There can be no doubt that careful selection, modification, and depacking of foreign technology played a vital role in the rapid industrialization of Japan. At the same time, however, it can be argued that this is only one part of the story of Japan's technological evolution, or indeed of the process of technological change as a whole.

The important point to emphasize here is that the acquisition of technology[1] from overseas can take any one of a number of forms:

1) It may simply involve the introduction of a new production process from overseas in the form of imported machinery, blueprints, etc. If the imported process is operated and controlled by foreigners, it will add to the nation's industrial output, but will not necessarily improve local skills and know-how, and it is likely that a large share of the profits generated by increased production will be repatriated overseas.

2) A somewhat more far-reaching form of technology acquisition is the development of local capacity to operate or control imported

production systems. At the most basic level, this simply involves the ability of workers to run imported machinery (2a), but at a more advanced level it also implies the ability to supervise and manage the production process and to repair and maintain equipment (2b).

3) Once acquired techniques are fully absorbed, local technicians may be able to modify and adapt them to suit the changing demands of the market or the changing supply of factors of production.

4) Adaptation cannot in practice be rigidly demarcated from innovation. At a certain point, however, fine tuning of production processes may lead to changes that are novel enough to be recognized as innovations in their own right. Broadly speaking, inventions can be divided into those which create new variants of existing processes or products (such as more powerful silicon chips) (4a) and those which create radically new products (such as the concept of the silicon chip itself) (4b).[2]

In addition to these four categories, which essentially represent the "top-down" introduction and assimilation of more sophisticated techniques from overseas, there is also a fifth, often neglected, form of technological acquisition which involves "bottom-up" modification of indigenous technology:

5) In this form of technology acquisition, basic scientific and technological ideas imported from abroad are used by local producers as a means of increasing the productivity of existing indigenous techniques. (For example, knowledge of chemistry may be used to analyze and improve traditional dyestuffs, etc.)

Industrialization inevitably involves the acquisition of technology in one or all of the forms outlined above. But the five forms of technology acquisition are not equally evident in all countries at similar stages of industrialization. Instead, each country has its own particular pattern of acquisition, which will be influenced by factors like the industrial structure of the economy, the degree of reliance on foreign capital, the export dependence of the economy, and local levels of education. It is particularly important to notice that the fifth form of technology acquisition means that, in traditional craft-based industries, active and deliberate innovation may be as important as the imitation of foreign techniques even in the early stages of industrialization.

Looking at Japanese industrialization before World War II, it is evident that several sorts of technological change were occurring simultaneously. On the one hand, Japan was acquiring foreign technological knowledge through the processes described as types 1, 2, and 3, that is, through importing techniques, learning how to operate and maintain them, and adapting those techniques to the particular circumstances of the Japanese economy. Japanese firms were able to develop this adaptive capacity relatively quickly, both because of the rather high levels of education and technical skill within Japan, and because the technologies imported (particularly in areas like the textile industry) were fairly simple. Machines such as the power loom could be taken apart and examined by Japanese technicians, who were then able to construct simplified local versions using cheaper raw materials (Nakaoka 1986). Even in more sophisticated areas like the chemicals industry, Japanese engineers in the 1920s and 1930s were able to devise modified, less capital-intensive versions of Western production systems.

On the other hand, however, Japan was also simultaneously modifying indigenous techniques through the process described as type 5. Rather than simply seeing Japan as going from being an imitator and adaptor to being an innovator of technology, therefore, we need to recognize the role of innovation in indigenous technology as a basis for the development of innovative capacity. Even in the earliest stages of industrialization, it should be noted, Japanese inventors were actively putting forward new ideas for patent protection. As the historian Uchida Hoshimi observed, some 23,000 patents were granted between 1885 (when the first patent law was introduced) and the end of the Meiji Era (1912), most to Japanese inventors, and the majority of those to improvements or innovations in traditional industries such as silk farming, printing, and saké brewing (Uchida 1990).

The process of bottom-up innovation and technological change in traditional industries was particularly important because it helped Japan gradually to acquire an infrastructure of inventive capability that was to support the later push toward innovation in advanced technologies. This infrastructure was reinforced by institutional developments within Japan. Whereas the import of advanced foreign technology was mainly the work of central government and large corporations, the upgrading of technology in traditional industry was achieved mostly through the efforts of small enterprises, often assisted by local authorities. In the 1930s Japan already had several dozen local research laboratories established by prefectural governments and devoted to encouraging technological change and technological innovation in traditional industrial sectors.

By this stage, traditionally based inventions were beginning to be joined by more sophisticated innovations. A modified diesel engine for small boats and a magnetic alloy of nickel and aluminum were among Japanese inventions that were granted patents in several industrialized countries during the 1930s. Between 1928 and 1932 just under 24,000 patents were granted in Japan, of which 66% went to Japanese inventors (*Japan-Manchukuo Year Book* 1939). The relatively low representation of foreigners might be attributed to the rise of nationalistic and xenophobic economic policies during the 1930s, but it is significant that the figure is similar for the postwar era of rapid growth, during which the import of technology was at its height (66% of the 17,800 patents issued in 1965, for example, were granted to Japanese citizens) (Kagaku Gijutsu Cho 1983). The prewar experience, both of adapting imported technology and of upgrading indigenous techniques, therefore helped to lay the foundations for the expansion of innovative activity in leading edge industries during the second half of the twentieth century. By 1960 Japan already had some 86,000 scientific and technical researchers (or about 93 per 100,000 population) and possessed an institutional basis for the very large expansion of corporate research which was to occur during the high growth era and beyond.

A significant feature of this bottom-up innovation was its role in helping small firms in Japan to adapt to technological change, and in many cases to become sources of parts and supplies for the modern industrial sector. Although some small subcontracting firms "spun off" from large industrial enterprises, taking with them modified pieces of imported know-how, others developed from a small-scale, traditional basis. A good example is to be found in the ceramics industry, where some enterprises in the early twentieth century used traditional knowledge of porcelain technology as a basis for developing the production of ceramic industrial components (such as electrical insulators). The spread of technological change throughout Japanese industry, therefore, was not simply the result of a trickle down of imported know-how from large to small firms, but was also made possible by an indigenous innovative process within traditional industry.

THE DIVISION OF LABOR AND ITS TECHNOLOGICAL IMPLICATIONS

The development of an ability, not just to acquire and operate imported techniques (what we have termed technological acquisition types 1 and 2), but also to modify and innovate (technological acquisition types 3, 4, and 5) plays an important part in the industrialization process. For one thing, in the process of modifying imported techniques or adapting and refining traditional know-how, it is often possible to create hybrid technologies that make profitable use of locally available resources. For countries in the early stages of industrialization, this generally means creating techniques that are more labor intensive and less technically complex than those used in the developed world. It should be emphasized that these "appropriate technologies" are not always benign in terms of their social effects. Labor-intensive forms of cotton spinning in Japan, for example, were profitable because they took advantage of the low pay and very hard work of women factory hands. Locally developed chemical technologies, like those introduced by the Chisso Corporation before and during World War II were also designed for a social environment that lacked health and safety regulations (Ui 1976). There can be no doubt, however, of their significance in promoting growth and supporting the expansion of technological capacity within Japan. Ability to innovate in more advanced areas of technology may give local enterprises a lead in expanding industries, and thus a strong position in world markets. Besides, as Richard Nelson observed, research and development activities are important, not only in generating major technological breakthroughs, but also in enabling domestic enterprises to keep abreast of worldwide technological developments (Nelson 1990).

From this perspective, it might seem that the development of innovative capacity in Japan has significant lessons for present-day industrializing Asian countries. I would suggest, however, that the main point to be emphasized is the very great difference that exists between the circumstances of Japan's industrialization and those of the contemporary Asian industrial revolution. Rather than using Japan as a model for emulation, therefore, I should like to use the *contrasts* between Japan and the Asian NIEs (including the ASEAN nations) as a basis for highlighting some features of technological change in contemporary Asia.

The most obvious, and often remarked, contrasts concern technology gaps and reliance on foreign capital. In the first place, the gulf between the leading edge technology of the most developed nations and the traditional techniques of the least developed is now much greater than it was when Japan embarked on its industrialization 100 years ago. Second, while Japan pursued a deliberate policy of avoiding dependence on overseas finance during its industrialization, all the rapidly industrializing Asian nations today have encouraged inflows of foreign direct investment (Shishida 1981). In the case of South Korea, for example, it was estimated in 1978 that 19.5% of manufacturing output and 22.7% of exports were produced by subsidiaries of foreign multinational companies (*Tsusho Hakusho* 1986). The large-scale presence of foreign capital means that a substantial share of technology transfer takes place within the structure of multinational enterprises, rather than through the licensing of technology to independent local firms. In Thailand, 80% of all technology transfer agreements in 1982 were made by local subsidiaries or affiliates of foreign firms (Tsuneishi 1990). As a result, it may be difficult for industrializing economies today to imitate the adaptation of imported technology which was a characteristic feature of Japan's industrial development.

I would argue, however, that an even greater constraint on technological independence comes from the contemporary international division of labor. Industrialization in East and Southeast Asia today has been described as being part of the emerging process of "peripheral intermediation": a process that can be defined as "the production of goods and services in a given country, *predominantly* utilizing inputs from *abroad* for the *principal* purpose of *export* to other countries" (Mirza 1986). The main characteristics of peripheral intermediation, in other words, are the increasingly international nature of production and the complex division of labor, in which a large share of international trade is made up of parts, components, and other semimanufactured goods. The outstanding example of this international system of production is, of course, provided by the electronics industry, although other branches of machinery manufacture (such as car production) also demonstrate similar features.

The pattern of industrialization in Japan was one that placed relatively heavy reliance on the domestic market. Although Japan's export dependence rose sharply in the interwar years, exports never exceeded 24% of GDP (Nakamura 1983), and by the 1950s the ratio had fallen to around 11%. Moreover, the Japanese economy was a classical "processing economy," where raw materials were imported, processed, and then exported either as basic semimanufactures like silk and cotton yarn or as finished manufactured goods. Until the 1950s these were largely consumer goods, but from then onward the export of machinery expanded rapidly. Until very recently, however, that machinery was normally wholly domestically made, with the semimanufactured inputs being supplied by local firms.

Table 1. Ratio of Exports to GNP, Various Asian Countries, 1988 (%).

South Korea	40.4
Taiwan	49.0
Thailand	29.0
Malaysia	66.8

The new industrial nations of Asia, on the contrary, are highly export dependent (Table 1), and a large and growing share of their exports are made up either of machine components or of finished equipment assembled from imported parts. This is particularly true of the more rapidly industrializing Southeast Asian countries. The share of machinery in Thai manufactured exports (SITC categories 5-8) rose extremely rapidly during the 1980s, reaching 28% by 1988, while the cases of Singapore and Malaysia are even more striking: over 60% of Malaysia's manufactured exports in the late 1980s consisted of machinery and equipment (a large share of that being accounted for by exports of integrated circuits) (Table 2). The pattern of industrialization in these Southeast Asian countries is thus not only different from Japan's experience, but also differs somewhat from the experience of Northeast Asian NIEs like Taiwan and South Korea, where textiles, clothing, and other simple manufactured goods provided the major share of exports in the first stages of industrialization.

Rapidly growing exports of machinery and machine components reflect the increasing integration of industry within the region. Large multinational companies are now extending their production networks throughout Asia, using more advanced industrial economies such as Japan, South Korea, and Taiwan as bases for the production of sophisticated components, and lower-wage countries such as Malaysia, Thailand, and the Philippines for assembly or for the production of simpler parts. Matsushita, for example, manufactures color televisions for worldwide export in Malaysia, with components being imported from a variety of other Asian industrial nations (*Asahi Shimbun*, June 4, 1988). The Mitsubishi Motor Company's Thai subsidiary uses car body parts produced in Malaysia and transmissions imported from the Philippines (*Asahi Shimbun*, June 22, 1988).

In these circumstances, the depacking or modification of technology to suit local needs becomes very difficult. The machine parts produced in various Asian countries all have to be made to precise specifications, in order to fit into the wider whole of a final product assembled elsewhere. Even in countries where labor is abundant, quite highly automated production techniques may be necessary because automation allows greater precision and accuracy in manufacturing. (Provided that large amounts of highly skilled labor are not needed, it may be profitable to locate fairly automated branches of production in low-wage countries because of the generous incentives provided by host governments, and because lenient labor laws permit capital to be worked for longer periods than in advanced industrialized countries) (Mirza 1986). Such constraints will limit the choice and adaptation of technology even if the factory is domestically, rather than foreign, owned. Indeed, constraints on the choice of technology are being reinforced by the growth of Original Equipment Manufacturer/Value Added Resaler agreements, under which local producers in lower-wage countries are licensed by famous "brand name" companies to make

Table 2. Manufactured Exports of Asian Countries, 1975 and 1988 (%).

	Manufactured Goods as % of Exports		Product as % of Manufactured Exports									
			Chemicals SITC 5		Basic Manufactures SITC 6		Machinery and transport equipment SITC 7		Miscellaneous Manufactures SITC 8		Unclassified	
	1975	1988	1975	1988	1975	1988	1975	1988	1975	1988	1975	1988
S. Korea	81.8	93.7	1.7	3.3	35.9	22.2	18.3	41.2	43.8	33.0	0.2	0.3
Taiwan	81.3	92.8	2.3	3.7	29.2	22.1	24.0	37.9	44.2	36.0	—	0.1
Singapore	50.2	76.1	7.4	8.7	16.9	10.9	45.2	63.1	13.7	11.8	16.7	5.5
Thailand	23.9	55.8	2.1	2.1	59.8	34.1	5.4	28.3	14.6	33.1	18.0	1.7
Malaysia	31.5	45.9	2.9	4.7	55.9	17.6	19.7	61.6	18.0	15.0	3.4	0.9

Source: Asian Development Bank, *Key Indicators of Developing Asian and Pacific Countries*, 1990.

their products under a strictly controlled set of specifications.

The more complex division of labor, therefore, limits the scope for the top-down adaptation of technology in today's industrializing countries. Although industrializing countries may acquire the capacity, not just to operate imported equipment (technology acquisition type 2a) but also to control and maintain imported production processes (type 2b), this capacity will not necessarily pave the way to local modification of techniques or to local innovation (types 3 and 4).

At the same time, the technology policies of the most recently industrializing Asian countries pay relatively little attention to the bottom-up development of indigenous craft-manufacturing techniques (technology acquisition type 5). Although some Southeast Asian institutions, like the Rubber Research Institute of Malaysia, have had considerable success in developing new agricultural techniques and new uses for domestic raw materials, these remain the exception rather than the rule. In general, attention tends to be focused on internationally recognized "high-tech" industries such as electronics and computer production, and in particular on the need to provide skilled workers and technicians to operate the high-tech production processes introduced by multinational firms.

Thus, for example, the Fifth Malaysia Plan of 1986-1990 referred briefly to the special importance of conducting "downstream research for resource-based industries," but proceeded to pay far more detailed attention to policies for improving the technological capacity of the microelectronics and computer sectors, and to the training of technicians and engineers (*Fifth Malaysia Plan 1986-1990*). In Thailand, the Sixth National Economic and Social Development Plan (1987-1991) emphasizes the need for greater screening of imported technology and for the development of local technical skills. A report by the Asian Development Bank observed, however, that strategies for the development of technological capacity are far less coherent than those pursued in Japan and the Northeast Asian NIEs, and points to the need for "the development of indigenous technological capability, which can never be improved without conscious and aggressive technological strategies." (Kakazu 1990).

The consequence of a developmental strategy based on peripheral intermediation in technologically complex areas of industry tends to be a widening gap between modern factories using imported technologies and small firms in traditional areas of manufacturing. This makes it hard for technology to trickle down through the economy, or for indigenous small firms to become suppliers of inputs to new industries. Significantly, when foreign multinationals in Asian NIEs decide to expand their local procurement of parts and components, they often do this by setting up their own parts-producing subsidiary, or (in the case of Japanese multinationals) by helping their home country subcontractors to set up factories overseas (Sato 1989). As a result, local government policies to encourage local parts procurement may lead, not so much to an expanded role for indigenous small enterprises, as to greater opportunities for foreign multinationals.

The Thai television industry provides a good example. By the mid-1980s, Thailand already had a rapidly growing television assembly industry, but the tubes and other vital components were mostly imported. To reduce this import dependence, the government decided to promote the local production of television tubes. Sure enough, by 1990 domestic production had reached a level of one million tubes per year, but this production was monopolized by Thai CTR, a joint-venture company in which 25% of capital was owned by the television assembly firms (themselves mostly subsidiaries of foreign multinationals) and 20% by the major Japanese producer, Mitsubishi Electric. The next step in the process was to encourage the domestic production of glass valves for use in the tubes. This is currently being achieved by the construction of a new factory owned by a joint venture between Thai interests and the leading Japanese producer Asahi Glass (*Kokusai Keizai* August 20, 1990). Eventually, these factories will not only supply local television makers but will also form part of the international production networks of the parent companies, exporting parts to factories elsewhere in Asia or even further afield.

In short, the pattern is one in which the growth and integration of the East and Southeast Asian economies is also leading to a functional specialization of different Asian industrial countries. In the consumer electronics area, for example, "Taiwan and South Korea specialize in the production of TVs, audio equipment, and video tape-recorders; Hong Kong in the production of radios, TV games, electronic watches, and more recently in video tapes; and the ASEAN-4 [Malaysia, Indonesia, the Philippines, and Thailand] in less sophisticated and lower value-added products" (Chen 1990). Similarly, less complex electronic parts like coils and condensers, and peripherals like audio speakers, are being produced in Southeast Asia while Japan and the Northeast Asian NIEs concentrate upon more sophisticated components (Tsuneishi 1990). As enterprises move through the product life cycle, so they steadily shift the areas of production which involve standardized and obsolescent technologies to lower-cost Southeast Asian countries, while concentrating newer and more technically complex branches of production in higher-cost countries like South Korea, Taiwan, or Japan itself. As a result, the contemporary industrialization process tends to lead, not to a steady diffusion of technology throughout all branches of industry, but to a widening gap between modern branches of industry (such as electronics) and traditional branches within the industrializing nations themselves.

THE NEW INTERNATIONAL DIVISION OF KNOWLEDGE IN ASIA

According to Yoshihara Kunio, the development processes that I have outlined are leading, as far as Southeast Asia is concerned, to "technologyless" industrialization. Yoshihara argues that East Asian countries, including South Korea and Taiwan as well as Japan, made efforts to absorb and master foreign technology, whereas Southeast Asian entrepreneurs are generally willing to leave technical details to their foreign business partners, and ASEAN nations as a whole have "failed to commit themselves to progress in science and technology" (Yoshihara 1988). "The basic reason for the technical weakness of industrial capitalist institutions in the region," concludes Yoshihara, "is the low overall level of technical competence. Because of this, capitalists who aspire to be industrialists have to depend on foreign technology even though it is extremely expensive. There is no effective local substitute for the technology needed for the advanced industrial activities the government is promoting" (Yoshihara 1988).

This analysis, I suggest, is rather too simple. Instead of speaking of technologyless industrialization, it may be more realistic to envisage Southeast Asian industrialization as being characterized by a particular form of technology acquisition. To put it another way, we can say that the emerging international division of labor is simultaneously giving rise to a new international division of knowledge. What is meant by a "new international division of knowledge"? As we saw in the previous section, the contemporary process of industrialization in East and Southeast Asia is essentially *internationally* rather than *nationally* based. As industrialization progresses, multinational firms (whether from within or from outside the region) are locating different parts of their production process in different countries. The result is a pattern of increasing functional specialization, with the various Asian industrializing countries concentrating on the production of particular manufactured goods or components. This specialization of *productive* activity also is reflected in a growing specialization of *technological* activity. The development of an ability to acquire and operate foreign technology is not necessarily leading, in each country, to an ability to adapt and innovate. Instead, innovative capacity is tending to be concentrated in a few parts of the East and Southeast Asian region.

There are good reasons why even foreign multinational corporations might wish to conduct part of their research activities within the East and Southeast Asian region. One reason is the increasing difficulty of recruiting research scientists in many major developed nations. Within the USA, a shortage of students interested in science has led to the growing recruitment of scientists from Asia. By 1990, the Massachusetts Institute of Technology had 748 Asian students (including 207 from China, 156 from Japan, and 98 each from South Korea and Taiwan) (*Asia Technology*, September 1990). For certain types of research and development, there may also be advantages in locating laboratories near production facilities or major markets. This is true both of research in consumer products like cosmetics and pharmaceuticals, where local markets may have specialized needs, and also of the development of producer goods such as computer software. Although the most advanced research tends to remain at home, therefore, some multinationals are beginning to locate part of their applied or developmental research overseas. The focus of this research, however, tends to be regional or global rather than national. In other words, it is concerned not with creating techniques that are specifically appropriate to the economy or society of the country where innovation occurs, but rather with developing techniques to suit the overall regional strategies of the innovating firms.

The ability to attract and foster this type of R&D activity depends, not just on the host government's technology policy per se, but also on a range of other factors such as quality of communications infrastructure and levels of general and technical education. This may favor not only the Northeast Asian NIEs (South Korea and Taiwan) but also countries like Singapore. Although its industrialization has been a classic case of peripheral intermediation, Singapore has the advantage of good education and communications, and of the use of English as an official language.

In recent years, the characteristic pattern of technological development in Singapore has involved the joint establishment of training or research establishments by the Singaporean government and foreign multinationals or governments. These include the Brown-Boveri Government Training Centre, the Philips Government Training Centre, and the French Singapore Institute of Electro-Technology. At the same time, a number of large foreign firms (including Nestlé and Ciba-Geigy) have chosen Singapore as a base for their Asian research laboratories, and the country is also emerging as a significant regional center for software development (Mirza 1986; Chew 1990). Although Singapore remains some way behind South Korea and Taiwan in terms of its research capacity, these trends were reflected in rapidly expanding research and development spending during the 1980s (Table 3).

Table 3. Research and Development in Selected Asian Countries.

	R&D Spending as % of GNP		Researchers per 100,000 Population
	1980	1987	
S. Korea	0.6	1.9 [b]	134.5(1988)
Taiwan	0.5	1.2	174.9(1987)
Singapore	0.3 [a]	0.9	125.9(1987)
Thailand	0.4	0.3 [c]	9.4(1986)
Malaysia	-	0.5 [c]	19.0(1986)

a 1981.

b 1988.

c 1986.

Sources: Kagaku Gijutsu Hakusho, 1990; Omichi Yasunori, " Ajia no Kogyoka to gijutsu iten no igi," in Taniura 1989; Asian Development Bank, *Key Indicators of Developing Asian and Pacific Countries*, 1990.

At the other end of the scale, countries like Thailand, despite their rapid recent industrialization, possess few of the attributes likely to encourage the development of research laboratories, either by domestic or foreign enterprises. Limited communications infrastructure and low levels of enrollment in secondary education are major problems. As a result, Thailand's industrialization is not being accompanied by any significant increase in R&D activity; in fact, industrialization may, in some respects, be producing a diminution of innovative capacity. A study by the Thai Development Research Institute (TDRI), which attempted to assess local industry's acquisitive, operational, adaptive, and innovative capacity in various branches of manufacturing, found that while *operational* capacity (i.e., technology acquisition type 2) in export-oriented firms such as the electronics companies was some 25% higher than in nonexport-oriented firms, *innovative* capacity (i.e., technology acquisition types 4 and 5) was some 10-14% lower (Tsuneishi 1990). It is, however, the export-oriented sector (and particularly the electronics industry) that has been responsible for the major share of Thailand's recent industrial growth. Extrapolating from the TDRI's research, then, it is possible to suggest that the present course of Thai industrializaiton, while it is strengthening the economy's ability to import and operate foreign technologies, may be resulting in a relative dilution of the country's potential for domestic innovation. This hypothesis is supported by the fact that the share of Thai GNP devoted to research activities stagnated at a low level during the rapid industrial growth of the 1980s.

Once this international division of technological knowledge emerges, it may be difficult to change. As Manuel Castells (1985) and other scholars have observed, research and development activities tend to become clustered into a few specialized centers where they can take advantage of informal flows of personnel and ideas from one laboratory to another. Innovation, in short, attracts innovation, and it seems likely that the dominance of a few specialized centers of East and Southeast Asian research and development will become increasingly evident over the coming decade.

CONCLUSIONS

The way in which an industrializing country acquires technological know-how is not something that can simply be determined by government through its technology policy. Rather, the pattern of technology acquisition is inseparably linked to the nature of the industrialization process as a whole. Japan's experience of technology acquisition reflected an industrialization strategy based on the creation of a "processing economy": a strategy in which the domestic market played an important role and in which intense economic nationalism limited the entry of foreign capital. The result was the widespread adaptation of imported techniques in ways that suited the structure of the domestic economy. Foreign machinery and processes were simplified, and made less energy and raw material intensive; at the same time, modern science was applied to indigenous technical know-how to enable small Japanese firms to compete in world markets. The adapted or hybrid techniques often placed great strains on the Japanese work force and environment. However, they also helped Japan to build up an infrastructure of research skills and institutions that were to play a vital part in the country's emergence as a technological leader in the late twentieth century.

The process of industrialization which is now engulfing Southeast Asia, by contrast, is essentially an international one, in which enterprises and industries are no longer confined within political boundaries. Technology, too, is becoming increasingly international. Certain parts of the East and Southeast Asian region are emerging as centers for the modification and development of technology, while others are being assigned the role of importers and operators of techniques developed elsewhere. These changed circumstances make it difficult for today's industrializing nations to derive useful lessons from the Japanese experience of technology acquisition. Instead, the Asian industrializing nations need to develop new strategies designed specifically to deal with the contemporary economic environment of the region. In the case of Southeast Asian nations like Thailand and Malaysia, if the object is to acquire an indigenous capacity for technological innovation, it may be necessary not just to develop new technology policies, but to reassess the whole framework of their industrialization strategy.

Notes

1. This paper follows Nelson's use of the phrase "the acquisition of technology" rather than "the transfer of technology," because the former expression emphasizes the active role played by the recipient in the international flow of technological know-how (Nelson 1990).

2. This four-fold division is a modification of the classifications "acquisitive capability," "operative capability," "adaptive capability," and "innovative capability," used in a number of studies (Tsuneishi 1990).

Referemces

Asahi Shimbun. June 4, 1988.

Asahi Shimbun. June 22, 1988.

Asia Technology. September 1990: 28.

Castells, M. 1985. High technology, economic restructuring, and the urban-regional process in the United States. In: M. Castells, ed., *High Technology, Space and Society*. Beverly Hills: Sage Publications.

Chen, E.K.Y. 1990. The electronics industry. In: H. Soesastro and M. Pangestu, eds., *Technological Challenge in the Asia Pacific Economy*. Sydney: Allen and Unwin.

Chew, S.B. 1990. Singapore: the information technology sector. In: H. Soesastro and M. Pangestu, eds., *Technological Challenge in the Asia Pacific Economy*. Sydney: Allen and Unwin.

Diehl, A. 1984. On Japanese creativity. In: H. Eto and K. Matsui, eds., *R&D Management Systems in Japanese Industry*. Amsterdam: North Holland.

Emmanuel, A. 1982. *Appropriate or Underdeveloped Technology?* New York: John Wiley.

Fifth Malaysia Plan 1986-1990.

Garnaut, R. and K. Anderson. 1979. ASEAN export specialization and the evolution of comparative advantage in the Western Pacific region. Paper presented to the Tenth Pacific Trade and Development Conference, Canberra, 1979.

Japan-Manchoukuo Year Book. 1939.

Kagaku Gijutsu Cho. 1983. *Kagaku Gijutsu Yoran*.

Kakazu, H. 1990. *Industrial Technology Capabilities and Policies in Selected Asian Developing Countries*. Manila: Asian Development Bank.

Kokusai Keizai. August 20, 1990: 195-196.

Mirza, H. 1986. *Multinationals and the Growth of the Singapore Economy*. London: Croom Helm.

Nakamura, T. 1983. *Economic Growth in Prewar Japan*. New Haven and London: Yale University Press.

Nelson, R.R. 1990. Acquiring technology. In: H. Soesastro and M. Pangestu, eds., *Technological Challenge in the Asia Pacific Economy*. Sydney: Allen and Unwin.

Nakaoka, T. 1986. Gijutsushi kara mita Nihon no keiken. In: T. Nakaoka et al., eds., *Kindai Nihon no Gijutsu to Gijutsu Seisaku*. Tokyo: University of Tokyo Press.

Okita, S. 1980. *The Developing Economies and Japan: Lessons in Growth*. Tokyo: University of Tokyo Press.

Okita, S. 1989. *Japan in the World Economy of the 1980s*. Tokyo: University of Tokyo Press.

Rosenberg, N. 1987. Keizai hatten to inobeshon soshiki. *Gendai Keizai*, May 1987: 64.

Sato, Y. 1989. *Taiwan—ukete kara dashite e no dainamizumu*. In: T. Taniura, ed. *Ajia no Kogyoka to Chokusetsu Toshi*. Tokyo: Ajia Keizai Shuppankai.

Shishida, T. 1981. Japan as a model for industrialization in Asia. In: World Peace Academy of Japan, eds. *Emerging Asia: The Role of Japan*. Tokyo: Riverfield Inc.

Toba, K. 1981. Asia in the 1980s and Japan's role. In: World Peace Academy of Japan, ed. *Emerging Asia: The Role of Japan*. Tokyo: Riverfield, Inc.

Tsuneishi, T. 1990. Tai—Nikkei kigyo shudo ni yoru gijutsu iten. In: Taniura T., ed. *Ajia no Kogyoka to Gijutsu Iten*. Tokyo: Ajia Keizai Shuppankai.

Tsusho Hakusho. 1986.

Uchida H. 1990. *Gijutsu iten*. In: S. Nishikawa and T. Abe, eds. *Nihon Keizaishi*, vol. 4. Tokyo: Iwanami Shoten.

Ui, J. 1976. A critique of industrialization. *Japan Quarterly*, 23 (1): 37-39.

Yoshihara, K. 1988. *The Rise of Ersatz Capitalism in Southeast Asia*. Singapore: Oxford University Press.

6 Moneyless Direct Investment and Development of Asian Financial Markets: Financial Linkages Between Local Markets and Offshore Centers

Shojiro Tokunaga

Faculty of Economics, Kyushu University

INTRODUCTION: "COMMON KNOWLEDGE" ABOUT FDI

"Common Knowledge": Japan Transfers FDI Funds to Host Countries

Foreign direct investment (FDI) is popularly believed to be the investing of funds in a foreign (local) business activity through which profit is obtained. Almost all money invested in a local business must be brought into the host country from the investing country. This is the usual popular understanding of Japanese, i.e., "common knowledge."

When the present author visited Thailand in autumn 1988, it was rumored that the Board of Investment (BOI) which selects and approves investment projects to be promoted was dissatisfied with the supply of funds from foreign firms. The reason the rumor started was that the equity capital of foreign (mainly Japanese) firms was only one-third of total investment capital. Many feel that the very fact of the high proportion of loans to equity indicates a considerable magnitude of money-lending by Japanese parent companies compared to acquisition of securities (equity); in other words, that Japanese companies should advance a lot of money to their overseas subsidiaries.

Generally speaking, the propensity to save in a developing country is much lower than that in an advanced country, and, in addition, the high proportion of loans to equity or owned resources is a characteristic of firms in the economic growth stage. Therefore, should Japanese parent companies lend large amounts of money to their subsidiaries? Are local subsidiaries unable to procure investment funds in their local financial markets?

The problem of the high ratio of loans to equity in Japan-based firms in Thailand is not due to the above-mentioned general situation. According to the Bangkok Center of the Japan External Trade Organization (JETRO), Japanese firms (manufacturers) who make new investments in Thailand raise on average two-thirds of the total investment in Thai currency (Baht) from local financial markets (JETRO 1988). Usually the balance (one-third) is provided by the parent companies as equity capital. During private interviews, one example was raised in which 20% of total investment was equity capital and the balance was procured locally.

Also, according to a survey by the Export-Import Bank of Japan (EXIM Bank 1991) the main source of Japanese subsidiaries' FDI funds is local financial markets in developing Asian countries, especially the ASEAN countries, as well as the USA and EC. Local financial institutions that extend loans and credits to Japanese subsidiaries include branches of Japanese banks, local banks whose management is controlled by Japanese, and special institutions such as finance companies and merchant banks that extend loans jointly with Japanese financial institutions.

Japanese banks have entered advanced countries (the USA and Europe) in various forms, in addition to establishing branches, in order to assist local Japanese subsidiaries. In Asian countries, however, their operations are restricted to the establishment of branch offices. For example, in Thailand where the activity of Japanese manufacturing firms has been and remains vigorous, only the Bank of Tokyo and the Taiyo-Kobe-Mitsui Bank, and in Malaysia only the Bank of Tokyo are allowed to engage in branch office business. In ASEAN countries, when Japanese subsidiaries seek loans it is impossible for them to rely solely on Japanese banks. Even if they borrow from Japanese banks, the funds come not from Japan but locally. Also, when borrowing from Thai-Japanese joint-venture finance companies or Malaysian-Japanese joint-venture merchant banks, those nonbank financial institutions restricted to collecting deposits and dealing in foreign exchange must obtain the funds from local banks or issue promissory notes for obtaining local funds directly. Therefore funds borrowed through local financial institutions by Japanese overseas subsidiaries originate not from Japanese but from local savings.

The "principle" of raising investment funds locally rather in Japan is not a peculiar phenomenon found only in Thailand and Malaysia. From multinational corporations' (MNCs) viewpoint, it is logical to procure necessary investment funds in local or offshore markets while minimizing the amount transferred directly from Japan.

What Is the Purpose of FDI: Transfer of Money to, or Effective Control of Local Juridical Bodies?

Another problem is the interdependence (action and reaction) between raising local funds by Japanese subsidiaries and modernizing local financial markets. Few Japanese scholars have been interested in the impacts of local fund-raising on the development of local Asian financial markets. This lack of concern toward local money-raising, and therefore FDI impact on the improvement of local financial markets, is due in part to the "common knowledge" theory of Japanese firms' motivations in establishing overseas business operations.

Professor Yoshikazu Miyazaki has argued that Japanese firms' internal reserves or undistributed profits create overseas investments or operations; in other words, the firms' excess savings over domestic investment motivate them to transfer investment funds to other countries for new opportunities to invest. This idea is popular among Japanese academics.

FDI is undertaken not only by large-scale but also by small- and medium-scale firms. In the case of the automobile industry, for example, Japanese firms are establishing overseas production facilities in "convoy." Also some parts manufacturers, so-called subcontracting firms, have combined with large assemblers and are making more positive progress in multinational production schemes. The reason Japanese firms are pursuing multinationalization is not that they have excess internally generated funds or inner reserves. At least under the present circumstances, Japanese firms' relative technological superiorities despite comparative cost disadvantages encourage them to establish overseas production facilities. The surplus internal funds of parent companies are employed in research and development (R&D) for new products or improved production processes rather than generally utilized as a source of FDI funds.

To discuss in more detail the nature of Japan's FDI in developing Asian countries, a clear definition of FDI is necessary. The term "FDI" in the manufacturing sector is basically defined as conduct to secure management control over local corporate bodies by transferring new technologies or new industries into the host (developing Asian) countries.

In relation to this definition of FDI, it is noticeable that in Japanese firms' FDI in Thailand, for example, the funds flowing into Thailand nearly correspond to the amount of capital stock (equity capital), since it is about one-third of total investment funds. Such equity capital is also used as payment for capital equipment, etc. that is purchased by Japanese firms' local subsidiaries. As a result of such transactions, the money to be paid for the capital equipment or machinery is nearly equivalent to the amount of capital equity. In other words, as the result of the transactions, the price of capital equipment, etc. can be regarded as equity capital transferred to local subsidiaries from Japanese parent companies.

The same transactions can also be considered as technology transfer and its control. If the equity capital flows return to Japanese parent firms as compensation for capital equipment, etc. that embody technology, then the following must be considered:

1) Japanese firms acquire equity in local juridical bodies by transferring equity capital from Japan, i.e., Japanese firms come into possession of local bodies and control their management.

2) Technology transfer is associated with the export of capital equipment, etc. to the local bodies, i.e., Japanese subsidiaries.

3) The equity capital is actually returned to Japan as the result of repayment for capital equipment, etc., and in addition parent firms acquire the right of management of the subsidiaries, including control of transferred technologies.

These are reasons why the acquisition of ownership and technology transfer constitute a harmonious whole in the case of Japanese FDI in Asia.

FDI is not in principle a method for Japanese firms to transfer money over national borders. It is instead a method for securing the ownership of firms established as foreign bodies in order to maintain or develop their comparative competitiveness or competitive advantage.

On the other hand, governments and business societies in host countries, who are eager to build self-reliant economies, do not approve of indiscriminate control by foreign firms of local ones. They impose stringent restrictions on the majority ownership of local juridical bodies by foreigners. The main reason why they approve FDI is that foreign firms foster innovative industries, and introduce new technology and know-how.

The purpose of Japanese firms' FDI in Asia is not to transfer surplus funds to the host countries, but to maintain or develop their competitive advantage, that is, to control their own technologies that are transferred to developing Asian countries. The following sections will focus on methods of Japanese subsidiaries' local fund raising and then on the modernization of Asian financial markets, centered on the ASEAN countries, especially Thailand and Malaysia. Finally, the interdependence of international Asian financial centers and nationwide financial markets is analyzed, and new developments are described and discussed.

JAPANESE FIRMS' METHODS OF RAISING FDI CAPITAL AND THEIR IMPACT ON LOCAL FINANCIAL MARKETS

Surveys on Sources of FDI Funds

According to the EXIM Bank, the breakdown of sources for FDI funds as planned by Japanese manufacturers in 1991 is shown in Figure 1. The bank sent a questionnaire in December 1990 to 506 Japanese manufacturers with three or more overseas facilities (production, sales, etc.), of which 277 firms responded. It is interesting that the parent company's own funds were reported as the source by only 26.1%. In contrast, both reinvestment and borrowing by the overseas subsidiary were the responses of 47.2% in the survey. FDI funds from abroad, including money raised overseas by the parent companies, were planned sources of 55.6% of respondents.

However, there was a big difference between the responses of large-scale firms (239), with capital stock of ¥1 billion or more, and small- and medium-scale firms (38). Large-scale firms reported that their largest source of FDI funds was outside funding to the overseas subsidiaries (34.1%), and, in addition, the subsidiaries' share of total FDI money was 47.7%. As far as fundraising for FDI is concerned, overseas subsidiaries of large-scale firms are independent of their parent companies.

In contrast, overseas subsidiaries of Japanese small- and medium-scale firms are basically dependent on their parent companies for funds. An overwhelming majority (79.1%) of such firms responded that FDI funds are raised by the parent firms on the Japanese domestic market. Since the parent companies' internal funding amounted to only 7.8%, they are reliant on the parent companies' credit standing with Japanese financial institutions and on the conditions of Japanese financial markets (Fig. 1).

To summarize the result of the EXIM Bank survey, FDI funds for Japanese firms are not basically covered by internal funding but supplied mainly by external sources. The overseas subsidiaries of large-scale Japanese firms tend to raise investment capital independently and in local financial markets, while small- and medium-scale firms' subsidiaries are dependent on Japanese financial markets.

It is known that 26.3% of the large-scale firms' resources are covered by internal funding, which appears to be used to acquire equity in or

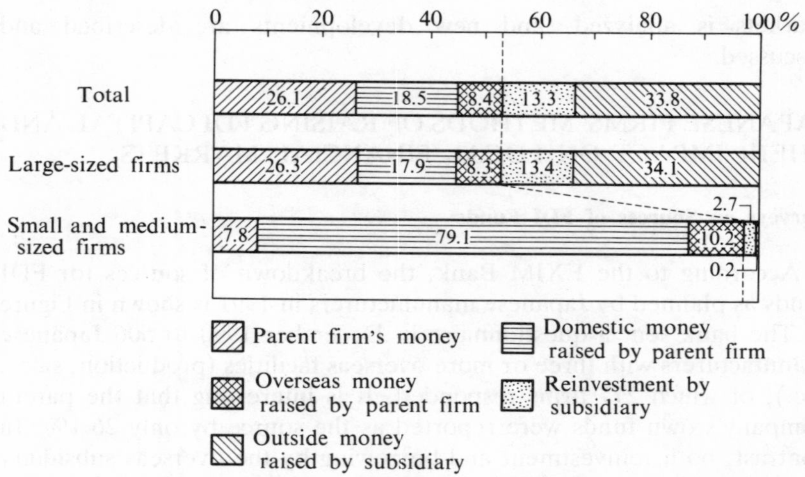

Fig. 1. Fund-raising Sources for Overseas Subsidiaries Planned in 1991.
Source: Export-Import Bank of Japan.
Notes: 1. The questionnaire was administered in December 1990.
2. Large-sized firms are those with ¥1 billion or more in equity capital.

ownership of overseas subsidiaries. According to a survey by the Economic Planning Agency of Japan (1990) on newly established overseas facilities, most Japanese firms regarded their own funds, sometimes including those raised in Japanese and overseas financial markets, as the most important source of FDI funds. In operating their subsidiaries, however, most Japanese firms regarded not only the parent company's funds but also local sources as the most important (Table 1). The difference in fund raising methods between newly established companies and those in operation for a longer period is often due to whether the parent companies need to acquire a larger share of capital stock (equity) or not.

The EXIM Bank conducted another survey on Japanese firms' overseas business activities in September-October 1989. They sent questionnaires to 437 Japanese manufacturing firms with three or more overseas subsidiaries, and received responses from 247. The firms were asked to name the three most common methods of raising funds for their overseas subsidiaries. The responses generally indicated that most overseas subsidiaries raise money independently through local financial institutions in both developing and developed regions. In analyzing fund-raising sources in four Asian NIEs and the five ASEAN countries excluding Singapore, more than three-fourths of those who raised

Table 1. Sources for Japanese FDI Funds.

Area of investment	Institution	No. Cas (%)	Sources	No. of Responses	(%)
1. Asian NIEs 300 cases (100.0%)	(1) Parent Company	72 (24.0)	(1) Japanese Domestic Bond and Debt, etc.	4	(1.3)
			(2) Borrowing from Japanese Domestic Financial Institutions	19	(6.3)
			(3) Local Bond and Debt, etc.	0	
			(4) Borrowing from Local Financial Institutions	15	(5.0)
			(5) Bond and Debt, etc., Issued in Third Country	5	(1.7)
			(6) Borrowing from a Third Country Financial Institution	0	
			(7) Leasing	2	(0.7)
			(8) Own Funds (Depreciation and Profit, etc.)	27	(9.0)
	(2) Local Subsidiary	226 (75.3)	(1) Japanese Domestic Bond and Debt, etc.	0	
			(2) Borrowing from Japanese Domestic Financial Institutions	4	(1.3)
			(3) Local Bond and Debt, etc.	5	(1.7)
			(4) Borrowing from Local Financial Institutions	170	(56.7)
			(5) Bond and Debt, etc., Issued in Third Country	0	
			(6) Borrowing from a Third Country Financial Institution	5	(1.7)
			(7) Leasing	4	(1.3)
			(8) Own Funds (Depreciation and Profit, etc.)	38	(12.7)
	(3) Financial Institution (subsidiary)	2 (0.7)	(1) Japanese Domestic Bond and Debt, etc.	0	
			(2) Borrowing from Japanese Domestic Financial Institutions	0	
			(3) Local Bond and Debt, etc.	0	
			(4) Borrowing from Local Financial Institutions	1	(0.3)
			(5) Bond and Debt, etc., Issued in Third Country	0	
			(6) Borrowing from a Third Country Financial Institution	1	(0.3)
			(7) Leasing	0	
			(8) Own Funds (Depreciation and Profit, etc.)	0	

Table 1. (cont.)

Region	Fund-raiser	Cases	Source of funds	No.	(%)
2. ASEAN Countries 249 cases (100.0%)	(1) Parent Company	43 (17.3)	(1) Japanese Domestic Bond and Debt, etc.	3	(1.2)
			(2) Borrowing from Japanese Domestic Financial Institutions	12	(4.4)
			(3) Local Bond and Debt, etc.	3	(1.2)
			(4) Borrowing from Local Financial Institutions	0	
			(5) Bond and Debt, etc., Issued in Third Country	4	(1.6)
			(6) Borrowing from a Third Country Financial Institution	4	(1.6)
			(7) Leasing	1	(0.4)
			(8) Own Funds (Depreciation and Profit, etc.)	16	(6.4)
	(2) Local Subsidiary	203 (81.5)	(1) Japanese Domestic Bond and Debt, etc.	0	
			(2) Borrowing from Japanese Domestic Financial Institutions	9	(3.6)
			(3) Local Bond and Debt, etc.	5	(2.0)
			(4) Borrowing from Local Financial Institutions	161	(64.7)
			(5) Bond and Debt, etc., Issued in Third Country	0	
			(6) Borrowing from a Third Country Financial Institution	9	(3.6)
			(7) Leasing	2	(0.8)
			(8) Own Funds (Depreciation and Profit, etc.)	17	(6.8)
	(3) Financial Institution (subsidiary)	3 (1.2)	(1) Japanese Domestic Bond and Debt, etc.	0	(1.3)
			(2) Borrowing from Japanese Domestic Financial Institutions	0	(6.3)
			(3) Local Bond and Debt, etc.	0	
			(4) Borrowing from Local Financial Institutions	0	
			(5) Bond and Debt, etc., Issued in Third Country	1	(0.4)
			(6) Borrowing from a Third Country Financial Institution	2	(0.8)
			(7) Leasing	0	
			(8) Own Funds (Depreciation and Profit, etc.)	0	

Table 1. (cont.)

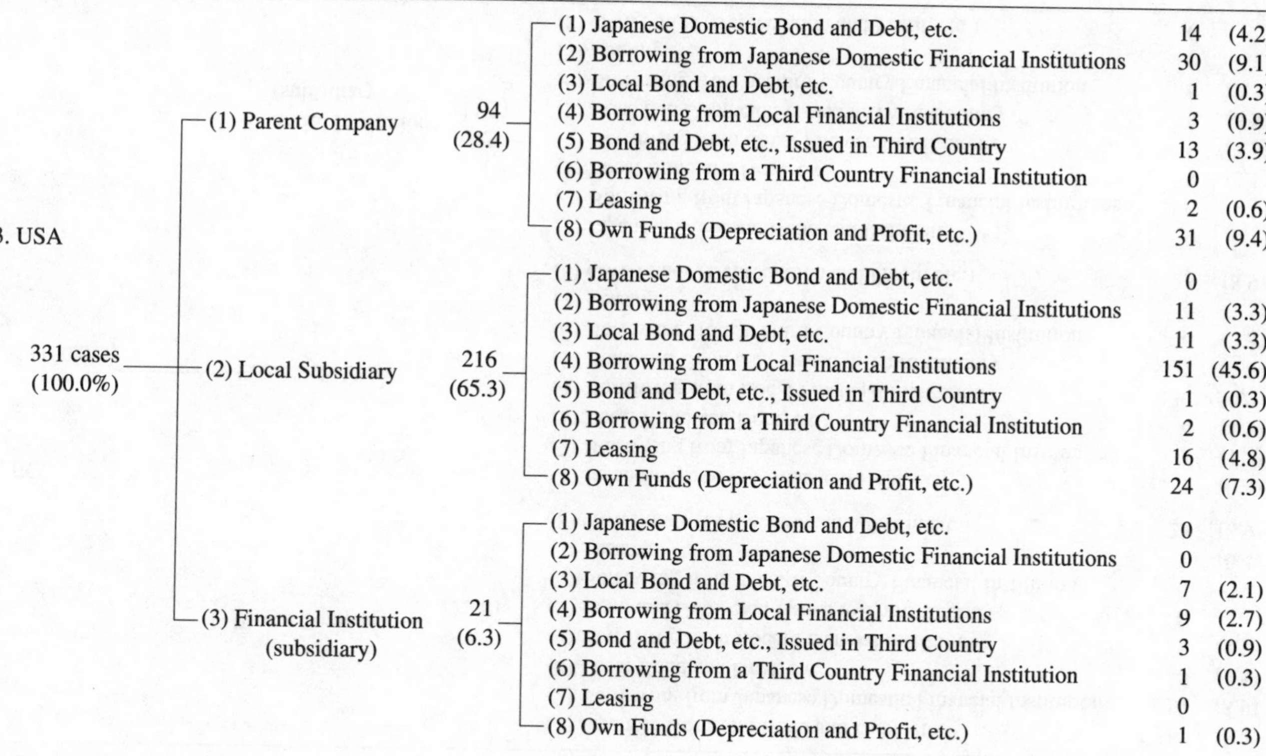

Country	Total	Fund-raising entity	Cases (%)	Source of funds	Cases	(%)
3. USA	331 cases (100.0%)	(1) Parent Company	94 (28.4)	(1) Japanese Domestic Bond and Debt, etc.	14	(4.2)
				(2) Borrowing from Japanese Domestic Financial Institutions	30	(9.1)
				(3) Local Bond and Debt, etc.	1	(0.3)
				(4) Borrowing from Local Financial Institutions	3	(0.9)
				(5) Bond and Debt, etc., Issued in Third Country	13	(3.9)
				(6) Borrowing from a Third Country Financial Institution	0	
				(7) Leasing	2	(0.6)
				(8) Own Funds (Depreciation and Profit, etc.)	31	(9.4)
		(2) Local Subsidiary	216 (65.3)	(1) Japanese Domestic Bond and Debt, etc.	0	
				(2) Borrowing from Japanese Domestic Financial Institutions	11	(3.3)
				(3) Local Bond and Debt, etc.	11	(3.3)
				(4) Borrowing from Local Financial Institutions	151	(45.6)
				(5) Bond and Debt, etc., Issued in Third Country	1	(0.3)
				(6) Borrowing from a Third Country Financial Institution	2	(0.6)
				(7) Leasing	16	(4.8)
				(8) Own Funds (Depreciation and Profit, etc.)	24	(7.3)
		(3) Financial Institution (subsidiary)	21 (6.3)	(1) Japanese Domestic Bond and Debt, etc.	0	
				(2) Borrowing from Japanese Domestic Financial Institutions	0	
				(3) Local Bond and Debt, etc.	7	(2.1)
				(4) Borrowing from Local Financial Institutions	9	(2.7)
				(5) Bond and Debt, etc., Issued in Third Country	3	(0.9)
				(6) Borrowing from a Third Country Financial Institution	1	(0.3)
				(7) Leasing	0	
				(8) Own Funds (Depreciation and Profit, etc.)	1	(0.3)

Table 1. (cont.)

Region	Fundraiser	Number (%)	Source of funds	Number	(%)
4. EC (100.0%)	(1) Parent Company	57 (22.0)	(1) Japanese Domestic Bond and Debt, etc.	14	(5.4)
			(2) Borrowing from Japanese Domestic Financial Institutions	10	(3.9)
			(3) Local Bond and Debt, etc.	4	(1.5)
			(4) Borrowing from Local Financial Institutions	5	(1.9)
			(5) Bond and Debt, etc., Issued in Third Country	0	
			(6) Borrowing from a Third Country Financial Institution	0	
			(7) Leasing	1	(0.4)
			(8) Own Funds (Depreciation and Profit, etc.)	23	(8.9)
	(2) Local Subsidiary	173 (66.8)	(1) Japanese Domestic Bond and Debt, etc.	1	(0.4)
			(2) Borrowing from Japanese Domestic Financial Institutions	3	(1.2)
			(3) Local Bond and Debt, etc.	4	(1.5)
			(4) Borrowing from Local Financial Institutions	130	(50.2)
			(5) Bond and Debt, etc., Issued in Third Country	2	(0.8)
			(6) Borrowing from a Third Country Financial Institution	6	(2.3)
			(7) Leasing	4	(1.5)
			(8) Own Funds (Depreciation and Profit, etc.)	23	(8.9)
	(3) Financial Institution (subsidiary)	29 (11.2)	(1) Japanese Domestic Bond and Debt, etc.	0	
			(2) Borrowing from Japanese Domestic Financial Institutions	0	
			(3) Local Bond and Debt, etc.	8	(3.1)
			(4) Borrowing from Local Financial Institutions	6	(2.3)
			(5) Bond and Debt, etc., Issued in Third Country	9	(3.5)
			(6) Borrowing from a Third Country Financial Institution	6	(2.3)
			(7) Leasing	0	
			(8) Own Funds (Depreciation and Profit, etc.)	0	

Source: Export-Import Bank of Japan.

Note: The survey asked for the three most common fundraising sources.

money were reported to be "local subsidiaries," while only 24% and 17.3% were "parent companies," respectively. In contrast, in the USA the category of "parent company" was reported by 28.4% and in the EC "financing subsidiaries" by 11.2% of respondents, while the share of "overseas subsidiaries" was 65.3% and 66.8%, respectively.

Local subsidiaries themselves finance investment money almost totally through local financial institutions, in addition to a small amount of leasing services in the USA. In cases where parent companies raised funds, the methods centered on internal funding and borrowing through Japanese domestic institutions.

Noticeably, the so-called parent-child loans, for example, when a parent company issues a convertible bond (CB) in foreign and/or offshore markets to raise money needed by a subsidiary, are included in the category of "funds raised by the parent." Therefore, it is surprising that ASEAN overseas operations by Japanese MNCs are reliant on local ASEAN financial markets where the propensity to save is lower, but not on Japan where the propensity is much higher.

Local Short-term Loans as FDI Funds for Japanese Subsidiaries

Generally, the financial markets of developing countries where industrialization is in its infancy are based on short-term loans, especially for wholesale and retail sales. Even in Asian countries where industrialization has progressed rapidly, such as Thailand and Malaysia, long-term financial markets have not yet developed. Nevertheless, Japanese firms which contribute investment funds in the form of equity capital or "parent-child" loans must raise a considerable portion of long-term funds, as well as working capital from local financial markets.

Table 2 shows sources of loans to Japanese manufacturing subsidiaries in ASEAN countries. The table divides loans into long-term and short-term ones as of 1983. Japanese subsidiaries in ASEAN had different modes of access to local financial markets compared with subsidiaries in the rest of the world, especially those in the USA and the EC. One impressive characteristic is that they were heavily reliant on short-term loans. The share of "loans from local financial institution" to total loans was about 75% or a little more in ASEAN, Asia, the USA, and EC. At the same time, the proportion of "short-term loans from local financial institutions" to the total was 58% in ASEAN, and only 42.8% in the USA.

In Thailand, large amounts of funds for capital equipment are often raised by rolling over short-term loans (overdrafts on commercial banks, loans on deeds of finance companies, etc.). In the course of such

Table 2. Borrowing Sources of Japanese Manufacturing Subsidiaries (data as of March 1984).

(amt. outstanding; ¥ million)

	ASEAN			Asia		
	Long-term Loans	Short-term Loans	Total	Long-term Loans	Short-term Loans	Total
Loans from Investors	109,035	9,536	118,571	119,273	18,970	138,243
(Japanese)	(59.2)	(3.4)	(25.7)	(41.5)	(4.5)	(19.5)
	(100,230)	(8,796)	(109,026)	(110,133)	(10,236)	(120,369)
Loans from Local Financial	75,018	267,396	342,414	167,968	402,354	570,322
Institutions	(40.8)	(96.6)	(74.3)	(58.5)	(95.5)	(80.5)
[of which, Japanese banks]	[19,742]	[104,527]	[124,269]	[24,976]	[123,474]	[148,450]
Total	184,053	276,932	460,985	287,241	421,324	708,565
	(100)	(100)	(100)	(100)	(100)	(100)
	United States			EC		
	Long-term Loans	Short-term Loans	Total	Long-term Loans	Short-term Loans	Total
Loans from Investors	57,266	9,249	66,515	12,301	9,218	21,519
(Japanese)	(33.7)	(6.4)	(21.2)	(33.3)	(15.2)	(22.1)
	(51,345)	(8,389)	(59,734)	(7,821)	(7,475)	(15,296)
Loans from Local Financial	112,670	134,353	247,023	24,679	51,370	76,049
Institutions	(66.3)	(93.6)	(78.8)	(66.7)	(84.8)	(77.9)
[of which, Japanese banks]	[18,544]	[89,710]	[108,254]	[3,990]	[23,383]	[64,373]
Total	169,896	143,602	313,498	36,980	60,588	97,568
	(100)	(100)	(100)	(100)	(100)	(100)

Source: MITI, The 2nd Fundamental Survey on Japanese Firms' Overseas Business Operations: General Statistics of Japan's Overseas Investments (in Japanese).

Note: No data on " Short-term Loans " after the 3rd Survey (1986).

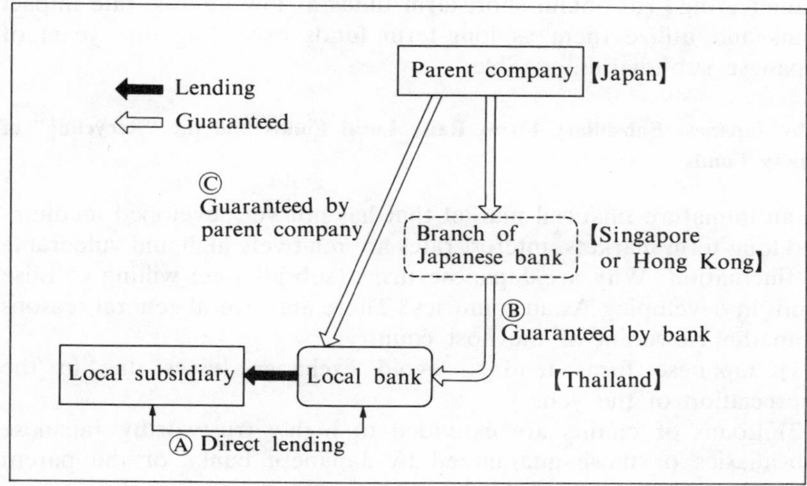

Fig. 2. Local Fund-raising Based on Guarantee by Bank or Parent Company.

transactions, Japanese subsidiaries usually enjoy the same low interest rates as on interbank transactions. Working capital is also raised by means of overdrafts and/or promissory notes.

Local subsidiaries of well-known Japanese firms such as household electrical appliance manufacturers or those which have long histories of local operations obtain loans from local commercial banks on their own reputations (Fig. 2-A). Other subsidiaries which are not well known and have lower credit standing procure low interest rate loans from local commercial banks based on guarantees provided by the Hong Kong or Singapore branches of the Japanese banks through the medium of their local representative offices (Fig. 2-B). Loans are also obtained on the basis of direct guarantees by the parent companies (Fig. 2-C). Although the short-term loans with local banks are rolled over as "long-term" funds, this is risky for firms due to interest rate fluctuations, since banks demand higher rates when markets become tight.

Japanese subsidiaries do have some options in terms of financing, however. They can, for example:

1) raise such foreign currency-dominated funds as the US dollar linked with the local currency in Singapore or in Hong Kong offshore markets, which local commercial banks and foreign bank branches convert to local currency-denominated funds; and

2) receive "parent-child" loans from parent companies in Japan or from Asian operational headquarters in Singapore or Hong Kong. Only the existence of these financing options makes the "financial

maneuvering" (to obtain short-term funds as low interest-rate impact loans and utilize them as long-term funds exceeding one year) of Japanese subsidiaries possible.

Why Japanese Subsidiary Firms Raise Local Funds and the "Recycling" of Equity Funds

In an immature financial market that has not yet developed medium- and long-term markets, interest rates are relatively high and vulnerable to fluctuation. Why are Japanese firms (subsidiaries) willing to raise funds in developing Asian countries? There are several general reasons from the viewpoint of the host country:

1) Japanese firms tend to avoid exchange losses due to the appreciation of the yen.

2) Loans or credits are extended to highly trustworthy Japanese subsidiaries or those guaranteed by Japanese banks or the parent companies almost at interbank rates.

3) Concessional (low-interest) export-promoting financing such as "packing credits" in Thailand and "export credit refinance" in Malaysia are very attractive to Japanese export-oriented subsidiaries.

4) Borrowing of offshore funds is regulated.

From the viewpoint of Japanese firms that raise local money, the sudden change in the economic environment caused by yen appreciation, escalating economic friction, formation of regional free trade areas (the expanded EC, US-Canada Free Trade Agreement), and domestic scarcity of blue-collar workers, make the establishment of offshore production bases and the formation of worldwide production networks necessary. The amount of equity capital needed is huge, as are total investment funds. Firms that intend to build up worldwide production and sales networks and place them under their own control are reluctant to issue their subsidiaries' stocks publicly. If they control the management of subsidiaries completely or by majority ownership, the parent companies must cover equity funds from internal reserves or by borrowing. If such investments are made in the form of debenture issuance or loans from financial institutions, their balance sheets are naturally deleterious.

In addition, in the case of operations in developing countries, there are time limits on investment incentives offered by local governments. The content or conditions of the incentives often change. Under such circumstances or due to other changes in an uncertain business environment, it is sometimes necessary to modify management policies and resite production bases to other countries. This is one of the reasons

Japanese parent companies that invest in developing countries tend to avoid loans to their subsidiaries. This same reason often leads to the incentive to recover quickly and completely even the equity capital in the form of remittance of returns, while retaining ownership. Moreover, it can sometimes be an inducement to develop new forms of FDI in which local (non-Japanese) firms are controlled by lending production equipment, parts, and materials rather then investing money as equity capital (see the Introduction).

If investment projects are approved by a government or its agencies in the ASEAN countries, various privileges such as exemption or reduction of corporate tax and customs duty imposed on imported materials, and accelerated depreciation of fixed capital are granted. Therefore, those approved Japanese subsidiaries that rapidly generate internal funds can remit some of these funds to their parent companies as returns or profits for investment. Such remittances mean that the funds invested by the parent companies as equity capital at the time of establishment of their overseas subsidiaries are "recycled."

IMPACT OF JAPANESE FDI ON MODERNIZATION OF LOCAL FINANCIAL MARKETS

Immature Local Financial Markets and Methods of Raising Funds: Thai and Malaysian Examples

Thailand

Thailand's financial markets consisted, at the end of 1988, of the Bank of Thailand (central bank), 15 commercial banks (2,078 domestic branches), 14 foreign banks including two Japanese, four government-affiliated special banks, and 94 finance companies. Of those financial institutions, commercial banks have a 60% or more share of the total assets, approximately 60% of which is dominated by four big local commercial banks. The four major commercial banks have been gaining superiority over other commercial banks and financial institutions (Table 3).

Figure 3A, in which Thai financial markets are divided into money and capital markets, shows the relationship between these conventional markets and the actual Thai credit market. When local firms raise funds in Thailand, the most common procedures include loans, overdrafts, bills discounted, and leasing. Direct loans, both short- and long-term, are made directly from various financial institutions, mainly commercial banks, to borrowers. In the latter half of the 1980s, loans from commercial banks accounted for about one-third of total commercial

Table 3. Thailand's Financial Markets (on the basis of assets as of the end of May 1989).

	(million bahts)	
Bank of Thailand	323,331	(16.8%)
Commercial banks	1,257,170	(62.8%)
4 Special Banks	217,879	(10.9%)
Finance Companies	199,644	(9.9%)
Total	2,004,044	(100.0%)

Source: Bank of Thailand.

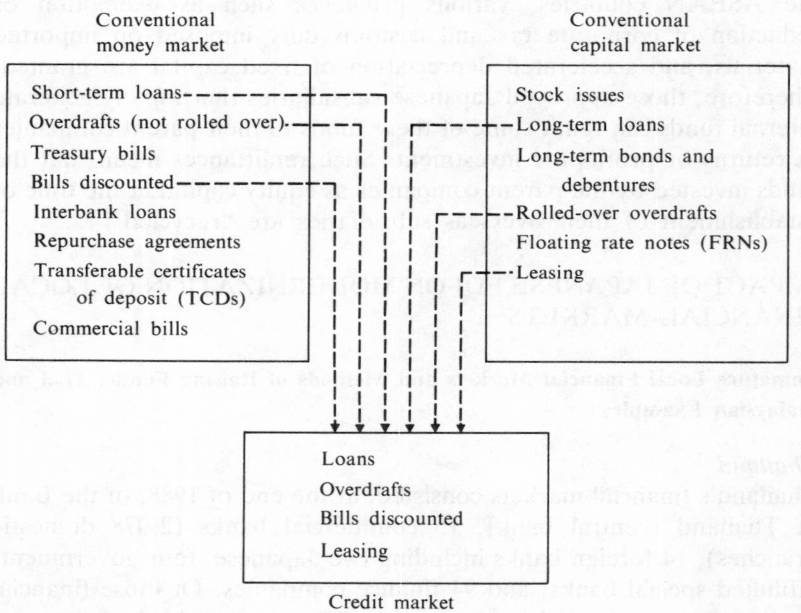

Fig. 3A. Classification of the Credit Market in Thailand.
Source: Bank of Thailand, *Financial Institutions and Markets in Thailand*, December 1988, p. 25.

bank credits. However, long-term loans have not been popular. Maturities of so-called term loans are usually within one year.

Overdrafts are revolving credit commitments, backed by some collateral, extended by commercial banks to their customers. Maturities of such credit commitments vary on a case-by-case basis, but they usually are within one year, and they can rolled over regularly. Before 1985, when the Bank of Thailand limited the amount of overdrafts given to a customer to 500 million baht, the large proportion of extended overdrafts remained unused and created a great deal of financial strain

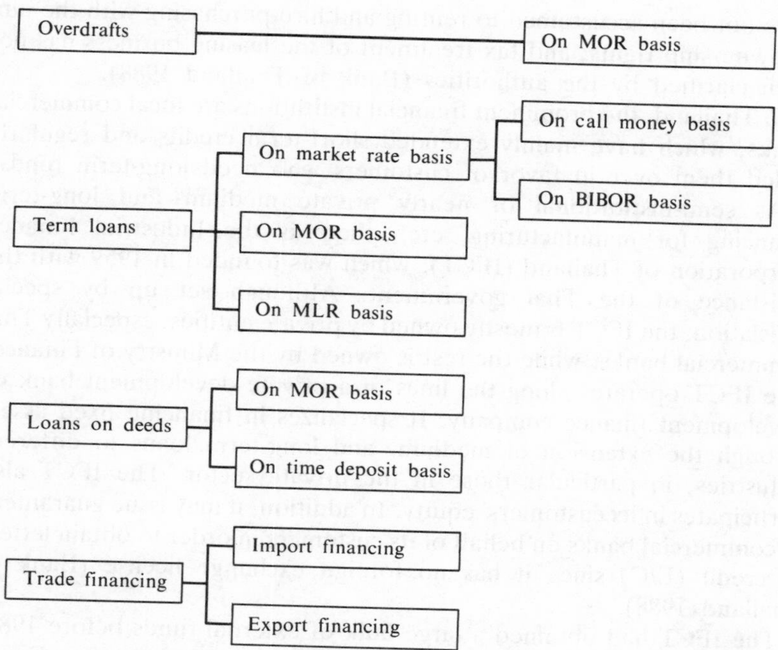

Fig. 3B. Forms of Financing through Commercial Banks and Finance Companies in Thailand.

Notes: 1. The minimum overdraft rate (MOR) is equal to the conventional prime rate.
2. The minimum lending rate (MLR) is adopted for a period of one year.
3. BIBOR, Bangkok Interbank Offer Rate.

on commercial banks. (Even at the end of 1987, unused overdrafts accounted for a substantial 36% of total overdraft commitments.) As a result, the share of overdrafts decreased to 33.4% of total commercial bank credits at the end of 1987 from 45.4% at the end of 1987.

Firms in need of short-term funds may sell postdated checks, promissory notes, or bills of exchange to commercial banks or finance companies at a discount, and with recourse. Those documents are called bills discounted. Maturities of bills are within one year. At the end of 1987, bills discounted at commercial banks accounted for about one-third of total commercial bank credits.

Leasing has been in existence in Thailand since 1978. Under a leasing agreement, a lessor acquires certain property or equipment and leases it to a lessee for a specified period of time, which is generally within seven years. Leasing is a kind of long-term financing that has not matured in Thailand. It is not used as a financing procedure because Thai firms have not been accustomed to renting and hire-purchasing with the aim of ownership rights; and tax treatment of the leasing business has not been clarified by the authorities (Bank of Thailand 1988).

In Thailand, the prominent financial institutions are local commercial banks, which have mainly extended short-term credits and regularly rolled them over in favor of customers who need long-term funds.

As semi-institutional or nearly private medium- and long-term financing for manufacturing, etc., there is the Industrial Finance Corporation of Thailand (IFCT), which was founded in 1959 with the assistance of the Thai government. Although set up by special legislation, the IFCT is mostly owned by private entities, especially Thai commercial banks, while the rest is owned by the Ministry of Finance. The IFCT operates along the lines of a private development bank or development finance company. It specializes in financing fixed assets through the extension of medium- and long-term loans to different industries, in particular those in the private sector. The IFCT also participates in its customers' equity. In addition, it may issue guarantees to commercial banks on behalf of its customers in order to obtain letters of credit (L/C) since it has no foreign exchange license (Bank of Thailand 1988).

The IFCT had obtained a large bulk of external funds before 1988, especially from the Overseas Development and Cooperation Funds (ODCF) of Japan in the form of so-called two-step loans. As the result of the rapid appreciation of the yen after the Plaza Accord in 1985, it experienced huge foreign exchange losses. Since then the IFCT has switched its borrowing source to the local market to take advantage of the general low level of interest rates, and to reduce exchange risk on foreign loans. Thus even semi-institutional financing for fixed assets tends to rely on local money.

Malaysia

The Malaysian financial market differs from that of Thailand due to the stronger influence of government regulation and the presence of foreign banks. As shown in Table 4-A and 4-B, the 62% share of foreign banks in 1970 has been lowered to the present share of about 25%. Government policies to nurture local (domestic) banks have played an important role in the present high status of Malaysian banks.

The financial markets for firms to raise funds are divided into domestic money markets, offshore money markets, and domestic capital markets. Under the foreign exchange control law, a firm in which a foreigner or foreignentity has majority ownership (nonresident controlled company, NRCC) must raise 60% or more of its funds from

Table 4. Foreign Banks' Share in Total Assets of Malaysian Commercial Banks.

(Unit: Malaysian Dollar)

Year	Foreign Banks	Local Banks	Total
1970	2,796 (62.1)	1,691 (37.9)	4,460 (100.0)
1980	12,224 (38.0)	19,962 (62.0)	32,186 (100.0)
1985	20,776 (28.0)	53,457 (72.0)	74,233 (100.0)
1989 (April)	24,994 (24.5)	77,066 (75.5)	102,060 (100.0)

Source: Bank Negara Malaysia, *Quarterly Bulletin*, 1989, No.1.

the financial institutions (commercial banks, merchant banks, finance companies, etc.) established in Malaysia and majority-owned by Malaysians.

For short-term financing, the utilization of overdrafts on commercial banks and revolving credit from merchant banks is popular. The term "revolving credit" means a financing method of obtaining a credit for a certain amount as a unit for the period of one, two, three, or six months, and then renewable on the due date if necessary. Therefore, it is utilized as the base of long-term funds and working capital as well. The interest rates for such financing is equal to the interbank rate plus the merchant bank's margin, and it is sometimes lower than the prime rate of commercial banks. Many firms use overdrafts and revolving credit jointly in order to minimize the cost of raising funds. (Since 1982 a 1% penalty has been imposed on the unused balance of overdrafts provided by commercial banks.)

For the purpose of raising working capital backed up by real transactions it is possible to utilize bills discounted, banker's acceptance (B/A), and factoring. B/A is issued in amounts of 30,000 ringgits or more at 1,000 ringgit pitch for a duration of 30 to 200 days. In general, the B/A rate is set in accordance with the interbank rate but is sometimes lower.

Both commercial banks and merchant banks provide medium-term and long-term loans for a duration of two to five years to private firms, and of eight to ten years to the government or similar agencies. The interest rate is fixed or floats with the prime rate in the case of commercial banks. In the case of merchant banks, however, it is often linked with the interbank rate to take advantage of the revolving credit form. Stable sources of medium- and long-term funds are limited in Malaysia as well as in Thailand, however. Medium- and long-term financing is, therefore, often accommodated in the form of continued short-term financing (overdrafts, revolving credit, etc.).

As institutional financing, the "New Investment Funds" (NIF) system was established in 1985. Through this facility, medium- and long-term funds for new investment in manufacturing, agriculture, tourism, and mining industries are provided, the maximum limit of which is 75% of necessary funds excluding the cost of acquiring real estate and for a maximum term of five years.

Another institutional medium- and long-term financing option is "Malaysia Industrial Development Finance" (MIDF), which supplies medium- and long-term funds for procurement of plant or equipment which is taken in mortgage. This financing is open to NRCCs that utilize the loans for the purpose of economic development of Malaysia. In reality, however, it is not easy for NRCCs to be approved since a large number of applications have been filed to obtain this advantageous financing.

Borrowing Sources of Japanese Subsidiaries for Fixed Capital: Impact on Establishment of Long-term Markets

Japanese manufacturing subsidiaries usually utilize their own funds as a source of fixed capital investment. According to the MITI surveys shown in Table 5, the main source of investment funds for equipment and machinery is not the parent companies but their subsidiaries' own funds. Where do those funds originate?

First, Japanese subsidiaries in ASEAN countries as well in more developed countries have their own funds for capital equipment and machinery, since their parent companies newly invest in and add money as equity capital to the subsidiaries. Parent companies cannot secure ownership or management control of subsidiaries until they pay the latter's equity capital. In addition, the equity capital is usually utilized as payment for equipment and machinery imported from Japan.

Second, ASEAN governments permit subsidiaries to accelerate the depreciation of equipment and abate or exempt their corporate tax, etc. in order to promote foreign investment. They locally reinvest such money in new projects. Since the latter half of the 1980s "loans from local financial institutions" has been a significant source of investment for capital equipment and machinery in ASEAN; 32.1% in 1989 compared to 11.8% in 1983. In addition, "loans from investors," most of which came from Japan, rapidly decreased to 8.4% in 1989 from 36.3% in 1983. In line with ASEAN industrialization, Japanese subsidiaries are locally raising capital equipment funds in local financial markets.

It marks a turning point in the development of ASEAN financial markets for Japanese subsidiaries to fund their fixed capital locally, and that will spur ASEAN countries to organize long-term financial markets as part of financial modernization.

Table 5. Borrowing Sources of Funds of Fixed Capital: Subsidiaries.

(amt. outstanding; ¥ million)

	ASEAN			Asia			USA			EC		
	1983	1986	1989	1983	1986	1989	1983	1986	1989	1983	1986	1989
Own Funds	40,725	41,950	–	60,508	81,680	–	35,454	53,418	–	13,158	13,049	–
	(39.7)	(76.8)	(43.6)	(43.8)	(56.2)	(51.2)	(62.1)	(61.7)	(43.4)	(48.6)	(64.8)	(46.1)
(from Japan)	[7,220]	[1,663]	[–]	[8,876]	[4,483]	[–]	[10,122]	[19,363]	[–]	[3,615]	[2,418]	[–]
	(7.0)	(3.0)	(–)	(6.4)	(3.1)	(–)	(17.7)	(22.4)	(–)	(13.4)	(12.0)	(–)
Local Government Subsidy	391	0	–	401	135	–	0	2,085	–	1,427	236	–
	(0.4)	(0.0)	(–)	(0.3)	(0.1)	(–)	(0.0)	(2.4)	(–)	(5.3)	(1.2)	(–)
Loans from Investors	37,240	2,438	–	38,916	3,176	–	8,564	4,880	–	1,422	355	–
	(36.3)	(4.5)	(8.4)	(28.2)	(2.2)	(5.9)	(15.0)	(5.6)	(18.4)	(5.3)	(1.8)	(27.0)
(from Japan)	[33,730]	[760]	[–]	[34,531]	[1,483]	[–]	[8,408]	[3,827]	[–]	[1,120]	[319]	[–]
	(32.9)	(1.4)	(–)	(25.0)	(1.0)	(–)	(14.7)	(4.4)	(–)	(6.6)	(1.6)	(–)
Loans from Local Financial Institutions	12,142	9,481	–	25,760	41,848	–	11,953	18,097	–	10,508	2,510	–
	(11.8)	(17.4)	(32.1)	(18.6)	(28.8)	(31.7)	(20.9)	(20.9)	(27.7)	(38.8)	(12.5)	(31.2)
Other	12,109	754	–	12,649	18,436	–	1,116	8,045	–	539	3,991	–
	(11.8)	(1.4)	(15.9)	(9.2)	(12.7)	(11.1)	(2.0)	(9.3)	(10.5)	(2.0)	(19.8)	(13.7)
Total	102,607	54,623	–	138,234	145,275	–	57,087	86,525	–	27,045	20,141	–
	(100.0)	(100.0)	(100.0)	(100.0)	(100.0)	(100.0)	(100.0)	(100.0)	(100.0)	(100.0)	(100.0)	(100.0)
(from Japan)	[41,027]	[2,885]	–	[43,651]	[6,746]	[–]	[18,715]	[23,383]	–	[4,735]	[2,737]	[–]
	(40.0)	(5.2)	(–)	(31.6)	(4.6)	(–)	(32.8)	(27.0)	(–)	(17.5)	(13.6)	(–)

Source: Same as Table 3 (1986, 1989, 1991 editions).
Note: (1) No data on amounts raised from 1991 edition.
(2) This survey is conducted every three years.
(3) ( ) indicates percentage of the total for each year.

According to Robert E. McBain (1989), the aggregate balance of Asian firms is changing steadily from a heavy weighting of short-term borrowing toward a balance between short-term sources of debt. Newer than the introduction of long-term bank loans in most Asian countries is the emergence of bond markets. Virtually nonexistent at the end of the 1970s, bond markets in local currencies now constitute an important option for corporate financing in most Asian countries and are attracting the attention of many nonbank financial institutions (Table 6).

Table 6. Asian Bond Markets.

	Year Bond Market Established	Government Bonds Outstanding (end 1988)	Corporate Bonds Outstanding (end 1988)
Hong Kong	1975	Nil	HK$8,188 million*
Indonesia	1983	N.A.	Rp.935,718,000.00
Malaysia	1961	M$55.8 billion	M$521.2 million
Philippines	1902	P193,331 million	P2,170.3 million
Singapore	1985	S$7.4 billion	S$824.95 million
South Korea	Mid-50s	Won7,358.9 billion	Won1,635.2 billion
Taiwan	1978	NT$566,995 million	Nt$7,675 million
Thailand	1975	Baht203.81 billion	Baht1.62 billion

Source: Robert E. McBain, *Corporate Finance: The Asian Trends* (Asian Finance Publications, 1989).
*Includes commercial papers, FRNs, etc.

New Linkages of Export-promoting Financing with Money Markets: Thai and Malaysian Examples

Packing Credits as Local Export-promoting Financing

A typical example of modernization of Thai money markets induced through the medium of local funding by Japanese subsidiaries is closely related to "packing credits," or more precisely, "rediscount under packing letter of credit or sales contract or usance bill of exchange." The Thai government has explained packing credits as follows: Rediscount of the exporter's promissory note by the Bank of Thailand under a packing letter of credit, or sales contract, or usance (term) bill of exchange is a kind of financial assistance or loan of export advance granted by the Bank of Thailand to the exporter at very low interest in order to promote export business in the country. Rediscount must be made through commercial banks. The export merchandise accepted for packing can be either agricultural products, or agricultural and industrial products.

The procedure to apply for rediscount is divided into two parts:

1) The applicant, usually a judicial body, who wishes to receive financial assistance from the Bank of Thailand by means of rediscounting a promissory note under a packing letter of credit, sales contract, or usance bill of exchange, should first submit an application through a commercial bank, which usually is the applicant's bank. The Bank of Thailand upon receipt of the application will examine all documents submitted and approve the application if all evidence is complete and appears satisfactory.

2) The applicant will be registered as a qualified exporter, and the promissory note will be accepted for rediscount. The longest term for rediscount is up to the expiry date of the letter of credit, the shipment date mentioned in the sales contract, or the due date of the usance bill of exchange, but not over 180 days. The amount of rediscount is 80% of the amount of the letter of credit, 70% of the amount of the sales contract, and 90% of the amount of the usance bill of exchange.

The packing credit is a kind of export concessional financing established in the early 1970s especially to promote the export of important agricultural products. In the beginning, approximately 85% of this concessional credit went to exports and a few export items absorbed most of the export subsidies. Concessional funds granted to four export commodities (rice, maize, tapioca, and sugar) added up to roughly one-half of the total export credit refinancing provided during 1972-1985 (Fig. 4) (*Business Review* 1989).

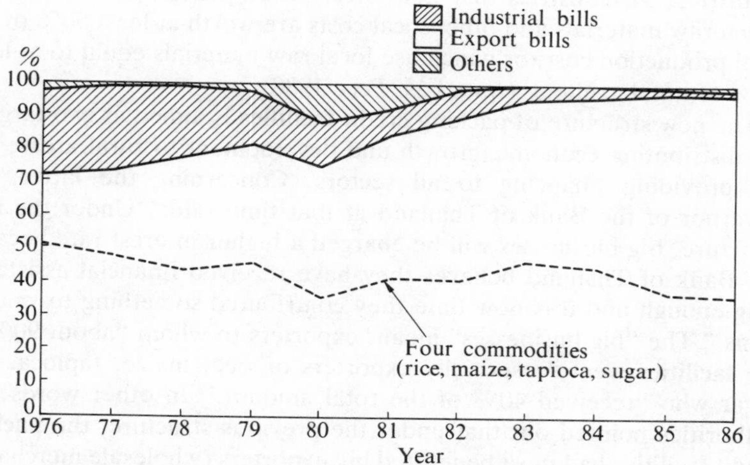

Fig. 4. Percentage Share of Refinanced Bills.
Source: *Business Review,* March 15-31, 1989.

In Malaysia as well as in Thailand, from the government's standpoint of promoting exports, the system called "export credit refinance" (ECR) has been successfully implemented. The period of credit extended is four to six months before and after shipping, respectively, and the interest rate is very low.

Export-promoting Investment and Its Impact on Development of Discount Markets

In the course of rapid industrialization based on introducing export-oriented investment by foreigners, in 1988 the USA and the EC labelled packing credits as "subsidies" for large exporters including Japanese subsidiaries. In other words, they charged that Thai export products are priced competitively on foreign markets due to interest rate subsidies provided by the governments. Therefore, the Bank of Thailand revised packing credit guidelines to stifle such criticism. However, external political pressure was not the only reason; the rapidly changing structure of the Thai economy also provided impetus.

The revision of the credit ruling focused on giving more credits to support expansion of industries both occupied by small- and medium-scale exporters and located in rural areas, that is: 1) industries that use local agricultural materials amounting to at least 20% of the combined value of all raw materials; 2) industries that export at least 20% of their total sales; 3) industries that use local raw materials equal to at least 50% of the combined value of all raw materials; 4) labor-intensive industries; 5) industries that help local development; 6) industries in which raw materials and other local costs are worth at least 50% of the total production cost, or which use local raw materials equal to at least 50% of total content (*Bangkok Post* 1988).

The new structure of packing credit facilities is aimed at two targets: (1) distributing economic growth and development to rural areas; and (2) providing financing to all sectors. Concerning the latter, the governor of the Bank of Thailand at that time said: "Under the new structure, big businesses will be charged a higher interest rate because the Bank of Thailand believes they have received financial assistance long enough and it is now time they contributed something to smaller firms." The "big businesses" meant exporters to whom "about 90% of the facilities went," especially exporters of rice, maize, tapioca, and sugar who "received 40% of the total amount." In other words, the authorities pointed out that under the previous structure, the packing credit facilities had most benefitted big exporters (wholesale merchants) and big manufacturers such as Japanese subsidiaries, and therefore, they would have to be spread out to local manufacturers nationwide.

The new wave in packing credits appears to be aimed at the

modernization of the Thai discount market to promote the spread of the nationwide rediscount system and to transform the so-called discount markets that operate under the market mechanism on the condition of the rediscount rates of big businesses (big manufacturers or international trading firms that export industrial goods) moving toward the market rates.

Development of Capital Markets

As Asian economies grow in credit-worthiness, and therefore as Asian firms improve their debt/equity ratio and rapidly expand activity in Asian stock markets, more investors from local and overseas markets will seek equity investments. Table 7 indicates that the number of listings and aggregate market value have grown significantly in the process of Thai and Malaysian industrialization. With the coming of age of equity finance, nonbank financial institutions such as merchant banks and finance companies have been increasingly playing important roles. Particularly in Thailand, commercial banks have committed substantial resources to their stockbroking subsidiaries (finance companies). Recently Thai commercial banks have become significant players in the brokerage industry in addition to money-lending (McBain 1989).

There were signals that Thai financial markets were changing in the middle of the 1980s. Portfolio investments shot up to 12 billion baht in 1987, six times as much as the 2 billion baht in 1983. Such trends paralleled the sharp increase in FDI. At the same time, Thai financial institutions increasingly offered noninterest financial services (Tables 8A and B).

According to the Bangkok Bank's analysis of the income structure of financial institutions for five years from 1983 to 1987, a change was already underway. In 1983, about 95% of the income of commercial banks and finance companies was based on dividends and interest. In 1987, however, commercial banks and finance companies earned 10.1% and 19.4%, respectively, of their income from brokerage business, up from 5.6% and 4.4%, respectively, in 1983.

Finance companies, a considerable number of which work as subsidiaries of commercial banks, generate their noninterest income from brokerage fees and profits in stock transactions. The introduction of foreign or offshore funds to Thailand such as the Bangkok Fund, the Siam Fund, the Thai Growth Fund (founded by Nikko Securities Co., Japan), the Thai Prime Fund (Nomura Securities Co., Japan), and the Thai Investment Fund (Yamaichi Securities Co., Japan), among others, provided a major boost to this sector (Silavatkul 1989).

Table 7. ASEAN Stock Markets.

	Singapore			Malaysia			Thailand			Indonesia		
Year	87	88	89	87	88	89	87	88	89	87	88	89
Listed companies	321	327	333	291	295	305	109	141	177	24	24	56
Value of listed companies (US$10 Billion)	42.7	53.2	71.8	29.7	36.4	57.8	5.5	8.9	25.7	0.07	0.26	2.29
Transaction values (US$10 Billion)	10.7	6.3	20.0	4.0	25.8	6.8	4.8	6.2	14.7	0.00	0.02	0.56
Index	824	1,039	1,481	1,306	1,815	2,831	285	387	899	83	305	400
	ST Index			NST Index			SET Index					
PER Times	21.3	21.9	20.6	30.7	24.1	31.6	10.5	12.6	18.2	—	—	—

Source: Daiwa Bank (Singapore Branch).

Basic Stock Market Data (for reference).

Country	Data Stock Exchange Founded	No. of Listed Companies			Value of Listed Companies		
		1978	1983	1988	1978	1983	1988
Hong Kong	1914	265	277	304	HK$65.9b	HK$141.8b	HK$580.4b
Indonesia	1977	3	23	24	UD$75.1m	Rp100,743.3	US$242.5m
Malaysia	1976	253	271	291	M$18.3b	M$53.1b	M$99.1b
Philippines	1927	184	154	143	P18.4b	P88.6b	P19.5b
Singapore	1973	266	301	327	S$22.7b	S$98.6b	S$103.6b
South Korea	1956	356	328	502	Won2,893b	Won3,489b	Won64,544b
Taiwan	1961	86	119	163	NT$153b	NT$306.06b	NT$3,383b
Thailand	1962	61	88	141	Baht33.1b	Baht34.8b	Baht223.7b

Source: Robert E. McBain, *Corporate Finance: Asian Trends* (Asian Finance Publications, 1989).

Table 8. Income Sources of Thai Financial Institutions.

(A) Income of Financial Institutions

(million Baht)

		CBs*	FCs	CFCs	GSB	GHB	BAAC
1983	Interest-based	61,748.5	13,411.6	564.9	4,990.2	1,328.9	2,626.1
	Fee-based	3,653.2	628.9	169.6	20.7	1.8	110.7
1984	Interest-based	77,675.2	14,802.6	540.1	6,162.6	1,507.8	2,784.9
	Fee-based	4,073.2	635.6	92.9	17.0	3.6	104.1
1985	Interest-based	86,490.9	14,724.6	522.9	7,372.6	1,559.5	3,148.4
	Fee-based	4,683.4	416.5	51.7	16.2	8.3	154.8
1986	Interest-based	77,269.7	14,239.0	469.8	8,838.8	1,366.7	3,404.2
	Fee-based	6,926.4	972.3	49.8	16.9	7.8	45.8
1987	Interest-based	74,652.2	11,289.6	358.7	10,071.0	1,268.9	3,451.2
	Fee-based	8,382.2	2,708.2	62.1	30.9	15.9	47.5

*15 Thai commercial banks.

Notes: CB, commercial bank; FC, finance company; CFC, credit finance company; GSB, government savings bank; GHB, government housing bank; BAAC, Bank of Agriculture and Agricultural Cooperatives.

(B) Proportion of Income of Financial Institutions

(% of total income)

		CBs	FCs	CFCs	GSB	GHB	BAAC
1983	Interest-based	94.4	95.6	76.9	99.6	99.9	96.0
	Fee-based	5.6	4.4	23.1	0.4	0.1	4.0
1984	Interest-based	95.0	95.9	85.3	99.7	99.8	96.4
	Fee-based	5.0	4.1	14.7	0.3	0.2	3.6
1985	Interest-based	94.9	97.2	91.0	99.8	99.5	95.3
	Fee-based	5.1	2.8	9.0	0.2	0.5	4.7
1986	Interest-based	91.8	93.6	90.4	99.8	99.5	98.7
	Fee-based	8.2	6.4	9.6	0.2	0.5	1.3
1987	Interest-based	89.9	80.6	85.2	99.7	99.8	98.6
	Fee-based	10.1	19.4	14.8	0.3	1.2	1.4

Source: Bangkok Bank Monthly Review, May 1989.

Commercial banks have increased noninterest income due to commercial banking laws that allow them to operate foreign exchange, open letters of credit, issue credit cards, and act as agents of the government or of government agencies in collecting funds as entrusted. Those businesses have been rapidly expanding in line with the upsurge in export-promoting investments.

At the end of 1988, however, in recognition of the rapid growth of the

Thai economy and in order to accommodate the increasingly important role of commercial banks in such economic development, the Bank of Thailand allowed commercial bank investment in a firm to exceed the previously prescribed limit. This permission is given on a temporary basis, each time for a period of not more than three years. After three years the Bank of Thailand reviews the situation to determine whether the commercial bank's holdings should be reduced and if so by what percentage. In any case the commercial bank is required to reduce its equity to the prescribed limit within five years from the date that it begins to make a profit. Firms that commercial banks can invest in beyond the prescribed limit must be newly established firms that can promote business and investment in the country and must be a commercial bank debtor with a financial position requiring equity participation by the creditor bank, without which the firm may become insolvent. The investment bank must ensure that the firm applies for a listing on the stock market within three years from the date the firm begins to realize a profit (Sutuntivorakoon 1962).

In the process of rapid Thai industrialization, the commercial banks have begun to play the role of "venture capital" sources for newly established firms, as well as the role of brokerages through their own finance companies. After its heavy foreign exchange losses in 1987, the IFCT has entered capital markets. The Mutual Fund Co. (MFC), which is an IFCT subsidiary, has been encouraging foreign investors to invest in the Thai capital market. The MFC deals with offshore funds such as the Thai Prime Fund, which was the fifth international fund project approved by the Thai central bank. The fund, with an initial value of $155 million with a duration of 25 years, was founded with the cooperation of the MFC, Nomura Securities Co. of Japan, the International Finance Corporation, and others. Its main purpose is to mobilize funds extended from foreign countries, in particular from Japan, for long-term investment such as equity securities for Thai firms. During bullish periods the fund may increase its holding of equity securities. In contrast, during downturns, it may reduce the holdings of equity securities and invest in bonds, debentures, short-term debt obligations, etc., in local (Thai) currency.

Thailand's successful economic growth based on export-oriented investments has attracted foreign money for equity finance. As a result, both stock and bond and debenture markets will have to expand, although these securities markets are now very small. Another impact on the development of Thai equity finance is the move to privatize the big government corporations. In addition, it is possible that the Thai BOI will ask foreign newcomers to list their stocks on the Stock

Exchange of Thailand as a condition for investment approval.

In Thailand and Malaysia, furthermore, several Japanese subsidiary firms have listed their stocks. The evaluation of Japanese firms is favorable and the stocks are popular. In addition, especially in Malaysia, the participation of native Malays in foreign firms and an increase in the proportion of their share has been requested by the government. It is expected, therefore, that the number of Japanese firms listed on the local stock exchange will continue to increase in the near future.

DEVELOPMENT OF ASIAN INTERNATIONAL FINANCIAL MARKETS: NEW TRENDS IN SINGAPORE

Competitiveness or Interdependence: Japan and Singapore Offshore Markets

In December 1986, the Japan Offshore Market (JOM) was established with three motivations: the need for Japan to carry out its global financial responsibility in recycling funds, the desire to ease foreign (especially US) demand for the liberalization of its financial market, and to add prestige to Tokyo as an international financial center.

As a result of the establishment of the JOM, the Hong Kong and Singapore offshore markets did not shrink. The opposite is actually true. Hong Kong and Singapore, respectively, had only a 10.5% and 12.3% share of world offshore markets excluding the UK, USA, and Japan at the end of 1980, but expanded to 25% and 21.8%, respectively, at the end of June 1987 (Fig. 5A).

According to the Development Bank of Singapore, Singapore and Hong Kong had a 10.3% and 13.1% share, respectively, of offshore lending in major centers, and 10.4% and 10.0%, respectively, in 1986. Japan's share was up to 9.4% in 1987 from 5.7% in 1986 (Fig. 5B).

The JOM strictly segregates domestic and offshore accounts, and therefore restricts the number of eligible participants. The authorities, who fear the possible mix of Euro-yen and domestic yen, have set JOM regulations to strengthen the effectiveness of domestic monetary policies. In this situation, foreigners and overseas subsidiaries of Japanese firms, except those for foreign exchange, are not willing to participate in the JOM.

In contrast, the free banking policy of Singapore provides a favorable background for the Singapore offshore market, the so-called Asian dollar market (ADM). Deregulation of exchange and financial controls and various tax concessions and fiscal measures have prompted the ADM to develop principally as a short-term market, with the Asian

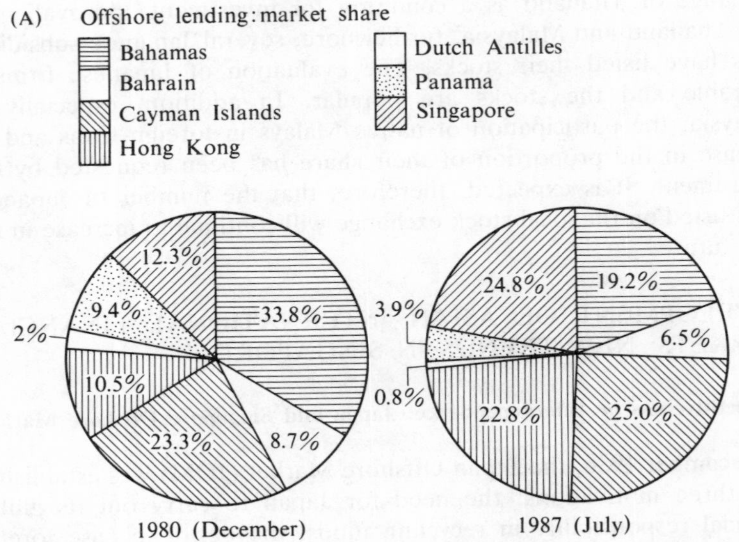

Fig. 5A. Market Shares of Singapore and Hong Kong Offshore Markets.
Source: Bank of England, *Quarterly Bulletin*, May 1988, p. 216.

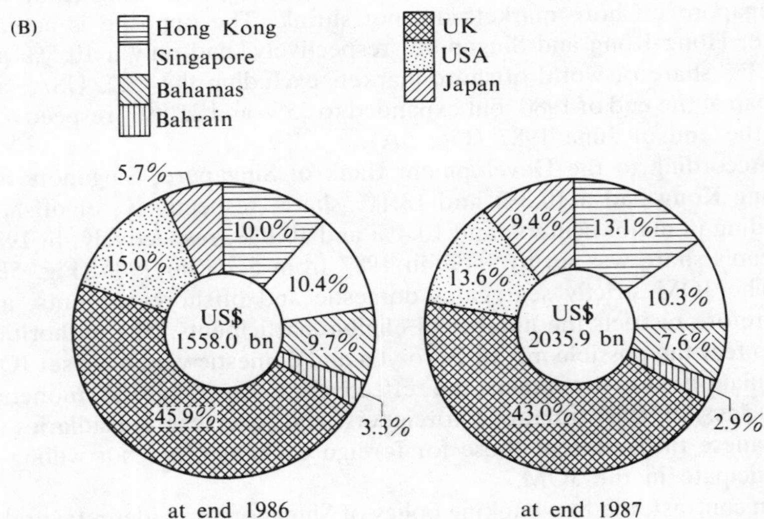

Fig. 5B. Offshore Lending: Market Shares in Major Centers.
Source: Development Bank of Singapore, *The Emergence of the Japan Offshore Market: Implications for Hong Kong and Singapore,* 1988.

bond market (ABM) as the medium- and long-term capital market.

The Asian currency unit (ACU) is essentially a locally licensed operational entity within a financial institution to deal with offshore money without reference to the exchange control authorities. ACUs are mainly used in offshore (foreign) banks and merchant banks.

The impetus for the establishment of the ADM was the development of Asian countries and the increasing number of MNCs in the region. Since the 1970s offshore funds have been channelled from London, the Middle East, and now Japan for investment in this region. The predominant share of "outside Singapore" (interbank funds) to total liabilities of ACUs shown in Table 9 confirms this trend. Recently "deposits of nonbank customers" includes mainly deposits of MNCs, governments, etc. in the Asian region.

Table 9. Asian Dollar Market: Singapore.

(A) Assets in Asian Currency Units.

(US$ million)

End of Period	Total Assets	Loans to Non-Bank Customers	Interbank funds				Other Assets
			Total	In Singapore	Inter-ACUs	Outside Singapore	
	(1)=2+3+7	(2)	(3)=4+5+6	(4)	(5)	(6)	(7)
1986	200,601.8	38,741.8	146,609.7	4,926.5	30,603.8	111,079.4	15,250.3
1987	244,868.5	55,010.8	171,092.9	5,079.7	26,055.8	139,957.4	18,765.0
1988	280,477.2	66,550.7	194,755.5	5,254.2	25,800.6	163,700.7	19,171.1
1989	336,581.8	86,393.5	228,725.2	7,329.6	27,565.9	193,829.7	21,463.1
1990	390,395.5	125,516.0	239,119.8	8,744.6	34,440.2	195,935.0	25,759.6

(B) Liabilities in ACUs.

(US$ million)

End of Period	Total Liabilities	Deposits of Non-Bank Customers	Interbank funds				Other Liabilities
			Total	In Singapore	Inter-ACUs	Outside Singapore	
	(1)=2+3+7	(2)	(3)=4+5+6	(4)	(5)	(6)	(7)
1986	200,601.8	33,804.6	159,368.9	4,860.9	30,603.5	123,904.5	7,428.5
1987	244,868.5	41,575.5	192,485.3	6,538.7	26,056.6	159,890.0	10,807.6
1988	280,477.2	47,453.9	221,803.6	8,444.2	25,801.4	187,558.0	11,219,7
1989	336,581.8	55,019.4	269,582.1	12,620.3	27,566.5	229,395.3	11,980.4
1990	390,395.5	66,885.5	309,427.1	11,955.8	34,438.1	263,033.2	14,082.8

Source: Monetary Authority of Singapore, *Monthly Statistical Bulletin*, April 1991.

"Loans to nonbank customers" comprise a considerable percentage of total assets of the ACUs. The ADM maintained robust growth during 1990. Total assets/liabilities of ACUs registered a 16% growth to reach

US$390 billion by the end of 1990. Local firms (including MNC subsidiaries) and governments in ASEAN countries such as Malaysia, Indonesia, the Philippines, and Thailand have been making use of the ADM and ABM in borrowing and depositing.

Therefore, Singapore has become an international financial center of Asia, especially ASEAN, and has promoted ASEAN business societies to form financial networks (Lee 1990, Tan 1989, Development Bank of Singapore 1988, Ministry of Trade and Industry of Singapore 1991). Since it plays an important role as a center of ASEAN financial networks, Singapore has competitive advantage over Japan. In addition, there exists a pool of hard currencies, especially US dollars, in the Singapore offshore market, because the currencies of ASEAN and other Asian countries are linked with the US dollar. The Singapore financial market coexists with the JOM.

Asian Bond Market and Booming Venture Capital Firms in Singapore

The issuers and underwriters of Asian dollar bonds are from different countries worldwide. They include private firms, banks, securities or finance companies, and governments and regional institutions. In particular, Japanese banks and securities companies play an active role in the Asian Dollar Bond Market (ADBM).

As mentioned previously, Japanese securities companies raise investment funds such as the Thai Prime Fund in the Asian Dollar Bond Market, which they invest in unlisted local firms (joint ventures) in ASEAN countries. In this sense, Singapore is a financial pool that distributes equity capital to local firms or joint ventures with foreigners in ASEAN countries.

In addition, a new type of foreign investment, venture capital, is being attracted by flourishing ASEAN. Japanese venture capital firms are eagerly establishing representative offices in Singapore as well as in Hong Kong. The Japan ASEAN Investment Co. (JAIC) opened a representative office initially in Singapore in 1988 and then in Bangkok, Kuala Lumpur, Manila, and Jakarta. JAIC is a semiprivate, semigovernmental venture capital firm established in cooperation with the Japanese government and the Japan Committee for Economic Development (Reidanren).

JAIC invests its funds, which are procured by the JAIC Investment Fund and in principle operate as venture capital, in unlisted companies in the ASEAN member countries to assist their development and growth. The JAIC Investment Fund was established under the Civil Code of Japan. Its assets are jointly owned by its members based on the ratio of the initial investment in its investment fund. The investment fund exists for a duration of 10 years from the date of its establishment. As of July 1990, the amount of the five JAIC Investment Funds had reached ¥71.6 billion. JAIC had invested in 50 companies (eight in Singapore, nine in Malaysia, 20 in Thailand, seven in the Philippines, five in Indonesia, and one in Hong Kong), whose investment amount totalled about 17.8 billion yen as of the end of January 1991 (Table 10).

Table 10. Investment Portfolio of JAIC (January 31, 1991).

Country	No. of Companies	Local Currency	Yen (1,000s)
Singapore	8	S$44,233	3,301,879
Malaysia	9	M$33,358	1,713,051
Thailand	20	B1,523,821	8,352,932
Philippines	7	P579,780	3,368,114
Indonesia	5	US$2,284 and Rp6,255,000	801,749
Hong Kong	1	US$2,375	318,036
Total	50	***	17,855,762

Source: JAIC.

The large Japanese venture capital firm, Nippon Godo Finance Co. (JAFCO), started Nomura-JAFCO Investment Asia jointly with Nomura Securities Co. in Singapore in 1990, after establishing a Hong Kong subsidiary, JAFCO International (Asia), in 1983. Therefore, JAFCO has two bases to invest in unlisted companies in Asia and Australia and promote them to become listed on stock exchanges. Nikko Capital Co. opened a representative office in Singapore, whose main purpose is to seek unlisted firms with bright business prospects.

The Singapore government offers generous tax concessions to firms receiving venture funds. These include exemption from the corporate tax for up to 10 years for some firms. In addition, the government's venture capital incentive scheme encourages investment in higher-risk ventures such as technology firms. According to *Asian Venture Capital Journal* (AVCJ), the number of Singapore venture capital firms rose to 20 in 1991 from 12 in 1989. These firms managed funds worth about US$765 million in early 1991, up from US$330 million at the end of 1989 (*Business Times* 1991).

Singapore Foreign Exchange Market and the MNC Intracompany Regional Settlement System

Since 1986 Singapore's foreign exchange market has grown rapidly.

Average daily turnover rose to US$61 billion in 1989 from US$13 billion in 1985. In the first quarter of 1990, average daily turnover rose further to US$72 billion. Increased global foreign exchange activity and the growing shift of treasury activities to the Asian time zone with the rise of Tokyo as a major financial center continues to benefit Singapore's market. Recently, however, an increasing amount of business has also originated from the surrounding region as strong growth in regional economies has boosted activity (Monetary Authority of Singapore 1990).

Singapore is a very important regional short- and long-term financial market as well as a center of the global financial network. Therefore, in line with the rapid growth of international financial transactions, nonbanks as well as banks transact foreign exchange. The existence of Singapore as the center of the ASEAN or Asian financial network is predominantly based on ASEAN industrialization and the formation of ASEAN production networks.

In the process of the formation of regional and worldwide production networks, Singapore is beginning to take on the following new functions, mainly for MNCs in the ASEAN region.

1) Many MNCs are establishing regional operational headquarters that serve as an international procurement office (IPO) for production subsidiaries in the surrounding region. In other words, the IPO sets up procedures to collect materials, parts, and semifinished products that are supplied to the subsidiaries and then distributes them to other subsidiaries worldwide. The procurement operations are conducted through a central distribution center (CDC). The IPO with CDC functions as a kind of headquarters of an MNC's regional distribution network with computerized worldwide information and telecommunications facilities.

2) The same regional headquarters that operates as IPO serves as the core of the regional settlement system. For example, SONY International Singapore (SONIS), Asian regional headquarters of SONY, uses local currencies (or the linked US dollar) as an invoicing currency when it sells to or buys from each subsidiary in the region, and as a result no exchange losses are incurred. SONIS mixes various local currencies and then hedges unmarried portions through foreign exchange and/or offshore currency markets.

3) The regional headquarters operates as a financial control center to raise investment funds for subsidiaries and uses their surplus funds in offshore financial markets. In other words, it plays the role of an intracompany finance company, as Fujikura Densen Co. (Singapore) does. Hitachi Asia has subsidiaries and branch offices in Hong Kong,

Malaysia, Thailand, Taiwan, Korea, and the People's Republic of China to cover the region and was awarded operational headquarters status in April 1990. The headquarters signed with 20 financial institutions a S$45,000,000 guaranteed note issuance facility (NIF) to provide financial support to the subsidiaries and 28 Hitachi, Ltd. related firms in Singapore.

The Singapore government has an incentive scheme for operational headquarters (OHQ), defined as an entity incorporated or registered in Singapore (including legitimate branches of companies incorporated overseas), for the purpose of providing management and other headquarters-related services to subsidiary/associate-related companies in other countries. Thus, for a foreign firm to acquire the status and privileges of a licensed "headquarters," it must have a substantial level of headquarters operations in Singapore to support the OHQ's network in the region. Such operations may include: (1) administration, business planning, and coordination; (2) sourcing of raw materials and components; (3) R&D services and product development; (4) regional technical support and maintenance; (5) marketing control and sales promotion; (6) regional training and personnel management; (7) treasury and fund management; and (8) any other activities of economic benefit to Singapore approved by the Economic Development Board (EDB).

As of April 1991, 37 MNCs including seven Japanese had been awarded OHQ status by the EDB. However, many other foreign firms that have subsidiaries or affiliated firms in Asia have set up what could be called regional headquarters in Singapore to facilitate intracompany networks in ASEAN or Asia. The expanding regional intracompany production, distribution, settlement, and financing networks have thus made Singapore the most important regional financial center, including foreign exchange activities.

CONCLUSIONS: IS AN ASIAN REGIONAL OR SUBREGIONAL MONETARY AREA POSSIBLE?

An article in the widely read *Business Review* (Thailand) (1989) made the following interesting proposal:

> With the emergence of new trading blocs throughout the world, e.g., US-Canada Free Trade [Area] and European Free Trade [Area] in 1992, it is not too far-fetched to imagine an Asia-Pacific Free Trade [Area] starting with ASEAN and in due time incorporating other major economies such as Japan and Australia. In line with this prospective development of free trade [areas], concurrent adjust-

> ments in exchange rate regime may be expected to materialise....
>
> The US-Canada Free Trade [Area] is a US-based area which may stretch to cover Latin America. [The] European Monetary System (EMS) ... may evolve into a full-fledged central banking system for one Europe in 1992. As for Asia-Pacific, similar evolution may lead to certain exchange rate management that can be coined the yen-currency area.

Can a yen-currency area be established under the present conditions? Such proposals, including the Malaysian prime minister's proposal of an "East Asia economic grouping," are based on ASEAN economies steadily industrializing, modernizing, and establishing nationwide economic and social infrastructures. Such modernization has been confirmed in the financial sector. In line with Japan's and Asian NIEs' FDI and securities investments, ASEAN countries are modernizing their own financial markets. In particular, Singapore is building an international financial center that organizes an ASEAN-wide regional financial network linked with the Japan and Hong Kong offshore markets, mainly based on the US dollar.

If more ASEAN countries can introduce the same basket currency system, there is a strong possibility of establishing a subregional, integrated monetary system. The more Asian countries become relatively independent of the US dollar, the stronger the potential to organize a new type of regional monetary and financial system. The potential is related to Asian industrialization, and therefore to Japan's and Asian NIEs' foreign investment and aid in the region.

Bibliography

Bangkok Post. 1988. September 16.

Bank of Thailand. 1988. *Financial Institutions and Markets in Thailand*. Bangkok: Bank of Thailand.

Business Review (Thailand). 1989. March 15-31, p. 51.

Business Review (Thailand). 1989. June 1-15.

Business Times (Singapore). 1991. April 24.

Development Bank of Singapore. 1988. *The Emergence of the Japan Offshore Market: Implications for Hong Kong and Singapore*. Singapore: Development Bank of Singapore.

Export-Import Bank of Japan. 1991. *Kaigaitoshi Kenkyushoho*. Tokyo: Export-Import Bank of Japan.

Japan External Trade Organization. 1988. *Tsusho-koho*. Tokyo: Japan External Trade Organization.

Lee, S.-Y. 1990. *The Monetary and Banking Development of Singapore and Malaysia* (3rd edn.). Singapore: Singapore University Press.

McBain, R.E. 1989. *Corporate Finance: Asian Trends*. Asian Finance

Publications Ltd.
Ministry of Trade and Industry (Singapore). 1991. *Economic Survey of Singapore 1990*. Singapore: Ministry of Trade and Industry.
Miyazaki, Y. 1981. *Gendai sekaikeizai to Takokuseki Kigyo*. Tokyo: Iwanami Shoten.
Monetary Authority of Singapore. 1990. *Annual Report 1989/90*.
The Nation (Thailand). 1989. July 8.
Silavatkul, J. 1989. Thai financial institutions: An attempt to switch to non-interest income. *Bangkok Bank Monthly Review,* May.
Sutuntivorakoon, P. 1989. Banking regulation in Thailand: an overview of the Commercial Banking Act B.E.2505 (1962) and its amendments. *JIBL,* Vol. 4 (5): 230.
Tan, C.H. 1989. *Financial Markets and Institutions in Singapore* (6th edn.). Singapore: Singapore University Press.

Part II

Case Studies

7 Foreign Direct Investment in Malaysia: Technology Transfer and Linkages by Japan and Asian NIEs

Chan-Onn Fong

Vice Minister, Ministry of Education, Malaysia

INTRODUCTION

Foreign direct investment (FDI) has played a major role in the economic development of Malaysia. In the colonial era, FDI was responsible for the extensive development of the rubber and tin sectors. After independence, Malaysia (then Malaya) launched a purposeful program of rapid industrialization and agricultural modernization based on utilization of FDI. By definition, the expertise and technology provided by FDI involves not only the transfer of capital, but also the transfer of a package of resources including technological and managerial expertise. FDI refers to investment made to acquire a lasting interest and an effective voice in the management of an enterprise in a host country.

In general, all capital flows provided by direct foreign investors, including equity capital, reinvested earnings, and net lending, are classified as FDI (Goldsborough 1985). Types of FDI include (Kulasingam and Tan 1982):

a) Private FDI—private outlays for the establishment of a new enterprise or extension of an existing enterprise controlled by foreign investors;

b) Private foreign portfolio investment—bank loans (in the lender's currency) to an enterprise in Malaysia or purchase of bonds issued abroad by a Malaysian public authority or enterprise; and

c) "New forms" of foreign investment—investments where a foreign investor has no controlling interest in terms of equity participation, such as in turnkey operations, licensing agreements, subcontracting agreements, management contracts, or those that have a 50% foreign equity in joint ventures.

An important feature of the open Malaysian economy has been the extent of foreign participation in the modern sectors of the economy. This foreign investment has been actively encouraged by the Malaysian government and is considered to be an important means of promoting industrial growth through technology transfer, skill development, and better access to foreign markets.

HISTORICAL PERSPECTIVE ON FOREIGN DIRECT INVESTMENT

Prior to Independence in 1957

A detailed examination of the distribution of foreign capital by industry and country of origin is not possible for this period due to the unavailability of data. The UK was the main source of private capital; in 1913, it was estimated that British investment in Malaya amounted to M$33 million. This increased to M$108 million by 1930; of which 93% was in agriculture and mining (Saham 1980, Table 2.8). Virtually all private foreign capital invested in pre-independent Malaya was of British origin and concentrated in the extraction and production of raw materials and primary commodities. The argument for such a lop-sided investment pattern was that Malaya's comparative advantage then lay in the production of primary commodities and mineral products.

Along with the capital in the primary sector were investments in commerce and trade to facilitate the export of the primary products to, and imports of manufactured goods from the UK. During this period there was a deliberate curtailment of manufacturing activities since Malaya was deemed to be an importer of British manufactured goods. Further, the rationale that Malaya's comparative advantage was in the primary sector led to the British colonialists' pursuance of and indifferent attitude towards the indigenous manufacturing sector. The manufacturing activities then were mainly in the primary processing of agricultural products and manufacture of nontraded goods that enjoyed natural protection. Consequently, as trade pushed inland from the ports, the number of British bankers increased and this led to the development of the familiar control pattern of trade and investment to serve the needs of the UK; thus the birth of a so-called colonial pattern of foreign investment.

The investment of British multinational corporations (MNCs) in local manufacturing was only evident in the late 1950s. These MNCs were engaged in industries associated with the processing of rubber, tin smelting, manufacturing of cement, food, beverages, tobacco, and light engineering works subsidiary to plantations, mines and ports (Allen and Dornithorne 1962). Some of the British MNCs that initiated investments in the manufacturing sector in anticipation of the independent Malayan government's import-substitution industrialization program included Fraser and Neave, UniLever, and Bata (Lim 1980).

Participation by other foreign nations during the preindependence era was negligible. However, unlike natural rubber, trade, and banking, foreign ownership in the tin mining industry was more evenly spread out among developed countries, although here again the bulk of the ownership was British. The tin mining industry attracted some US, Australian, and French interests. About 70% of the tin production was by foreign-owned mines. These mines used processes that were more sophisticated and capital-intensive, and was therefore more labor productive. Japanese investment came to Malaya in the 1930s also to exploit the extraction of minerals, but it was concentrated on the iron mines that are now declining in importance primarily due to the Japanese being assured of supplies from the huge deposits in Australia and elsewhere. Foreign investment in manufacturing industries during the preindependence period was negligible and, even with local manufacturing investment, accounted only for a very small proportion of the total investment then.

1957 to 1970

The domination of the primary sector by foreigners immediately after independence is a legacy of Malaysia's colonial past. This strong presence was still evident immediately after independence. In the early 1960s, more than 50% of the capital stock was either owned or controlled by foreigners and about 70% of the profits earned by all companies in Malaysia were netted by foreign companies. Pretax profits of all companies were about $678 million in 1968. Of this amount, about $455 million was netted by foreign companies. Rubber, tin, palm oil, and manufacturing industries and banking, insurance, shipping, and wholesale trade continue to be dominated by foreign interests (Table 1). In other sectors of the economy, foreign ownership is lower than that in the primary sector, but still high in absolute terms.

Under the strong encouragement of the newly independent government in the early 1960s, FDI began to flow into import-substitution industries. This was due partially to the perceived needs of foreign MNCs to protect their markets in Malaysia. The inflow of this FDI

Table 1. Investment in Fixed Assets in Malaysia, 1968 ($ million).

Sector	Limited Companies Incorporated in Malaysia (Locally Controlled) (1)	Limited Companies Incorporated in Malaysia (Foreign Controlled) (2)	Malaysian Branches of Foreign Companies (3)	Total (4)	% Foreign Control (2)+(3) / (4)
Rubber	265.0	203.0	575.0	1043	74.6
Other Agriculture	107.0	54.0	70.0	231	53.7
Tin Mining	119.0	70.0	114.0	303	60.7
Other Mining	23.0	105.0	20.0	148	84.5
Manufacturing	489.0	426.0	47.0	962	49.2
Construction	32.0	4.5	8.5	45	28.9
Wholesale Trade	120.0	75.0	155.0	350	65.7
Retail Trade	45.0	20.0	1.0	66	31.8
Other Industry	428.0	84.0	83.0	595	28.1
All industries	1,628.0	1,041.5	1,073.5	4046	56.5

Note: Figures represent book values of net assets.
Source: Malaysia, *Financial Survey of Limited Companies in Malaysia,* 1967, and other official sources.

resulted in the high annual growth rate of 12.2% from 1961 to 1965 registered by the manufacturing sector. The separation of Singapore from Malaysia in 1965 temporarily reduced the inflow of investment. This partly explains the drop in the growth rate from 12.5% in 1966 to 8.6% in 1968. Local investors, as in most developing economies, did not go all out to invest in industries, partly because of their lack of experience, the brand-consciousness of the consumer public for imported manufactured goods, and the reluctance of foreigners to enter into joint ventures with them. Another major reason is that the retail trade, mineral-extraction industries, and property development were considered to be more attractive investments to them. Early opportunities in industrialization were therefore taken up by foreign investors. There was a marked influx of foreign capital with the British moving in quickly to be the largest foreign investor in Malaysia in the early 1960s. By 1968, the total fixed assets of foreign-controlled companies had reached 56.5% (Table 1) of the total assets of all limited Malaysian companies. Dominance of foreign investment in agriculture was still evident.

1970 to Present

A detailed analysis of foreign investment by country of origin and subsector was not possible prior to 1968 due to the lack of published data. The first comprehensively disaggregated data analysis on foreign investment by country of origin was the 1968 Census of Manufacturing Industries. There is, however, a lack of data on foreign investment by country of origin in the manufacturing sector.

The Malaysian government implemented the New Economic Policy (NEP) in 1970 with the aims of eradicating poverty irrespective of race and restructuring society to eliminate identification of race with economic functions (Government of Malaysia 1971). The restructuring goal involved reducing foreign corporate ownership from 61% in 1970 to 30% by 1990, and simultaneously increasing the share of *Bumiputeras* (Malays and other natives) from 2% to 30%, and that of other Malaysians from 37% to 40%. This implies the need to nurture a class of *Bumiputera* industrialists and entrepreneurs. Since domestic capital is relatively scarce and Chinese dominated, and local technology inherently low level and comparatively unproductive, FDI was urgently needed to bridge this gap.

In the early 1970s, Malaysia had a large surplus of labor. Export-oriented industries with high labor absorption capacity were therefore encouraged in order to absorb the rapidly expanding labor force. The coincidence of foreign capitalists seeking low production-cost bases to maintain their competitiveness fits into the government's industrial promotion strategy. This brought in labor-intensive, export-oriented industries from advanced countries (such as the USA and Japan) into especially the textile and the electronic industries.

The change in industrial development strategy to one of increasing the value added of agro-based, export-oriented industries and heavy industries in the 1980s marked the graduation of Malaysia into the next stage of industrialization. To spearhead heavy industrialization, the Heavy Industries Corporation of Malaysia (HICOM) was established in 1980. The advancement into high-technology industries intensified Malaysia's dependence on foreign investors for their "magical" package of capital, technological advancement, management expertise, and market sophistication.

In summary, the traditional role of FDI as supplier of capital rather than loans or grants continued to be significant through the passage of time. However, since independence and with the emergence of the indigenous industrial sector, foreign capital not only participated in the promotion of foreign-controlled companies but also facilitated the growth of joint ventures and provided loan capital to companies controlled by Malaysians.

FDI FROM JAPAN

The UK, the major traditional source of FDI in Malaysia in the 1950s and 1960s, has declined in relative importance in recent years. FDI from the USA, Japan, and Germany, on the other hand, has grown most rapidly since the 1970s. Globally, the stock of Japanese direct investment in developing countries, such as Malaysia, Singapore, Mexico, and Brazil, grew at an average of 21% per annum over the period 1970-1982 (Goldsborough 1985). Since the early 1970s FDI from Japan was concentrated in the industrial sector, in particular the export-oriented subsectors like electronics and textiles and the capital-intensive subsectors like iron and steel. This study focuses attention on FDI from Japan and the Asian newly industrializing economies (NIEs) like Singapore, Taiwan, and South Korea.

Malaysia's electrical and electronics sector evolved in the early 1960s. In 1966, Matsushita Electric Company was established as a local subsidiary of the Japanese MNC for the assembly of TV sets. Malaysia's efforts in attracting Japanese FDI in the electronics industries were so successful that by 1980 the country had become one of the world's major exporters of electronics components, particularly integrated circuits (ICs). The majority of electronics firms were established after 1970 when the 1968 Investment Incentive Act and the 1971 Free Trade Zone (FTZ) Act were actively used to encourage foreign investments in the sector. FDI was mostly concentrated in the assembly of electronic devices for export or assembly of consumer products and industrial equipment for both the domestic and international markets (Table 2).

Since the United Nations Technical Assistance Board sent a study mission to Malaysia in 1961 to do a feasibility study on the development of the iron and steel industry in Malaysia, FDI has been flowing into the country to establish iron and steel mills (in collaboration with large foreign steel companies). Malayawata—a joint venture of local capital with Nippon Steel Corp.—in 1966 was the first of such companies. By 1985, the iron and steel sector had evolved into a broad-based sector with extensive foreign investment (Table 3). The major investors in this sector include those from Japan in the Terengganu Integrated Steel Mill and the Labuan Sponge Iron Plant.

The textile subsector is another sector with a large inflow of FDI. The origin of the Malaysian textile industry can be traced back to 1957, with

Table 2. Activities of Malaysian Electronics Establishments [1], 1980(No. of Establishments [2]).

Product	Country of Ownership [3]				Total
	Malaysia	Japan	USA	Other	
Consumer Appliance Assembly	10	6	2	5	23
Radio and Stereo Equipment	4	2	3	5	13
Television Sets	1	3	—	—	4
Other Consumer Products	8	11	—	—	19
Electronics Components	6	12	16	5	39
Semiconductor Components	1	5	15	5	26
Capacitors	2	2	—	—	4
Inductors and Transformers	1	3	—	—	4
Computer Components	2	—	1	—	3
Resistors	2	2	—	—	4
Condensors	1	—	—	—	1
Industrial Equipment	6	2	—	2	10
Industrial Control Equipment	6	1	—	—	7
Communication Equipment	—	1	—	2	3
Other	4	1	—	1	6
Medical Equipment	1	—	—	1	2
Records and Cassettes	3	1	—	—	4
All establishments: Total Number	26	21	18	13	78
Percentage by Country	33.3	26.9	23.1	16.7	100

Notes: 1. Data collected from a survey of 78 electronics establishments located throughout Peninsular Malaysia in 1980.

2. Since one establishment may produce more than one product, the total number of establishments in each product group is not necessarily equal to the sum of the number of establishments producing each product.

3. Country of ownership refers to the country that owns more than 50% of the paid-up capital of the establishment.

the setting up of the first mill producing gray cotton fabric for the domestic market. The early 1970s saw the rapid expansion of the industry with the implementation of the 1968 Investment Incentives Act. By 1980, the industry had evolved into a thriving one encompassing a wide variety of activities, ranging from garment manufacturing to man-made fiber. By 1979, FDI had a strong presence in the sector, controlling 16 (24.6%) of the 65 firms surveyed (Table 4).

To examine in greater detail the nature of FDI from Japan, we have conducted a number of case studies of FDI from Japan and Asian NIEs in these subsectors. These case studies are summarized in Appendix A.

Table 3. Number of Products and Effective Capacity in the Malaysian Iron and Steel Industry, 1978-1981.

Type of Product	Number of Producers			Effective Capacity ('000 tonnes/year)				Future Additional Capacity (Year)
	1979	1980	1981	1978	1979	1980	1981	
Crude iron (excl. foundries)	1	1	1	120	120	200	200	600 (1985)[1] 715 (1985)[2]
Crude steel (excl. foundries)	4	4	45	n.a.	230	230	680	576 (1985)[3]
Hot-rolled nonflats:								
Wire rods	2	2	2	n.a.	120	150	150	
Bars	5	5	6					
					260	260	540	560 (1986)[3]
Other light sections	5	5	6					
Cold-rolled flats	0	0	0	0	0	0	0	150 (1986)[3]
Steel pipes & fittings	5	5	5	n.a.	140	144	144	
Wires	11	11	11	n.a.	130	130	130	

Notes: 1 Proposed integrated steel mills in Telok Kalong, Terengganu. The crude steel (in billets) is for the domestic market.
2 Proposed sponge iron plant in Labuan, Sabah. The sponge iron is mainly for export.
3 Expansion plants of Malayawata, Antara, Southern, and Malaysia Steel.
n.a., not available.

Source: Southeast Asia Iron and Steel Institute.

FDI FROM ASIAN NIEs

Since the 1970s, there has been a marked increase in the growth of exports of capital goods and related services from several relatively advanced developing countries to other developing countries. Major developing countries that have exported investment-related technological services to Malaysia include South Korea, Taiwan, Singapore, and India.

Taiwanese and Singaporean manufacturing firms have invested in Malaysian joint-venture firms since the 1960s as a result of the industrialization drive initiated by the Malaysian government through the granting of pioneer status. It is mainly through these joint-venture firms that technology acquired by the Taiwanese and Singaporean firms has been transferred to Malaysia. The South Koreans are relatively new investors in Malaysia. They are mainly involved in the construction of infrastructural works and have made an impact in the construction and civil works sector only since the late 1970s. Taiwan and Singapore are

Table 4. Ownership and Activities in the Malaysian Textile Industry, 1979.

Textile Subsector	More than 50% Local Ownership	More than 50% Foreign Ownership	Total No. of Establishments	As % of Total No. of Establishments
Man-made fiber manufacturing	0	1	1	1.5
Spinning and weaving	3	6	9	13.8
Dyeing, printing ,& finishing	3	1	4	6.2
Final products subsector				
textile goods manufacturing (e.g., gloves, nets, etc.)	2	3	5	7.7
Knitted apparel manufacturing	23	2	25	38.5
Wearing apparel manufacturing	18	3	21	32.3
Total	49	16	65	100.0

Source: Data collected from a survey of textile establishments located throughout Peninsular Malaysia in 1979.

involved mainly in joint-venture manufacturing concerns.

The participation of foreign establishments in Malaysian manufacturing concerns is relatively important. Singapore is mainly involved in food processing and textile manufacturing, while Taiwan is principally involved in textiles and electronics manufacturing.

FDI from Asian NIEs to Malaysia has been mainly engineering technology embodied in infrastructural construction or industrial projects. Being a developing country, infrastructural works and new industrial plants are of prime importance as a basis for major development programs to be implemented. Engineering technology for the construction of roads, bridges, water supply networks, electricity transmission lines, high-rise buildings, and new townships in Malaysia was supplied by construction firms from these newly industrializing countries. The provision of engineering construction technology by these countries is a relatively new phenomenon in Malaysia, dating back to the late 1970s, with the influx of South Korean and Japanese contractors into the local construction scene. This sudden influx was largely encouraged by the Malaysian government's pursuance of the "Look East" policy in its attempts to emulate the Japanese and South Korean "economic miracles." The Malaysian industrial sector was encouraged to model itself on Japanese and South Korean technology, work ethics, and industrial strategies. As a result of the Look East policy, many major infrastructural and construction projects undertaken by the government have been awarded to South Korea, such as the construction of the Penang Bridge, the Kenyir Dam, and part of the Peninsular Malaysia North-South Expressway. The engineering construction technology provided by firms from industrializing countries is, however, standard engineering construction technology.

In the case of the many joint-venture manufacturing industrial projects implemented in Malaysia, FDI is both in "embodied" and "disembodied" forms. Industrial engineering with the supply of machinery and equipment and recommendations on the acquisition of the relevant modern and advanced machinery and equipment as well as consulting services or technical aid agreements are the main components in these manufacturing joint ventures. Upon successful implementation, the operations are normally handed over to local personnel with minimal foreign specialists being retained. However, as a shareholder, the foreign partner continues to receive a share of the profits from the use of the technology. There are, however, many instances where the shareholdings are Malaysianized after a number of years of operation. Areas of joint ventures between foreign firms from industrializing countries and Malaysia are diverse and range from textiles to food processing. Many of these joint-venture firms have been initiated by the import-substitution industrialization drive actively promoted by the Malaysian government in the early 1960s. At that time, projects were in the manufacturing of textiles, footwear, food products, and electrical and transport machinery that were previously imported.

It must be noted that in the manufacturing industries, a number of firms in the industrializing countries acquired their production technology from a third country, usually a developed country, before the technology was transferred to Malaysia. Even after the technology has been transferred to Malaysia, the firms maintain close contacts with the producer of the technology so that standards and quality of products are continuously upgraded.

To understand better the characteristics of FDI from industrializing countries, a number of case studies have also been conducted. The details of these studies are contained in Appendix B.

CONCLUSIONS AND POLICY IMPLICATIONS

During the colonial period and in the early years of independent Malaya, the relationship between FDI and the host environment was such that the former was the dominant factor in determining the type and form of investment. However, the implementation of the 1968 Investment Incentive Act and the NEP since 1970 with its policy guidelines on the equity structure of foreign investment, the balance of power has shifted in favor of national interests. In this respect, foreign investors have shown particular willingness to comply with the requirements of the NEP. Investors from Asian NIEs were quick to impart their technologies, as well as to Malaysianize the key posts in their joint ventures. Investors from developed countries, especially Japan, however, were less forthcoming in terms of technology transfer and Malaysianization of key posts. This could be because FDI from Asian NIEs is mainly involved in domestic-oriented activities with technologies that were purchased (or copied) from advanced countries. Hence, it does make economic sense for such FDI to comply with both the intent and spirit of the NEP. FDI from Japan is generally in export-oriented areas using technologies innovated by the parent companies. Thus, although they could be willing and able to comply with the work force structure requirements, they have to maintain managerial or equity control to ensure that their innovated processes are well guarded.

Notwithstanding the NEP regulation with regard to the equity structure for foreign investments, the inflow of FDI from Japan and Asian NIEs to Malaysia has continued unabated since the early 1970s.

This could be attributed to both push and pull factors—push factors such as the need for portfolio diversification, high home labor wage rates, strict home environmental regulations, and penetration of the Malaysi69 market; and pull factors such as investment incentives for foreign investments, relatively cheap labor, good infrastructure, and the rapidly expanding Malaysian domestic market. In this respect, much FDI from Asian NIEs has taken advantage of the pull factors of the country's textile quota (to advanced countries) still unused by domestic textile establishments. Such FDI was less concerned with investment incentives, fiscal support accorded to the FTZs, or the cheap labor available. Investors from Japan were more attracted by the country's incentives for export and the various subsidies provided to the FTZs, as well as the cheap surplus labor available, since most of their investment was in the electronics subsector.

The Malaysian economy, particularly the primary, financial, and trade sectors, was once dominated by British colonial masters. However, they are now increasingly being overshadowed by the Japanese and other foreign investors. Investors from the Asian NIEs and, to some extent Japan, have shown a readiness to participate in joint ventures with local majority equity ownership. Most of the FDI from Japan and Asian NIEs operates side by side with the domestic economy.

The strong presence of FDI from Asian NIEs implies that joint ventures on a foreign minority basis have evolved to become a new form of foreign investment in Malaysia, particularly in the manufacturing sector. This new form of investment obviously is beneficial to the host country in terms of technology transfer and control of the national wealth. As part of its industrialization strategy in the coming decade, it is important that policy measures be implemented to encourage FDI from Japan to come to the country in the form of joint ventures with Malaysians eventually acquiring effective control. This is particularly true for FDI in manufacturing subsectors where the technologies are fairly standardized, as well as in the plantation agricultural sector where Malaysia still possesses strong international comparative advantage.

Notwithstanding the emergence of the new form of international investment, from the case studies it is clear that transfer of technologies and skills from the FDI to the domestic economy is still lacking. This is particularly true for FDI from Japan. While FDI from the Asian NIEs has better records in technology transfer, their technologies are generally not as advanced as that from Japan. In its future industrialization policies, the Malaysian government must draw up new guidelines to ensure better and more effective transfer of technology and expertise from Japanese MNCs to the domestic economy.

Most of the foreign-owned companies interviewed—particularly subsidiaries of investing companies from Japan—did not view technology transfer as part of their goals. This is understandable since their original objective for establishing their plants was to take advantage of the surplus cheap labor in the country. With rapid economic development and a tightening of the labor market since then, there now appears to be a divergence of the needs of the companies and that of the host economy. Policies should be implemented to make the two sets of objectives more consistent and to encourage a greater flow of technology transfer.

To achieve the above, specific incentives are needed to encourage the purchase of parts and components by Japanese MNCs from domestic ancillary suppliers. This could be attained through the provision of tax credits or double deductions on expenses spent on purchase of parts and services from the domestic ancillary firms. The ancillary suppliers themselves should also be given specific tax incentives for the supply of parts and components to MNCs, as well as for the exporting of these parts and components to the rest of the world. The enhancing of linkages between these modern MNCs and the domestic economy would greatly facilitate technology upgrading and advancement.

Some guidelines on the continued reliance on expatriates for company management and training of domestic staff should also be formulated. In particular, all MNCs should be given incentives to impart fully the needed technology and managerial responsibilities to domestic engineers and to terminate slowly the services of the expatriates. On the other hand, protection should be given to companies to ensure that the information and expertise imparted to the domestic work force would not be detrimental to the company. This includes the strict implementation of patent rights and copyright legislation to the extent that the technological information acquired by domestic managers would not be abused.

Besides technology transfer and technological upgrading, greater emphasis should also be given to encourage the development of indigenous R&D facilities. Most of the MNCs from Japan found no necessity or incentive to decentralize R&D facilities to local subsidiaries. This is a pity, as some R&D work, such as adaptation of the major core processes to the domestic economy, could be done locally and should be encouraged.

There is now a need for the government to formulate a coherent national science and technology policy, listing the specific areas and means by which the country's industrial technology should be upgraded.

This could include critical areas that Malaysia has traditionally depended on, such as electronics, wood-based industries, and textiles. Incentives could then be given to companies in related areas to retrain and upgrade their work force and to use up-to-date, appropriate technologies in their enterprises. Further, the provisions of the Investment Incentive Act should also be made applicable to the modernization of existing plants, as well as the establishment of new plants. This would result in a more rapid rate of plant modernization among existing industrial establishments in the country. In particular, investors from the Asian NIEs have involved themselves in many of the domestic-oriented industrial subsectors without much plant modernization and expansion. These investors should be encouraged to adopt policies similar to those of Japanese FDI—i.e., to be export-oriented, using the most up-to-date technologies and processes.

APPENDIX A
CASE STUDIES OF FDI FROM JAPAN

Case Study A

Company A, a Japanese MNC subsidiary, was set up in Malaysia in 1972 to manufacture electrical consumer products (electric cookers, fans, washing machines, and hair dryers) and industrial equipment (air conditioners and compressors) with an initial capital investment of M$15 million and 100% foreign equity. Capital investment was increased to M$20 million in 1982 with 94.1% foreign and 5.9% local equity. Products manufactured by the company were mainly for domestic consumption, with only 1% of the M$98 million worth of products manufactured in 1982 exported.

Among the factors that had influenced the location of this Japanese subsidiary in Malaysia were the abundant supply of easily trained labor, relatively low wage rates, easy accessibility to the domestic market, and favorable industrial climate with good potential for further improvement. Political stability and government tax incentives also played important roles in attracting the MNC subsidiary to Malaysia.

Company A has a technical collaboration agreement with its parent company in Japan. The company had to pay a certain amount of "technology fees"; for example, the total technology fees paid by the company in 1982 was M$5 million. These fees included a 4% royalty payment for license and technical assistance from its parent company. Company A also sent its local technical personnel to Japan for training, ranging from 2-6 months. Foreign engineers were also despatched to Malaysia to assist in plant installation and other operating processes.

The company's record of technology transfer was poor. In spite of having operated in Malaysia for over a decade, with the domestic market absorbing the major bulk of its sales, the company made no serious attempt to transfer the basic core processes of the manufacturing technology to the domestic work force or managerial personnel. The basic "core" technology (i.e., the design of circuit boards required for the industrial equipment and the basic critical processes of consumer product manufacturing) was innovated and developed in Japan. The trainees sent for training were given exposure in operating the equipment needed for the assembly of the products. They were not given access to the patented technology contained in the core processes. This is notwithstanding the fact that the subsidiary had a technology agreement with its parent company which entitled the local company to be given access to all technology deemed "relevant" for the operation of Company A. From the viewpoint of the parent company the core processes were deemed not relevant. The expertise that was transferred to the local work force was that related to adaptation of the manufacturing processes to local conditions, such as the needed adjustments to the machinery to suit the more fluctuating humidity conditions. The parent company felt that given Malaysia's existing status of manpower and infrastructure these noncore processes were more relevant in improving the productivity of its Malaysian subsidiary.

There may be some truth in the company's assertion that the lack of domestic expertise had hindered the company's efforts in technology transfer. It could be that the local ancillary suppliers of electronic components were not on par with their Japanese counterparts. Nevertheless, this is only one side of the story. The ancillary firms that we interviewed suggested that this particular company might have been using the excuse of quality to limit their purchase of domestic parts and components. They pointed out that many of the ancillary firms were established by former employees of the company. Although they have the needed experience with respect to the quality requirements of the company, they have not been successful in bidding for subcontracts.

Case Study B

Company B was set up in 1962 as a private limited company in an industrial estate in Petaling Jaya. It commenced commercial production four years later and managed to increase the company's capital investment to M$2 million by 1982. It was a Japanese MNC subsidiary in 1962, but foreign equity had decreased to 90% by 1982. The company produced almost 2,905,000 units of products such as 45 G-drums, pails, and cans with the value of ex-factory sales amounting to M$10 million.

All the products manufactured by the company are sold domestically.

The company acquired its technology through importation of capital equipment and machinery. Technological expertise was also acquired through the training of personnel both in-plant and out-of-plant. When the company was first set up in 1962, there were three expatriates in the plant, but this was reduced to only one by 1979. The expatriates were responsible for the foreign majority interests in the firm.

Given that the firm's production processes consist mainly of low-level iron and steel fabrication activities, it is surprising that technology transfer was not as rapid and widely diffused as expected. In 1982, the company still needed the services of a foreign engineer. Besides looking after the interests of the majority foreign equity shareholders, the presence of the foreign engineer, an employee of the parent company, also ensured that the basic core (such as the detailed specifications including the hardness and brittle levels) of the processes was not imparted to the domestic work force. This safeguarding of the specifications had been so successful that 20 years after the firm's formation, most of its needed parts and components were still imported.

Case Study C

Company C was established as a Japanese MNC subsidiary and commenced production in 1975. Its initial capital investment was M$70 million. This remained unchanged in 1984. The establishment is involved in the manufacturing of man-made fibers such as polyester fiber. Its output value in 1982 was M$82 million; 24% was sold domestically and the rest exported to Hong Kong, Europe, North America, the Middle East, and other Southeast Asian countries.

The firm had extensive linkages with foreign establishments through its importation of capital equipment, raw materials, and components from its parent-associated companies. The company also had foreign professionals on its payroll. In 1984, out of 927 workers, 13 were expatriates, all holding major managerial responsibilities. The company regarded the level of technology required for the production of its major products as high, due to the nature of the activities involved. The three main processes of production are polymerization, spinning, and "after treatment" processes. The process of polymerization is a batch-wise process using terephthalic acid (TPA) and ethylene glycol (EG) as raw materials. After two successive chemical reactions in esterification and polymerization, polyethylene terephthalate (PET) is obtained. This is in the form of molten polymer, which is cut into chips after the cooling process. The spinning process begins with the chips being dried by a rotary drier after which the chips are melted in extruders and then extruded through spinnerets. The spun yarn is then cooled and carefully stored. In the "after-treatment" process, the spun yarn is passed through oil baths to the drawing zone. Drawn yarns are then crimped and run through heat treatment. The heat-treated yarn is then cut and the cut fibers put into bales.

The alternative techniques are more advanced technologies compared to the techniques used in the firm. Such techniques, however, are not readily available locally. Even present techniques used by the company rely on its parent company in Japan for all the technical know-how, such as managerial expertise, patents, and manufacturing.

The technological processes used by the company for the manufacture of man-made fiber are extremely capital intensive. It is also very skilled-labor-intensive, which makes the process rather inappropriate for the Malaysian environment. Thus, we find that the company still must rely on the services of Japanese engineers to maintain the plant.

This plant represents a network of off-shore man-made fiber plants maintained by the Japanese MNC in Southeast Asia. The other plants are in Korea, Taiwan, Hong Kong, and Thailand. The technology and patents required for the various processes were developed by the Japanese MNC, and this information is withheld from its subsidiaries, including the Malaysian plant.

The Japanese MNC felt that there was no necessity to pass on to the domestic work force the most current information on man-made fiber technology. The plant is a "turn-key" plant, and the company views its major responsibility to be one of employment creation rather than technology transfer. Further, the Japanese MNC feels that it is not in the company's interest to pass on all the technological information, which it had developed at great expense, to the domestic economy.

The above comments notwithstanding, it must be pointed out that the plant represents only the apex of a network of textile manufacturing establishments in Malaysia which the Japanese parent company helped to set up. Figure 1 presents this network of textile plants. Although the polyester plant is completely owned by the Japanese company, the others—ranging from manufacturing of yarn and gray fabric to dyeing and printing—were joint ventures with domestic entrepreneurs. The polyester plant serving as the apex of the network has extensive linkages with the other plants in the network. Its output is used as inputs by the yarn and gray fabric plants. Further, it also provides the needed expertise (leasing of personnel) and capital to these other member companies. Extensive assistance is also given by the apex plant to the other member plants in terms of exporting their products.

Interviews with these member companies indicated that although the

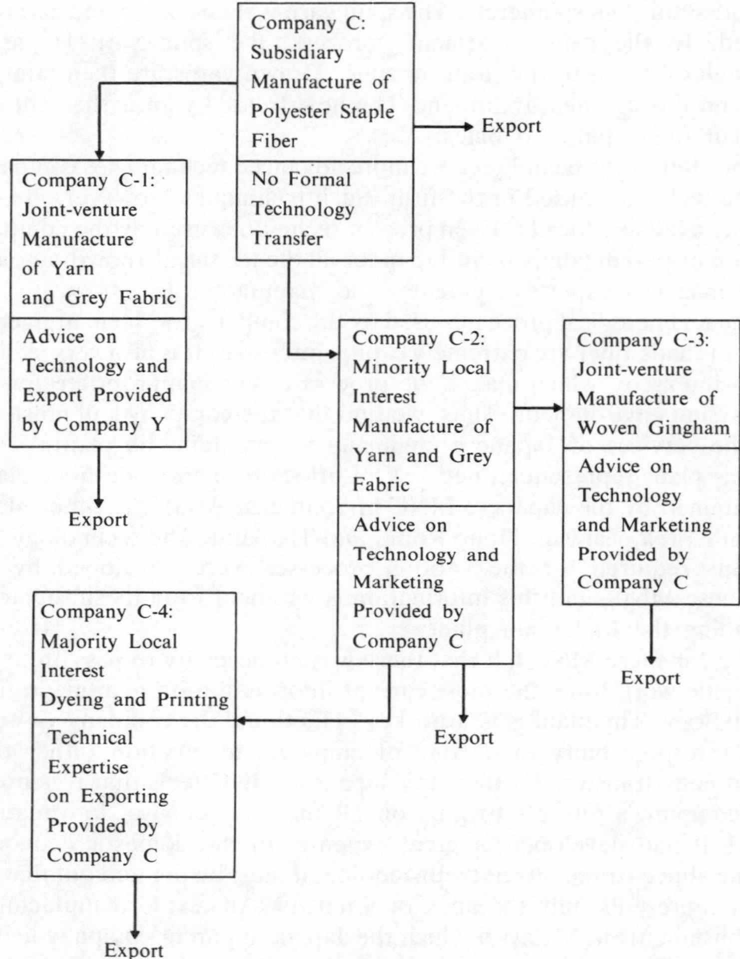

Fig. 1. Network of Malaysian Textile Plants Affiliated with Company C.

Japanese company jealously guarded its polyester staple-making technology, it is more generous in diffusing yarn-making, woven garment-making, and dyeing and printing technologies. Each of these member plants have received experienced personnel from the apex plant for periods of up to several months. In these member plants, there were considerable interactions between the leased personnel and the local work force. Advice was provided by these personnel on how best to make use of the polyester staple for manufacturing, and how best to adopt their processes to optimize the outputs of the finished products from the polyester staple. The story of technology transfer in one of these member plants is described in greater detail under Company D.

As a result of the assistance provided by the apex plant to its "subsidiaries," there has been a general upgrading in textile manufacturing technology, particularly in Penang where almost all the plants are located. Although polyester-staple technology was still kept away from the local work force, through the efforts of the apex plant, there has been a general diffusion of textile technology associated with yarn and fabric making and dyeing and finishing. Modern Japanese technologies used by these plants are also able to make efficient use of the polyester staple produced by Company C.

Case Study D

Company D was established in 1971 with an initial investment of M$20 million (this amount remained unchanged by 1982) and as a 90% foreign-owned subsidiary of a well-known Japanese MNC. Commercial production of yarn and fabric commenced in 1972.

The 1982 total sales value of the firm was M$99.2 million; about 56% of the products were sold locally and the rest exported to Australia, New Zealand, Europe, North America, Japan, Hong Kong, and Singapore. The capacity utilization of the company was over 75%. About 91% of the raw materials used by the company in 1982 were imported from Japan. The rest, mainly simple items, was purchased locally.

The company's products are generally regarded as high quality, and were in great demand locally and overseas. The firm uses fairly up-to-date technological processes for yarn and fabric making. The spinning and weaving plants have been continuously updated and modernized, to ensure that the outputs are up to the specifications of the parent company. To further ensure quality output, the parent company maintains three foreign engineers in the Malaysian plant. Their responsibilities include the adaptation of the Japanese technology to local conditions, maintaining the plant at its peak efficiency levels, and training of the domestic work force. The expatriate engineers return to Japan regularly to be briefed on the latest in textile technology. Some of the senior local staff were also sent to Japan for training, mainly in the basic processes of spinning and weaving.

This company acquired the needed technological expertise by recruiting foreign technical personnel, as well as by sending their own local personnel overseas for training. All the needed equipment was imported from the parent company. In 1984, the payment of capital equipment amounted to M$2.5 million. The firm has its own R&D unit consisting of 10 persons mainly to adapt the Japanese technologies to local conditions. Some of the activities include the adaptation of the spinning and weaving process to suit the more humid Malaysian environment, and appropriate mixture of synthetic and natural fiber in the production of its gray fabric which would be more suitable to its end users. The company's policy is to use the most up-to-date machinery and equipment.

The firm can be said to have made some attempts at transferring its technological and managerial expertise to the local work force. The fact that the company has set up an R&D unit clearly indicates this. However, even then, it is evident that all the technological expertise and information passed on to the locals are those associated with low-level, basic spinning and weaving processes—such as the adaptation of the invented technologies to the more labor-intensive environment of Malaysia, and methodologies for detecting inferior yarn and fabrics. The basic core processes of spinning and weaving (such as the speed of spin, and the directions of spin relative to the types of fabric and garments) were all innovated in Japan and kept as well-guarded company secrets. This technological know-how is critical for any well-run weaving and spinning plant, and the fact that this information is only available to the foreign engineers indicates the strong desire on the part of the parent company to maintain its technological lead.

APPENDIX B
CASE STUDIES OF FDI FROM ASIAN NIEs

Case Study E

A 30% local participation by local contractors was made mandatory as part of the award of the construction works of the Penang Bridge to Hyundai Engineering and Construction Co. Ltd. of South Korea. The local contractors involved in the projects were Syarikat Pembinaan Hashbudin Sdn. Bhd., Lim Kar Bee & Sons Sdn. Bhd., and Pembinaan Rahim Sdn. Bhd. Hyundai had also promised to effect the transfer of construction technology to local workers by providing training programs for 1,000 persons per year. Through these two measures, the transfer of construction technology from the South Koreans to Malaysians was effected.

About 100 South Korean engineers were involved in the construction of the Penang Bridge project. About 2,000 workers, over one-third of them South Koreans, were employed during the construction. Malaysian workers employed included engineers, technicians, helmsmen, scuba divers, heavy machinery mechanics for dredges and pile-driving vessels, crane operators, generator engine operators, riggers, and welders. However, these Malaysians were directly employed not by Hyundai Engineering and Construction Co. Ltd. but by the Malaysian joint-venture partners. Several South Korean engineers were assigned to work with these local partners and site meetings were held fortnightly to discuss the work. This appeared to be the only venue for technology transfer as Hyundai did not employ local engineers and all skilled work was done by the South Koreans.

Technology transfer in the construction of the Penang Bridge involved mainly the training of Malaysian engineering personnel in the various aspects of bridge construction through South Korean construction specialists. Subcontracting of the various packages to Malaysian contractors also enabled local contractors to gain experience in bridge building with their direct interaction with the South Korean technical experts as well as to reap the economic benefits accruing from this massive infrastructure project.

Local raw materials were also used in the construction of the bridge as part of the award of the contract to the South Korean firm. Only where materials were not available locally was the contractor allowed to import, and this only upon certification by local suppliers.

Case Study F

Company F is a Malaysian-Singaporean joint venture with a current paid-up capital of M$25.9 million. The Singaporean share is 37.9% of the paid-up capital. The nature of this joint venture is mainly in terms of the capital, management, and technical expertise provided by a Singaporean entrepreneur who has gained vast experience in the textile manufacturing industry in Textile Alliance, Hong Kong. Through his association with Textile Alliance, joint-venture textile manufacturing companies were formed.

Machines and equipment from the UK, the USA, Japan, and Germany are installed in the factories and Company F's mills are one of the most highly automated in Malaysia, requiring a relatively small work force. The majority of the workers are maintenance workers as not too many machine operators are needed. The textile mills are also fully air-conditioned to ensure the correct environment for the materials being handled and pleasant working conditions for the operators, which has been a contributing factor in the very good performance registered by the mill even in times of recession.

The establishment of the textile mills by Company F has resulted in training of workers in various aspects of textile manufacturing, from spinning, knitting, printing, dyeing, and bleaching to garment manufacturing. Operators have also been trained in the operation, management, and maintenance of highly sophisticated textile manufacturing equipment and machinery, which are the most advanced and capital intensive in the textile industry. Textile technology from the advanced textile producing countries such as Japan, the USA, the UK, and Germany was imported and has definitely helped to raise the level of textile technology in Malaysia.

Training of local workers in the various industries has also been effected. Local workers from Company F were sent to the Taiwanese principal companies for training, while qualified Taiwanese textile production workers are based in Company F to train local workers.

Case Study G

Realizing the potential for the development of cable and wire manufacturing in Malaysia, the Malaysian co-venture partners decided to venture into this new field of industry. Hence, Company G was set up to manufacture products previously imported. The two Taiwanese partners in this joint venture are both leading manufacturers of electric cables in Taiwan.

The joint venture was incorporated as a private company in November, 1966, and the production of copper and aluminum power cables, telephone cables, and underground cables started in 1968. In November 1969, the company was converted into a public company and expanded into copper refining and the production of enamel wires. The copper refinery set up was the only one of its kind in Southeast Asia while the enamel wire plant was the first in Malaysia.

In October 1975, Company G entered into a joint venture with the Malaysian National Electricity Board and a Japanese cable manufacturer to produce paper-insulated power cables. A technical assistance agreement was concluded, with the Japanese cable manufacturer to provide the technical know-how and expertise in the production of paper-insulated power cables with a view to establishing itself as a leading manufacturer of telecommunication cables in Malaysia. Sales of the paper-insulated power cables are made entirely to the National Electricity Board. The production facilities of this joint venture were greatly expanded under this technical assistance agreement with the Japanese cable manufacturer.

The manufacturing techniques employed in this project were derived from the Taiwanese co-venture partners and backed by a research organization. This research organization is staffed with highly skilled specialists who work in close technical cooperation with other electric cable manufacturing companies in the USA and Japan. Close contact is also maintained with the Taiwanese companies to remain abreast of the latest developments in the field of electric cable manufacturing to improve quality and reduce costs. Strict measures of quality control are also adopted and the most up-to-date equipment is installed in the laboratory to ensure quality in production.

Technology transfer in this joint venture is mainly in the form of the acquisition of technology for the manufacture of wires and cables by Malaysians. With the acquisition of this technology and continuous research and development, this joint venture has acquired the basic technology enabling it to diversify into nonrelated fields such as management services and property development.

Local raw materials are also utilized in the production. The success of this venture led to diversification into the manufacture of other related products that are technologically more advanced. The continued ties of this venture with its foreign partners will ensure that product advances continue to be made available to the Malaysian manufacturer.

Being a Malaysian-Taiwanese joint venture, several of the directors were seconded from Taiwan. However, with the continued Malaysianization of its operations, this component has been gradually decreased. In its initial stages of operation, Taiwanese experts were employed and valuable training in the manufacturing of electric cables was afforded to the Malaysians. However, with the availability of trained local workers in the field, Taiwanese specialists are no longer required by the company and with the continued Malaysianization of the company, Malaysians are the majority shareholders of the company.

This joint venture represents the import of FDI in a "disembodied" form by Malaysians. Knowledge and expertise in the wire and cable manufacturing processes were made available to Malaysians by the Taiwanese through this joint venture. Through this process, Malaysians have been trained in the production of these products and the latest and most advanced equipment and machinery made available. This joint venture has been successful and beneficial to both the Malaysians and the Taiwanese.

Case Study H

Being a relatively new industry where skills and precision are needed, there is still a lack of skilled manpower in the manufacture of cutlery and tableware. Company H was established in 1975 to produce tableware and cutlery for the domestic and export market through domestic joint ventures with FDI from Hong Kong and Taiwan. Experts from Hong Kong and Taiwan were employed in the factory, especially in the mould-making section, so as to enable the commencement of production as well as to train local workers in cutlery manufacturing.

The Malaysian partners were instrumental in initiating this joint venture and the Hong Kong and Taiwanese partners were chosen as they were able to offer the most modern and advanced tableware manufacturing machinery and equipment as well as the technology for the joint venture. This, combined with the traditional skills of Malaysians in handicraft production, culminated in the formation of a Malaysian-Taiwanese-Hong Kong joint venture to produce cutlery for both the local as well as the international market.

Skills and precision are prerequisites of the tableware industry if the products are to meet stringent international standards. As Malaysians lacked these qualities, Hong Kong specialists were initially employed by Company H to enable it to commence production. Local workers were then gradually trained in the skills of metalware manufacturing by these foreign experts. Eight employees were sent to Taiwan for training in the various aspects of tableware manufacturing and in the operational aspects of the machinery and equipment imported from Taiwan as well as in supervision and quality control.

The latest techniques in tableware manufacturing are constantly being monitored and supplied by the technical aid supplier, Taiwan, through a firm in Hong Kong. This has ensured that any advancements in tableware manufacturing achieved by the Taiwanese are made available to the joint venture.

The establishment of this joint venture represents the import of FDI by Malaysia in a "disembodied" form. Technical and marketing support in this venture were provided by the foreign venture partners. All other capital inputs were supplied by the Malaysian venture partner. This joint-venture manufacturing concern has generally been successful in the transfer of technology and expertise.

References

Allen, G.C. and A.G. Dornithorne. 1962. *Western Enterprise in Indonesia and Malaya*. London: George Allen and Unwin.

Goldsborough, David. 1985. Foreign direct investment in developing countries. *Finance and Development,* 22 (1): March.

Government of Malaysia. 1971. *Second Malaysia Plan, 1971-75*. Kuala Lumpur: Government Printer.

Junid Saham. 1980. *British Industrial Investment in Malaysia, 1963-71*. Kuala Lumpur: Oxford University Press.

Kulasingam, M. and Siew Ee Tan. 1982. *Changing Patterns of Foreign Investments in Malaysia: Determinants, Issues and Implication*. School of Social Sciences, Discussion Paper No. 9, Universiti Sains Malaysia, Penang.

Lim, Linda. 1980. *The Political Economy of Foreign Investment in Malaysia.* Paper presented at the Annual Meeting of the Association of Asian Studies, March 21-23, 1980.

Table A.1. Summary Statistics: Case Studies of FDI from Advanced Countries, 1982.

	Firms Interviewed[1]					
	A	B	C	D	E	F
1) Type of product	Consumer products & electronic components	Semiconductor components	Semiconductor components	Pails, cans, machinery	Polyester staple fiber	Yarn, fabric
2) Year of operation	1972	1972	1973	1966	1975	1972
3) Capacity utilization (%) 1982	78	–	83	86	77.5	77.5
4) Total employment, 31/12/82	3,500	1,138	3,200	185	927	n.a.
5) Salary[2] (M$) 1982	–	10,985,000	869,600	962,100	n.a.	n.a.
6) Total sales[3] (1982, M$ million)	98	41.343	60.4	10.0	82.0	99.2
7) Foreign equity (%) 1982	94.1	100	99.9	90	100	90
8) Fixed Assets (M$) 1982*	9,596,268	11,396,000	9,613,551	1,505,000	71,748,000	63,269
9) Method of technology transfer	1. On-the-job training 2. Apprenticeship 3. Technology agreement	1. Importation of capital equipment 2. Foreign professional technical personnel 3. Training of local personnel overseas	1. Importation of capital equipment 2. Foreign professional technical personnel 3. Training of local personnel overseas	1. Importation of capital equipment	1. Importation of capital equipment 2. Foreign professional technical personnel 3. Training of local personnel overseas	1. Importation of capital equipment 2. Foreign professional technical personnel 3. Training of local personnel overseas 4. Licence, techni-cal know-how from foreign firms

Table A.1.(cont.)

10) Cost of transfer (M$) 1982	5 million	n.a.	n.a.	-	n.a.	n.a.
11) Incentives & assistance	Pioneer status	Pioneer status	Investment tax credit	Pioneer status	Free trade zone Offshore facility	Free trade zone Offshore facility
12) Exports (% and M$) 1982	1%	Parent company, sister branch 100%	Parent company, sister branch 100%	Domestic	76% 62,000,000	44% 44,715,000

Notes: 1. Data gathered from a survey conducted in 1984.
2. Includes salary, wages and bonuses, cash allowances, and overtime.
3. Value of ex-factory sales.
*Net value at 31/12/82 ; n.a. denotes not available.

8 Characteristics of Foreign Direct Investment in Thailand*

Mikimasa Yoshida

Institute of Developing Economies

INTRODUCTION

The investment boom in Thailand reached its peak in 1988 and declined in the subsequent two years in terms of the number of applications and applications approved by the Board of Investment. The private investment index in 1990 was still much higher than the normal level, however. Despite some slowdown, investment was still active in 1990. It is important to note that foreign direct investment has played a leading role in the current investment boom. The same situation was seen in the 1960s, it being a well-known fact that foreign capital played a key role in the early stage of industrialization in Thailand during that period. Again in the latter half of the 1980s, a large inflow of foreign direct investment gave Thailand the chance to develop an advanced structure of industry and to attain the status of newly industrialized economy (NIE) in the near future.

The Thai economy began to show signs of recovery in the latter half of 1986 due to an increase in manufactured exports, the falling price of crude oil, a large inflow of foreign tourists, and a decline in interest rates. Moreover, due to the high appreciation of the Japanese yen after the Plaza Accord of September 1985 as well as the appreciation of Asian NIE currencies such as those of Taiwan and South Korea, many firms in those countries have started to relocate their production and export bases to Thailand. The large inflow of foreign direct investment also

This paper is a revised version of the author's chapter in a volume edited by Samart Chiasakul and Mikimasa Yoshida and published by the Institute of Developing Economies, Tokyo, in 1990.

contributed to the country's economic recovery, leading in turn to the recent investment boom and further progress in the field of industrialization.

The Thai economy has been undergoing rapid change, and the impact of foreign direct investment on this structural change is far-reaching. This chapter examines the structural change of Thai industry and the characteristics of foreign direct investment, after which the role of the Board of Investment will be discussed.

INDUSTRIALIZATION AND STRUCTURAL CHANGE

Thirty years have passed since the adoption of the National Economic and Social Development Plan. From the 1970s, industrial development strategy shifted from import substitution to the promotion of export-oriented industries. During that period, structural change in production was achieved. The share from the agricultural sector in gross domestic product (GDP) declined from 26% in 1970 to 15% in 1989, as shown in Table 1, and that of the manufacturing sector rose from 16% to 25%. In 1981, the share of manufacturing exceeded the agricultural share.

Table 1. Gross Domestic Product by Industrial Origin (Current prices, million Baht).

	1970	1980	1985	1988	1989
Agriculture	38,163	152,852	169,895	250,384	271,443
Industry	37,327	203,136	345,037	540,089	677,321
Manufacturing	23,503	139,936	224,456	373,326	455,228
Services	71,895	302,521	499,467	716,504	842,046
GDP	147,385	658,509	1,014,399	1,506,977	1,790,810
Share (%)					
Agriculture	25.9	23.2	16.7	16.6	15.2
Industry	25.3	30.8	34.0	35.8	37.8
Manufacturing	15.9	21.3	22.1	24.8	25.4
Services	48.8	45.9	49.2	47.5	47.0
GDP	100.0	100.0	100.0	100.0	100.0

Source: NESDB: *National Income of Thailand*, 1970-87 and 1989.

Furthermore, a major change was seen in the export structure. Agricultural commodities, which accounted for 51% of total export value in 1980, decreased to 21% in 1990, while that of manufactured goods doubled from 32% to 64% (Table 2). The value of manufactured exports, which exceeded that of agriculture in 1985, showed a rapid increase in the latter half of the 1980s. Among the manufacturing industries that have led economic growth in Thailand, labor-intensive light industries such as agricultural processing, textiles and garments,

Table 2. Distribution and Growth of Export by Sector (%, million Baht).

	Distribution			Growth Rate	
	1980	1985	1989	1980-1985	1985-1989
Agriculture	46.9	38.0	23.0	3.3	12.7
Fishing	4.2	5.5	5.5	13.8	28.1
Forestry	0.1	0.2	0.1	39.1	17.8
Mining	11.6	5.2	1.6	−8.1	−5.7
Manufacturing	32.3	49.4	68.6	17.3	38.7
Other	4.9	1.7	1.2	−13.1	18.2
Total	100.0	100.0	100.0	7.7	27.8
Total amount	133,197	193,366	516,315		

Source: Bank of Thailand, *Monthly Bulletin*.

and leather goods and footwear have greatly contributed to export growth. The top ten export items in terms of value in 1990 were as follows (in order): garments, computers and their components, gems and jewelry, rice, tapioca products, rubber, integrated circuits, footwear, canned seafood, and shrimp.

When the Thai economy, which had been in a recession after the second oil crisis, revived in 1987, the increase in external and internal demand for Thai products, the sharp rise of investment in plant and equipment, and the construction boom of offices, factories, and condominiums led to three years of double-digit economic growth. The average economic growth rate during the period of the Sixth Five-year Development Plan (1987-1991) is anticipated to be more than 10%. According to Table 3, the following manufacturing industries achieved relatively high growth in the latter half of the 1980s: garments, leather products and footwear, furniture, rubber and plastic, nonmetallic minerals, fabricated products, machinery, electrical machinery, and transport equipment. The economic expansion during this period concurrently stimulated an increase in capital goods imports, especially machinery imports from Japan (Table 4). A large influx of foreign direct investment was seen in the latter half of the 1980s, as shown in Table 5. The share of foreign direct investment (net inflow) in gross domestic investment was at the 3% level before 1986, then rose to 6.5% in 1988 and to 7.0% in 1989. As a proportion of gross private business investment it increased from around 4.1% in 1987 to 8.6% in 1989. The increasing importance of foreign direct investment will have various impacts upon the Thai economy.

First, since more than 60% of the promoted projects were export-oriented industries, the proportional share of manufactured exports will increase to a large extent when all the projects are producing in full

Table 3. Distribution and Growth of Manufacturing Sector (%).

	Share (Current Prices)				Growth Rate (1972 Prices)		
	1970	1980	1985	1989	1970-80	1980-85	1985-89
Food	19.9	12.7	15.5	11.5	8.4	7.8	9.2
Beverages	12.0	7.4	9.4	7.5	8.1	6.3	10.0
Tobacco	7.4	5.3	5.1	3.4	7.2	−1.2	6.8
Textiles	7.5	12.2	9.9	10.3	15.4	4.0	13.4
Garments	9.0	10.1	13.5	14.1	10.0	7.0	16.9
Leather & footwear	2.3	2.0	2.6	4.7	6.5	6.8	22.0
Wood	2.8	4.2	2.3	1.9	3.2	−2.5	−1.5
Furniture	2.1	2.1	1.6	2.1	5.6	3.7	14.8
Paper	1.6	1.5	1.4	1.4	13.0	3.0	11.6
Printing & publishing	1.4	1.6	1.6	1.2	11.7	7.3	3.1
Chemicals	3.6	3.4	3.5	3.0	11.7	7.0	10.1
Petroleum products	5.7	8.2	6.7	5.2	9.1	3.0	7.5
Rubber & plastic	2.9	3.0	2.6	2.8	10.8	2.2	16.3
Nonmetallic minerals	4.3	3.7	4.7	4.6	8.9	7.1	16.3
Basic metals	2.7	2.6	1.7	1.1	5.7	3.9	4.3
Fabricated products	3.2	2.8	2.8	2.6	4.6	4.4	14.8
Machinery	3.1	2.6	2.5	2.9	10.9	6.6	15.8
Electric machinery	1.9	2.4	2.6	4.0	14.7	4.9	20.2
Transport equipment	5.2	8.2	4.9	8.2	13.9	−8.9	30.6
Other manufacturing	1.5	4.0	5.2	7.4	21.0	10.6	25.4
Total value added	100.0	100.0	100.0	100.0	10.1	4.6	13.9

Table 4. Imports by Economic Classification (million Baht).

	Total Imports			Imports from Japan		
	1981	1986	1989	1981	1986	1989
Consumer goods	18,263	24,466	55,807	5,090	7,683	13,977
Nondurable	10,459	12,982	25,585			
Durable	7,804	11,484	30,222			
Intermediate products and raw materials	58,084	84,333	235,154	17,606	21,070	50,863
Chiefly for consumer goods	38,225	61,191	154,727			
Chiefly for capital goods	19,859	23,142	80,427			
Iron and steel	12,039	15,737	54,739	8,155	9,832	25,499
Capital goods	56,985	78,316	242,277	19,760	25,511	99,989
Nonelectrical machinery	25,842	32,299	119,917	12,024	14,364	56,912
Electrical machinery	11,080	25,561	67,985	2,989	5,354	25,016
Other imports	83,414	54,243	129,441	10,065	9,392	36,108
Vehicles and parts	9,568	8,939	40,031	8,579	7,303	32,560
Fuel and lubricant	65,100	32,354	59,819	839	395	550
Total imports	216,746	241,358	662,679	52,251	63,656	200,937

Source: Bank of Thailand, *Monthly Bulletin*.

Table 5. Foreign Direct Investment and Gross Domestic Investment (million Baht).

Year	FDI	GCF	FDI as % of GCF	GPBI	FDI as % of GPBI
1970	891	37,331	2.36	24,566	3.63
1971	808	37,136	2.18	25,482	3.17
1972	1,427	36,872	3.87	27,216	5.24
1973	1,605	59,958	2.68	38,526	4.17
1974	3,836	74,365	5.16	54,628	7.02
1975	1,745	81,134	2.15	53,676	3.25
1976	1,614	83,109	1.94	55,848	2.89
1977	2,164	108,480	1.99	74,870	2.89
1978	1,135	137,496	0.83	85,891	1.32
1979	1,127	152,050	0.74	100,434	1.12
1980	3,878	174,045	2.23	107,104	3.62
1981	6,414	199,723	3.21	120,059	5.34
1982	4,388	189,577	2.31	125,793	3.49
1983	8,225	236,090	3.48	144,808	5.68
1984	9,645	242,506	3.98	156,546	6.16
1985	4,403	243,949	1.80	148,363	2.97
1986	6,908	238,643	2.89	155,087	4.45
1987	9,049	299,790	3.02	218,868	4.13
1988	28,244	434,546	6.50	329,614	8.57
1989	39,000*	556,351	7.01	452,578	8.62

FDI, foreign direct investment; GCF, gross capital formation; GPBI, gross private business investment.
* Estimate.
Sources: Bank of Thailand; National Economic & Social Development Board.

swing. In June 1990, before the Gulf Crisis, the Governor of the Bank of Thailand predicted that Thailand's external trade position was expected to improve within two or three years and that the country would enjoy a current-account surplus for the first time in 1997. The high current account deficit will become lower starting in 1992, as the result of long-term productive investment that will help generate exports.

Second, a structural change in employment, which had been rather moderate compared with other sectors, can be expected as projects promoted between 1987 and 1989 plan to employ more than one million workers. Furthermore, it is anticipated that the demand for educated workers (not primary- but secondary-educated workers) will increase in the 1990s as well as the demand for engineers and technicians who are already in critical shortage. Third, a structural change in production is also expected in the future, since the increase in investment in industries such as machinery, electricals and electronics, and petrochemicals will lead Thai industry to a more advanced and diversified stage.

UPSURGE IN FOREIGN DIRECT INVESTMENT

Characteristics of Recent Investment Boom

The recent investment boom can be characterized by six different aspects as follows.

1) Foreign investors have played a leading role in investment. In terms of the projects approved by the Board of Investment (BOI) during 1987-1990, foreign investors dominate in around 60% of the total number of projects. Furthermore, in 1988, for the first time in the history of the BOI, the amount of foreign-registered capital exceeded that of Thai investors in terms of the number of projects approved.

2) There has been a shift from import-substitution and local market-oriented industries to export-oriented industries. Since 1985, as shown in Figure 1, export-oriented projects that export more than 80% of their output have exceeded nonexport-oriented projects in terms of the number of projects and the amount of investment. Two factors have contributed to this change. First, the BOI agreed in 1983 to promote wholly foreign-owned projects on the condition that more than 80% of their output be exported. The second factor was the appreciation of the currencies of Japan and Asian NIEs. A number of firms in those countries invested in Thailand to take advantage of low production costs, using it as their production base for exporting goods to their home country or to third countries.

3) Direct investment has spread to various parts of the industrial sector. This is particularly true of Japanese investment projects for various reasons. Some, losing their export competitiveness due to the strength of the yen, decided to relocate their production and export bases to Thailand. Manufacturers of spare parts and components, being subcontractors for larger companies in Japan, invested at the request of those companies already operating in Thailand to reduce the increased cost of importing parts and components from Japan. Some have adopted the production policy of horizontal division of labor, whereby Thailand is assigned the role of one of the parts and components suppliers. Moreover, expanded production activities required other types of supporting industries, thus providing new type of business opportunity. Accordingly, almost 50% of Japanese firms receiving BOI certificates between 1987 and 1989 were in the production of intermediate products or supporting industries.

4) Investment in medium-advanced or small- and medium-scale industries has increased. In the case of Japan, the recent increase in

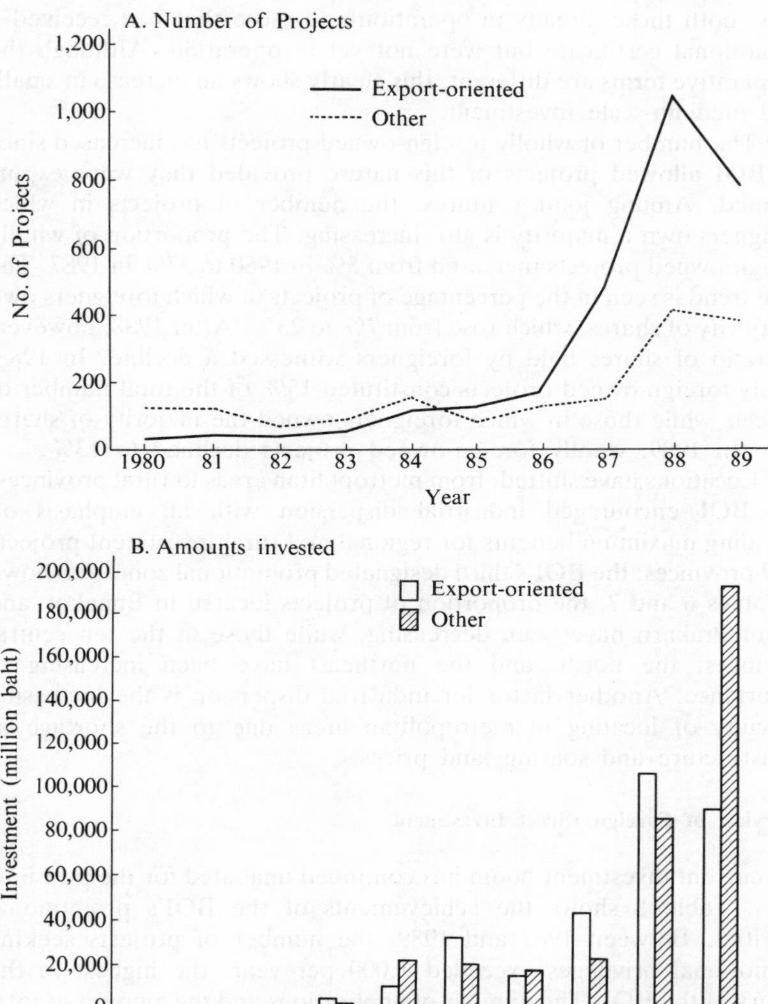

Fig. 1. Export-oriented Investment.

investment in various sectors of industry, as mentioned in (3), has been largely due to the medium-advanced or small- and medium-scale industries. As far as the average size of the work force in Japanese firms is concerned, 217 Thai workers were employed in the projects approved in 1988, while in 1982, 427 workers were employed by a total of 166 firms, both those already in operation and those that had received a promotional certificate but were not yet in operation. Although the comparative terms are different, this clearly shows an increase in small- and medium-scale investment.

5) The number of wholly foreign-owned projects has increased since the BOI allowed projects of this nature provided they were export oriented. Among joint ventures, the number of projects in which foreigners own a majority is also increasing. The proportion of wholly foreign-owned projects increased from 5% in 1980 to 37% in 1987. The same trend is seen in the percentage of projects in which foreigners own a majority of shares, which rose from 7% to 23%. After 1988, however, the ratio of shares held by foreigners witnessed a decline. In 1988, wholly foreign-owned projects constituted 15% of the total number of projects while those in which foreigners owned the majority of shares 22%. In 1989, wholly foreign-owned projects declined to 13%.

6) Locations have shifted, from metropolitan areas to rural provinces. The BOI encouraged industrial dispersion with an emphasis on providing maximum benefits for regional and rural investment projects in 57 provinces, the BOI's third designated promotional zone. As shown in Tables 6 and 7, the proportion of projects located in Bangkok and Samut Prakarn have been decreasing, while those in the ten central provinces, the north, and the northeast have been increasing in importance. Another factor for industrial dispersion is the increasing difficulty of locating in metropolitan areas due to the shortage of infrastructure and soaring land prices.

Overview of Foreign Direct Investment

The current investment boom has continued unabated for the past four years. Table 8 shows the achievements of the BOI's promotional activities. Between 1987 and 1989, the number of projects seeking promotional privileges exceeded 1,000 per year, the highest in the history of the BOI. The number of applications and the amount of total investment grew rapidly. In 1989, although the number of applications declined to 1,285 projects, the figures still surpassed the results of 1987. One of the reasons why more than 2,000 applications were submitted in 1988 was that investors rushed to apply to the BOI before new changes in promotional criteria came into force in January 1989.

Another investment scenario is seen from data of the Bank of Thailand. Table 9 shows trends in foreign direct investment since 1965. Foreign direct investment is composed of equity investment and direct investment loans from parent companies or associate concerns,

Table 6. Distribution of Projects by Location (number of projects; % share).

	1987	1988	1989	1990 (1~6)
⟨Applications⟩				
Bangkok & Samut Prakarn	437 (41)	550 (26)	386 (30)	137 (27)
4 provinces near Bangkok	231 (22)	333 (15)	161 (13)	85 (17)
10 central provinces	} 272 (25)	581 (27)	316 (24)	124 (24)
Other central provinces		226 (11)	125 (10)	54 (10)
North	35 (3)	66 (3)	93 (7)	35 (7)
Northeast	20 (2)	59 (3)	68 (5)	27 (5)
South	57 (5)	309 (14)	118 (9)	32 (6)
Unknown	25 (2)	28 (1)	30 (2)	20 (4)
Total	1,077 (100)	2,152 (100)	1,297 (100)	514 (100)
⟨Approvals⟩				
Bangkok & Samut Prakarn	290 (46)	429 (29)	335 (28)	131 (27)
4 provinces near Bangkok	160 (25)	232 (16)	201 (17)	80 (16)
10 central provinces	} 113 (18)	351 (24)	322 (27)	131 (27)
Other central		147 (10)	94 (8)	41 (8)
North	17 (3)	48 (3)	77 (6)	37 (8)
Northeast	12 (2)	33 (2)	57 (5)	23 (5)
South	40 (6)	241 (16)	−92 (8)	41 (8)
Unknown	3 (1)			
Total	635 (100)	1,481 (100)	1,179 (100)	486 (100)

Note: Total figures exceed the actual number of projects, because some projects are located in more than one region. *Source*: BOI.

Table 7. Distribution of Foreign Projects by Location in 1988 (number of projects; % share [in parentheses]).

	Total	Zone 1	Zone 2	Zone 3	Unknown
Japan	389 (100)	224 (58)	60 (15)	89 (23)	16 (4)
USA	136 (100)	60 (44)	34 (25)	19 (14)	23 (17)
UK	45 (100)	23 (51)	11 (24)	10 (22)	1 (2)
Taiwan	400 (100)	164 (41)	141 (35)	73 (18)	22 (6)
Hong Kong	126 (100)	60 (48)	29 (23)	31 (25)	6 (5)

Note: Based on current zoning effective January 1989. *Source*: BOI.

including capital funds from foreign commercial banks. The increase in the inflow of direct investment has continued uninterrupted, with the amount doubling every five years. The figures in 1987 and 1988 indicate that equity investment constituted the mainstream of recent foreign direct investment.

Foreign Direct Investment by Country

BOI data on registered capital, shown in Table 8, have frequently been

Table 8. Registered Capital by Country (million Baht).

	1984	1985	1986	1987	1988	1989	1990.1~6
(1) Applications							
No. of applications	376	325	431	1,058	2,128	1,285	505
Total investment	54,896	59,583	59,688	209,029	530,826	461,102	181,241
Registered capital	12,240	14,997	15,804	57,159	139,454	131,852	55,220
Thai	8,147	10,148	10,962	31,924	79,048	83,326	35,877
Foreign	4,093	4,849	4,842	25,235	60,406	48,527	19,342
Japan	1,199	443	1,690	9,386	21,292	16,636	7,747
Taiwan	305	445	602	2,078	9,610	6,311	1,748
USA	427	2,732	546	1,870	5,059	3,269	647
Hong Kong	249	183	87	850	1,633	3,964	2,969
Singapore	306	27	34	602	1,373	1,420	272
S. Korea	4	28	3	426	784	1,781	286
UK	390	112	193	233	2,306	1,636	2,106
Australia	127	36	100	843	3,618	51	99
Germany	141	9	98	75	230	1,506	109
Machinery & equipment	24,381	22,603	25,019	113,895	260,916	186,877	81,096
No. of Thai employees	118,774	76,420	100,681	332,568	532,602	409,701	149,900
(2) Approvals							
No. of approvals	266	210	295	626	1,464	1,176	483
Total investment	37,657	54,197	34,610	67,748	201,842	287,936	169,783
Registered capital	9,297	7,421	9,203	18,878	60,358	70,389	50,995
Thai	6,844	5,537	6,064	10,500	28,391	44,584	34,015
Foreign	2,453	1,884	3,139	8,378	31,967	25,805	16,980
Japan	904	169	1,675	3,665	18,234	9,964	4,957
Taiwan	248	111	46	1,540	3,983	3,949	1,718
USA	294	737	143	574	1,851	1,013	1,724
Hong Kong	181	163	230	350	894	1,239	1,803
Singapore	60	37	97	54	524	1,056	1,329
S. Korea	3	12	4	107	530	689	888
UK	101	45	291	112	1,651	1,027	161
Australia	125	13	16	38	240	205	86
Germany	39	11	121	31	179	304	29
Machinery & equipment	18,874	16,892	18,508	36,559	103,661	119,881	74,257
No. of Thai employees	64,845	59,374	60,231	204,113	352,964	332,194	162,330

Source: BOI, *Activity Report*, various issues.

Table 9. Flow of Foreign Direct Investment (million Baht).

Year	Inflow			Outflow			Net Inflow		
	Equity	Loan	Total	Equity	Loan	Total	Equity	Loan	Total
1965-1969	4,098.6	901.7	5,000.3	130.5	237.3	367.8	8,408.7	664.4	9,073.1
1970-1974	7,079.5	3,372.0	10,451.5	458.1	1,426.1	1,884.2	6,621.4	1,945.9	8,567.3
1975-1979	7,069.5	16,036.2	23,105.7	1,256.8	14,063.9	15,320.7	5,812.7	1,972.3	7,785.0
1980-1984	26,582.8	32,528.9	59,111.7	1,583.4	25,041.5	26,624.9	24,999.4	7,487.4	32,486.8
1985-1988	46,333.5	19,854.9	66,188.4	2,038.2	15,533.2	17,571.4	44,295.3	4,321.7	46,817.0
1980	3,703.8	5,555.2	9,259.0	132.7	5,248.1	5,443.0	3,571.1	307.1	3,878.2
1981	4,127.1	5,214.7	9,341.8	78.9	2,848.5	2,978.6	4,048.2	2,366.2	6,414.4
1982	3,884.0	5,712.5	9,596.5	505.3	4,759.8	5,292.8	3,378.7	952.7	4,331.4
1983	7,255.4	6,688.8	13,944.2	393.3	5,326.1	5,752.3	6,862.1	1,362.7	8,224.8
1984	7,612.5	9,357.7	16,970.2	473.2	6,859.0	7,332.2	7,139.3	2,498.7	9,638.0
1985	6,339.9	3,826.4	10,166.3	930.2	4,833.9	5,764.1	5,409.7	-1,007.5	4,402.2
1986	6,304.5	4,221.1	10,525.6	468.8	3,148.7	3,617.5	5,835.7	1,072.4	6,908.1
1987	10,621.0	1,915.0	12,536.0	373.2	3,119.0	3,492.2	10,247.8	-1,204.0	9,043.8
1988	23,068.1	9,892.4	32,960.5	266.0	4,431.6	4,697.6	22,802.1	5,460.8	28,262.9
1970-1988	87,065.3	71,792.0	158,857.3	5,336.5	56,064.7	61,401.2	81,728.8	15,727.3	97,456.1

Source: Bank of Thailand.

Table 10. Foreign Investment, Number of Projects and Total Investment (million Baht).

	1986		1987		1988		1989		1990 (1st half)	
	No.	Total Inv.	No.	Total Inv.	No.	Total Inv.	No.	Total Inv.	No.	Total Inv.
(1) Applications										
Total inv.	431	59,688	1,058	209,029	2,127	530,292	1,284	461,052	505	181,241
Total foreign investment	207	35,487	630	163,322	1,273	394,212	856	341,496	311	103,692
Japan	53	8,111	200	46,987	389	148,221	233	135,769	76	30,733
Taiwan	31	2,957	178	14,642	400	54,287	207	30,273	75	8,950
USA	24	13,998	61	19,214	136	92,767	76	31,497	34	10,301
Hong Kong	17	1,934	46	7,035	126	20,108	106	36,172	40	16,928
Singapore	9	330	37	5,129	90	16,954	45	18,483	16	3,546
S. Korea	2	20	16	2,303	40	3,679	39	9,482	17	2,255
Australia	6	528	22	7,331	30	29,851	9	386	5	1,366
Europe	42	16,292	110	33,131	148	73,569	128	52,163	51	6,901
UK	11	2,020	26	4,231	45	12,598	40	15,898	18	17,492
Germany	9	1,139	14	720	25	5,612	22	16,106	7	2,788
France	3	11,710	7	59	18	29,927	18	4,893	5	342
Belgium	4	878	12	15,407	15	3,616	9	736	3	411

Table 10 (cont.).

(2) Applications approved										
Total inv.	295	34,610	625	67,290	1,463	201,812	1,175	287,844	438	169,783
Total foreign investment	154	25,047	385	60,064	838	158,066	752	205,495	334	116,437
Japan	35	6,593	136	24,363	265	77,019	223	90,569	88	40,506
Taiwan	18	940	102	7,700	308	21,498	214	22,305	88	7,831
USA	20	1,067	34	4,431	106	17,028	68	14,123	42	19,501
Hong Kong	18	1,178	32	3,144	86	11,416	65	14,430	35	14,388
Singapore	6	250	17	1,630	59	6,924	45	10,460	21	12,086
S. Korea	2	23	7	333	36	2,758	26	4,387	17	5,155
Australia	4	297	12	984	19	1,325	17	2,342	4	1,312
Europe	35	5,185	51	6,901	110	26,257	120	40,163	55	15,503
UK	13	1,866	16	2,643	44	8,387	31	12,493	15	2,926
Germany	5	739	7	337	17	3,513	21	3,220	7	1,435
France	4	400	3	32	14	1,289	17	2,487	9	1,783
Belgium	4	79	4	1,472	15	11,697	10	819	2	137

Note: Total investment figures are for Thai as well as foreign investors. Firms with foreign investment from more than one country are doubly counted.

Source: International Division, BOI.

quoted in order to determine trends affecting foreign investment in Thailand. In terms of the amount of registered capital in applications approved, the following trends are observed. First, the top three investors, namely, Japan, the USA, and Taiwan, increased their capital to a large extent. Second, investment from Asian NIEs, such as Hong Kong, Singapore, and South Korea, grew rapidly. Third, investment from European countries, the main target in the BOI's attempts to attract investment in those three years, also increased satisfactorily.

In 1986, the proportion of projects in which foreigners participated to the total number of projects was 48% in terms of the number of applications and 52% in terms of the number of applications approved (Table 10). This proportion increased gradually to 60% and 62%, respectively, in 1987, 60% and 61% in 1988, 67% and 64% in 1989, and 62% and 76% in the first half of 1990. The figures in Table 10 cover all the projects in which foreign firms invested, including those with a less than 1% foreign shareholding ratio.

Table 11. Accumulative Registered Capital by Country (million Baht).

	Nov. 1985		June 1990	
	Amount	% Foreign Capital	Amount	% Foreign Capital
Total	36,486		148,399	
Thai	26,179		92,161	
Foreign	10,307	100	56,238	100
Japan	2,768	26.9	30,252	53.8
USA	1,698	16.5	3,716	6.6
Taiwan	926	9.0	6,306	11.2
UK	714	6.9	1,643	2.9
Hong Kong	510	4.9	1,887	3.4
Singapore	458	4.4	1,765	3.1
Australia	315	3.1	432	0.8
Netherlands	276	2.7	598	1.1
Switzerland	152	1.5	1,524	2.7
Malaysia	267	2.6	398	0.7
Germany	162	1.6	347	0.6
France	66	0.6	353	0.6

Source: BOI, *Activity Report*.

As regards the actual amount of registered capital, Table 11 shows the cumulative total as of November 1985, just before the recent investment boom, and as of June 1990 in terms of the number of projects receiving promotional certificates. During this period only three countries increased their shares of overall foreign capital, Japan, Taiwan, and Switzerland, although the last accounted only for a very small amount.

Table 12. Net Inflow of Foreign Direct Investment by Country (million Baht).

	1970-1974	1975-1979	1980-1984	1985-1988	1970-1988
Japan	2,383.8	2,584.1	8,367.2	22,443.0	35,778.1
USA	3,295.3	2,607.3	8,984.5	8,675.5	23,562.6
UK	462.8	638.5	1,649.9	1,587.1	4,338.3
Germany	69.5	348.2	878.3	1,396.1	2,692.1
France	143.2	117.2	162.1	649.9	1,072.4
Netherlands	239.8	96.9	2,138.7	265.3	2,739.7
Italy	109.2	384.0	385.3	126.3	966.2
Switzerland	49.2	275.0	400.7	1,703.8	2,428.7
Canada	51.2	-77.5	145.8	143.6	263.1
Australia	40.0	37.4	408.1	134.5	620.0
Hong Kong	942.0	394.7	3,253.1	5,454.8	10,044.6
Singapore	443.4	457.8	2,586.0	1,337.2	4,823.7
Malaysia	99.0	3.1	351.4	66.2	518.4
Taiwan	36.1	1.1	89.1	4,151.9	4,278.2
S. Korea	n.a	n.a	35.3	321.9	
China	n.a	n.a	1.5	382.5	
Total (includes other countries)	8,567.2	7,785.0	32,486.8	48,597.8	97,436.8

Source: Bank of Thailand.

The real inflow of foreign direct investment is shown in Table 12, from which the following five points can be observed. First, Japan is the largest souce of foreign investment, a fact also indicated by BOI data. However, it was not until 1987 that Japan replaced the USA to receive top ranking. The great US influence in Thailand is the second point. Third, unlike BOI data which designate Taiwan as the second highest investor, Table 12 suggests, surprisingly, that Taiwan's actual investment is quite small. Fourth, Hong Kong and Singapore invested a comparatively large amount during the 1980s. Finally, Taiwan, Korea, and China appear to be newly rising investors.

The form of investment from five countries, Japan, the USA, Taiwan, Hong Kong, and Singapore, can be seen from Table 13. First, Japan, the USA, and Taiwan invest mainly in equity, while Hong Kong and Singapore concentrate mainly on investment loans. Second, equity investment in the 1980s grew with Japan, Hong Kong, and Taiwan as sources of investment. The increase in equity investment from Hong Kong is particularly noteworthy due to its imminent reversion to China. On the other hand, equity investment from the USA underwent a decline after 1984. Third, Japan became the largest source of loans as well as of equity investment in the latter half of the 1980s, while investment from Hong Kong leveled off and Singapore marked a

Table 13. Inflow of Direct Investment (million Baht).

	Inflow			Outflow			Net Inflow		
	Equity	Loan	Total	Equity	Loan	Total	Equity	Loan	Total
Japan									
1970-1974	1,886	742	2,629	42	203	244	1,844	540	2,384
1975-1979	1,742	2,255	3,997	199	1,213	1,413	1,543	1,041	2,584
1980-1984	6,149	4,241	10,390	224	1,799	2,046	5,925	2,443	8,367
1985-1988	18,940	7,611	26,551	338	3,770	4,108	18,602	3,841	22,443
1970-1988	28,717	14,849	43,567	803	6,985	7,811	27,914	7,865	35,778
USA									
1970-1974	3,131	975	4,107	202	609	812	2,929	366	3,295
1975-1979	2,341	2,529	4,870	210	2,046	2,376	2,131	476	2,607
1980-1984	8,929	1,952	10,882	414	1,483	1,927	8,515	469	8,985
1985-1988	8,554	1,556	10,110	651	784	1,435	7,903	773	8,675
1970-1988	22,956	7,013	29,968	1,477	4,922	6,549	21,478	2,084	23,563
Taiwan									
1970-1974	36	0	36	–	–	–	36	0	36
1975-1979	8	–	8	7	–	7	1	–	1
1980-1984	81	8	89	–	–	–	81	8	81
1985-1988	4,032	131	4,163	11	–	11	4,020	131	4,152
1980-1988	4,157	140	4,297	18	–	18	4,138	140	4,278
Hong Kong									
1970-1974	684	388	1,072	33	97	130	651	291	942
1975-1979	810	2,622	3,432	187	2,850	3,037	623	−228	395
1980-1984	2,802	5,931	8,733	267	5,213	5,479	2,535	718	3,253
1985-1988	4,937	5,437	10,374	134	4,785	4,919	4,803	652	5,455
1970-1988	9,233	14,377	23,610	622	12,944	13,566	8,612	1,433	10,045
Singapore									
1970-1974	244	361	605	42	121	162	203	240	443
1975-1979	372	7,252	7,623	125	7,041	7,166	247	211	458
1980-1984	1,503	14,683	16,186	67	13,533	13,600	1,436	1,150	2,586
1985-1988	2,175	3,742	5,917	88	4,492	4,578	2,088	−750	1,338
1970-1988	4,294	26,037	30,332	321	25,187	25,508	3,973	851	4,284

Source: Bank of Thailand.

decrease after it reached a peak in the first half of the 1980s. Finally, although investment loans consist of medium- and long-term loans, those extended by Hong Kong and Singapore tend to be the short-term type compared with those from Japan and the USA. The cumulative total outflow of investment loans from these two countries accounted for 90% of the cumulative total inflow of loans.

Foreign Direct Investment by Sector

As shown in Table 14, based on the net inflow of direct investment, the

Table 14. Net Inflow of Foreign Direct Investment by Business (million Baht).

	1971-1974	1975-1979	1980-1984	1985-1988	1971-1986	1987-1988	1971-1988
Financial institutions	1,622.9	665.6	1,167.7	2,397.5	2,687.1	3,166.6	5,853.7
Trade	1,308.9	1,977.1	5,520.2	7,651.0	11,671.4	-785.8	16,457.2
Construction	767.4	1,032.1	4,604.7	6,108.0	9,223.8	3,287.8	12,511.6
Mining & quarrying	1,446.1	462.6	7,288.0	1,420.7	9,953.0	664.6	10,617.6
Oil exploration	1,362.6	306.2	6,457.7	1,316.7	8,792.9	650.3	9,443.2
Other	83.5	156.4	830.3	104.0	1,159.9	14.3	1,174.2
Agriculture	25.1	−10.5	348.6	872.3	642.3	593.2	1,235.5
Industry	2,058.5	2,889.2	10,506.3	24,576.1	18,935.9	21,094.2	40,030.1
Food	281.9	243.0	314.4	2,347.8	1,521.0	1,666.1	3,187.1
Textiles	1,023.9	884.1	852.8	2,260.8	2,906.4	2,115.2	5,021.6
Metal-based and Nonmetallic	140.4	95.1	1,420.7	2,176.9	1,507.9	2,325.2	3,833.1
Electrical appliances	222.8	907.1	3,136.2	8,342.7	5,163.1	7,445.7	12,608.8
Machinery & transport equipment	50.9	255.1	990.6	904.2	1,313.7	887.1	2,200.8
Chemicals	203.4	365.7	1,131.0	3,787.5	2,672.5	2,815.1	5,487.6
Petroleum products	17.9	97.9	2,054.2	826.0	2,178.2	817.8	2,996.0
Construction materials	46.3	−117.9	47.6	76.8	19.7	33.1	52.8
Others	71.0	159.1	516.5	3,853.4	1,611.1	2,988.9	4,600.0
Services	447.8	768.9	3,051.9	5,572.2	6,145.5	3,695.3	9,840.8
Transportation & travel	209.5	613.9	1,195.7	1,082.2	2,472.6	628.7	3,101.3
Housing & real estate	91.2	49.7	350.5	1,567.0	839.6	1,218.8	2,058.4
Hotels & restaurants	79.7	18.0	449.3	976.6	870.2	653.4	1,523.6
Other	67.4	87.3	1,056.4	1,946.4	1,963.1	1,194.4	3,157.5
Total	7,676.7	7,785.0	28,486.8	48,597.8	59,258.8	37,287.5	96,546.3

Source: Bank of Thailand.

manufacturing sector accounted for the largest share, as seen by the following statistics: 32% of total investment between 1971 and 1986 was invested in manufacturing, followed by 20% in trade, 17% in mining, 16% in construction, and 10% in services. Between 1987 and 1988, 57% of total investment was centered on manufacturing, followed by 13% in trade, 10% in services, 8.8% in construction, and 8.5% in financial institutions. These figures confirm the heavy investment in manufacturing in that two-year period.

In the manufacturing sector, investment between 1971 and 1986 was poured into electrical appliances, textiles, chemicals, petroleum products, and food, in descending order, and their respective shares of total investment were 27%, 15%, 14%, 12%, and 8%. Between 1987 and 1988 investments in the manufacturing sector ranked as follows: electrical appliances, chemicals, metal and nonmetallic products, textiles, and food, with respective shares of total investment of 35%, 13%, 11%, 10%, and 8%. This indicates heavy investment in the electrical appliance industry, although investment in miscellaneous aspects of the manufacturing industry has also grown considerably.

PATTERNS OF INVESTMENT

Japan and the USA

The combined share of direct investment from Japan and the USA accounts for 61% of the total in terms of net inflow. This share reached 75% in the latter half of the 1960s, when Thailand was still at the stage of launching its industrialization drive, but declined afterward. Nevertheless, it still maintained a more than 50% share of total foreign investment, accounting for 66% in the 1970s and 53% in the first half of the 1980s, and rising to 64% in the latter half of the 1980s due to the large increase in Japanese investment. Considering the importance of these two countries, the distribution of Japanese and US investment should be examined.

For investment from Japan (Table 15), the manufacturing sector ranks first, followed by construction. Heavy investment in the construction industry is one of the features of Japanese investment. Investment in construction was particularly prevalent in the first half of the 1980s; its amount at that time exceeded that of the manufacturing sector. Between 1987 and 1988, Japanese investment concentrated on the manufacturing sector, with 69% invested in manufacturing and 12% in construction. As a result, between 1971 and 1988, the manufacturing and the construction sectors accounted for 52% and 21%, respectively,

Table 15. Net Inflow of Direct Investment from Japan (million Baht).

	1971-1974	1975-1979	1980-1984	1985-1988	1971-1986	1987-1988	1971-1988
Financial institutions	261.4	266.1	237.7	1,206.3	845.2	1,126.3	1,971.5
Trade	569.0	440.3	2,019.7	2,195.6	4,439.6	785.0	5,224.6
Construction	113.4	339.1	3,053.3	3,872.3	5,168.4	2,209.7	7,378.1
Mining & quarrying	12.7	5.9	8.6	8.4	29.3	6.3	35.6
Oil exploration	7.6	5.5	8.1	2.1	23.3	0	23.3
Others	5.1	0.4	0.5	6.3	6.0	6.3	12.3
Agriculture	20.0	−17.9	83.8	447.7	235.0	300.2	535.2
Industry	1,026.5	1,302.9	2,813.7	13,258.1	6,009.5	12,391.7	18,401.2
Food	227.8	110.0	−314.3	484.4	197.0	310.9	507.9
Textiles	471.1	750.4	632.9	430.8	1,950.9	334.3	2,285.2
Metal-based and Nonmetallic	41.4	27.6	1,081.7	1,608.8	899.2	1,860.3	2,759.5
Electrical appliances	91.8	76.5	791.4	5,947.6	1,396.7	5,510.6	6,907.3
Machinery & transport equipment	29.1	105.2	352.6	792.8	457.4	822.3	1,279.7
Chemicals	145.3	174.1	229.5	729.1	627.0	651.0	1,278.0
Petroleum products	0.3	14.6	2.8	2,029.7	17.7	2,029.7	2,047.4
Construction materials	12.8	0.4	8.0	5.8	26.6	0.4	30.0
Other	6.9	44.7	29.1	1,229.1	437.6	872.2	1,309.8
Services	58.7	246.1	150.4	1,454.6	869.0	1,040.8	1,909.8
Transportation & travel	34.5	220.6	84.7	293.1	448.1	184.8	632.9
Housing & real estate	10.5	9.3	0.2	451.6	24.4	447.2	471.6
Hotels & restaurants	7.8	3.3	0	240.9	20.5	231.5	252.0
Other	5.9	12.9	65.5	469.0	376.0	177.3	553.3
Total	2,061.7	2,584.1	8,367.2	22,443.0	17,596.0	17,860.0	35,456.0

Source: Bank of Thailand.

of total Japanese investment. The proportion of Japanese investment to total foreign investment by sector is as much as 46% in the manufacturing sector and 59% in the construction sector.

Japanese investment in the manufacturing sector covers a wide range of products, with the exception of construction materials. Between 1971 and 1986, the Japanese invested mainly in textiles, electrical appliances, metal and nonmetallic products, chemicals, and machinery and transport equipment, in that order. Between 1987 and 1988, the following major advances were observed: electrical appliances accounted for 44% of the total investment in manufacturing and this was accompanied by a sizable investment in the petrochemical industry, a sector in which the Japanese had shown little interest in the past, as well as by an increase in investment in metal products, machinery and transport equipment, and the chemical industry. As a result, each sector's share of the total outstanding in manufacturing up to 1988 changed. They ranked as follows: electrical appliances, metal and nonmetallic products, textiles, petroleum products, machinery and transport equipment, and chemicals.

As far as US investment is concerned (Table 16), mining, manufacturing, and trade are the main sectors in which Americans have invested. Extensive investment in the mining sector, spurred by the development of oil and natural gas, is a special feature of US investment, exceeding that in manufacturing. Investment in mining accounted for 30% of all US investment during 1971 and 1988, while manufacturing accounted for 28%. The proportion of US investment in total foreign direct investment by sector is 66% in mining and 16% in manufacturing.

In the manufacturing sector, the emphasis was placed on electrical appliances, which accounted for 57% of US investment in manufacturing between 1971 and 1986. Investment in the first half of the 1980s focused mainly on the production of integrated circuits. During 1987 and 1988, investment in the manufacturing sector covered a rather wide range of products, such as electrical appliances, textiles, and food, while investment in miscellaneous manufacturing industry also increased. Thus, compared with the total investment in manufacturing up to 1988, the proportion invested in electrical appliances underwent a decline, falling to 47%.

Investment Patterns in 1988

The investment patterns of five major countries are shown in Table 17. It should be noted that the figures in Table 17 represent the number of

Table 16. Net Inflow of Direct Investment from USA (million Baht).

	1971-1974	1975-1979	1980-1984	1985-1988	1971-1986	1987-1988	1971-1988
Financial institutions	429.0	348.8	−558.1	488.3	807.7	35.8	843.5
Trade	330.9	754.7	832.7	1,926.3	2,507.7	1,336.9	3,844.6
Construction	385.0	61.9	615.3	418.4	1,255.0	225.6	1,480.6
Mining & quarrying	1,408.7	271.5	4,432.1	845.1	6,489.4	468.0	6,957.4
Oil exploration	1,339.9	224.0	4,449.2	7111.5	6,322.0	402.6	6,724.6
Other	68.8	47.5	−17.1	133.6	167.4	65.4	232.8
Agriculture	2.9	1.8	28.8	223.4	125.1	131.8	256.9
Industry	252.8	696.0	2,662.3	2,939.9	4,688.8	1,862.2	6,551.0
Food	17.6	28.5	232.2	553.3	528.5	303.3	831.8
Textiles	70.4	20.4	20.1	395.8	116.0	390.5	506.5
Metal-based and Nonmetallic	27.4	20.2	−64.5	82.5	-6.2	71.8	65.6
Electrical appliances	117.9	484.9	1,823.7	630.5	2,658.3	428.7	3,087.0
Machinery & transport equipment	3.1	115.6	68.8	67.6	218.5	36.6	255.1
Chemicals	−6.2	15.9	41.0	524.0	470.5	122.2	592.7
Petroleum products	9.1	83.2	416.7	1.3	509.0	1.3	510.3
Construction materials	6.0	−128.0	0	29.0	−122.9	29.0	−93.9
Other	8.4	25.5	124.3	637.7	317.1	478.8	795.9
Services	134.1	354.6	971.9	1,834.1	2,360.7	934.0	3,294.7
Transportation & travel	87.3	309.6	295.3	339.9	962.4	123.7	1,086.1
Housing & real estate	−2.5	–	90.5	411.2	338.6	106.6	499.2
Hotels & restaurants	12.1	0.7	68.6	224.1	248.6	56.9	305.5
Other	37.2	44.3	517.5	804.9	811.1	592.8	1,403.9
Total	2,943.4	2,489.3	8,984.5	8,675.5	18,216.4	4,994.3	23,210.2

Source: Bank of Thailand.

Table 17. Promoted Foreign Investment in 1988.
(1) Distribution of Employment Size

	No. of projects	More than 400	200-399	50-199	10-49	1-9	0[1]	Total Employment	Employment per Project
Japan	264	52 (20%)	58 (22%)	117 (44%)	36 (14%)		1 (0.4%)	69,108	217
USA	104	22 (21%)	31 (30%)	34 (33%)	17 (16%)			37,202	358
UK	43	3 (7%)	16 (37%)	18 (42%)	5 (12%)		1 (2%)	9,189	214
Taiwan	303	55 (18%)	107 (35%)	117 (39%)	24 (8%)			75,671	250
Hong Kong	86	20 (23%)	28 (33%)	27 (31%)	10 (12%)	1 (1%)		32,784	381

(2) Distribution of Investment Size

	No. of Projects	Total Investment per Project (Mil. B)	Total Invest-ment (Mil. B)	Distribution of Investment Size			
				More than 500 (Mil. B)	100-499 (Mil. B)	20-99 (Mil. B)	Less than 20 (Mil. B)
Japan	264	76,781	291	32 (12%)	89 (34%)	109 (41%)	34 (13%)
USA	104	16,745	161	8 (8%)	24 (23%)	55 (53%)	17 (16%)
UK	43	8,367	195	3 (7%)	6 (14%)	24 (56%)	10 (23%)
Taiwan	303	20,936	69	8 (3%)	32 (11%)	154 (51%)	109 (36%)
Hong Kong	86	10,244	119	3 (4%)	21 (24%)	48 (56%)	14 (16%)

Table 17 (cont.).

(3) Pattern of Ownership

	100% Foreign	Joint Venture with Thai	Joint Venture with Other Foreign	No Capital Increase[2]
Japan	47 (18%)	173 (66%)	13 (5%)	31 (12%)
USA	8 (8%)	70 (67%)	10 (10%)	16 (15%)
UK	1 (2%)	29 (67%)	5 (12%)	8 (19%)
Taiwan	78 (26%)	203 (57%)	15 (5%)	7 (2%)
Hong Kong	5 (6%)	67 (78%)	3 (4%)	11 (13%)

(4) Distribution of Export Ratio

	100%	80-99%	1-79%	0	Unknown	Total
Japan	123 (47%)	100 (38%)	20 (8%)	19 (7%)	2 (1%)	264
USA	57 (55%)	24 (23%)	11 (11%)	11 (11%)	1 (1%)	104
UK	22 (51%)	10 (23%)	1 (2%)	10 (23%)	43	
Taiwan	194 (64%)	71 (23%)	16 (5%)	22 (7%)		303
Hong Kong	39 (45%)	24 (28%)	11 (13%)	12 (14%)		86

Notes: 1. Equipment expansion project with no increase in workers.
2. Equipment expansion project without capital increase.
Shareholding ratio is not shown in BOI data.

Source: Compiled from BOI promoted project list by country.

projects rather than the number of firms, and multiple projects undertaken by the same company are counted separately. In addition, projects designed to expand existing firms are also included; the proportion of this latter type to the total number of projects is as follows: Japan 27%, the USA 18%, the UK 30%, Taiwan 5%, and Hong Kong 21%. As in Table 4, projects in which the investment originates from more than one country are double-counted. Therefore, the total number of employees, the average size of work force per company, and the average amount of total investment will be significantly affected, especially in the case of countries with only a small number of projects.

In employment, Taiwan had the largest number of Thai employees, followed by Japan, the USA, Hong Kong, and the UK. The average size of the work force per project is over 200 persons for each of the countries mentioned; by Thai standards any company employing such a large work force would be classified as "large." Hong Kong and the USA employ a large work force, 381 and 358 persons, respectively, indicating the extent of their investment in labor-intensive industries. Taiwan has also made a considerable investment in labor-intensive industries, but the average size of a company work force is rather small at 250 persons. For Japan and the UK, the average number of employees per project is almost the same: 217 and 214 persons, respectively. As for the size of the work force in terms of distribution, more than half of all US, Hong Kong, and Taiwanese projects employ over 200 persons, while Japan and the UK employ, on average, between 50 and 199 persons.

In contrast to the size of the work force in their employ, the Japanese account for the largest investment (291 million baht) in terms of the amount invested per project. They are followed by the UK, with an investment of 195 million baht, the US with 161 million baht, Hong Kong with 119 million baht, and Taiwan with 69 million baht. Compared with the other countries, the size of the Taiwanese investment is relatively small. As for the distribution of each country's investments, Japan invested 12% of its total in large-scale projects, which accounted for an investment of more than 500 million baht, and 34% (between 100 and 500 million baht) in medium-scale projects, a relatively large investment compared with that of other countries. This is partly because many Japanese projects are in industries engaged in the production of machinery and related products.

For investment from the other four countries, small-scale projects representing an investment of between 20 and 100 million baht accounted for more than 50% of the total number of projects. Taiwan placed particular emphasis on relatively small-scale projects; projects representing an investment of less than 20 million baht accounted for 36% of their projects. Based on the distribution in terms of investment size, Hong Kong's amount of investment per project should be greater than that of the UK. However, this is not the case because, although the number of UK-funded projects is relatively small, the petrochemical project on the Eastern Seaboard, representing an investment of 4,500 million baht, boosted the UK's average investment. Without this project, the average size of investment from the UK would amount to a mere 92 million baht, comparatively small in scale.

In sum, Japanese investment is large in terms of the amount invested, but relatively small in terms of the size of the work force employed. Taiwan, however, presents the opposite picture in that it has tended to concentrate on labor-intensive industries that require comparatively little investment to operate.

In structure of ownership, joint ventures with Thai capital predominate, accounting for two-thirds of the total, and Hong Kong has the highest proportion of 78%. As regards the proportion of wholly foreign-owned projects, Taiwan ranks highest among the five countries, with 26%, followed by Japan with 18%. Given the size of investment and structure of ownership, it can be said that, in general, wholly foreign-owned projects constitute a relatively small investment. The average investment of wholly foreign-owned projects is about half of that of joint ventures. In the first half of 1989, in terms of the number of applications, the average investment in wholly foreign-owned projects was even smaller than that in wholly Thai-owned projects. It appears that foreign small- and medium-scale firms prefer 100%-owned projects.

Projects exporting more than 80% of their output accounted for over 70% of the total number of projects undertaken by each country. Japan accounted for 85%, and Taiwan 87%. Typically, Taiwanese investors relocate their production and export bases; their projects exporting 100% of their output accounted for 64% of the total, the biggest proportion of all countries investing in Thailand. Furthermore, the investment sectors of Taiwanese consist mainly of labor-intensive light industries, thus leading to competition with Thai firms. On the other hand, the proportion of industry oriented toward the local market constitutes a relatively large part of investment from the UK, Hong Kong, and the USA.

In relation to the above-mentioned structure of ownership, Table 18 details changes in the shareholding ratio of original investors. To take the case of Japan, the shareholding ratio among those firms in operation

Table 18. Ownership Pattern of Promoted Firms by Country.

	Firms in Operation										Firms with Certificates but Not Yet in Operation				
	End of 1987					End of 1988					End of 1988				
		Registered Capital					Registered Capital					Registered Capital			
	No. of Firms	Amount (Mil. B)	Country of Origin (%)	Other Foreign (%)	Thai (%)	No. of Firms	Amount (Mil. B) (%)	Country of Origin (%)	Other Foreign (%)	Thai (%)	No. of Firms	Amount (Mil. B) (%)	Country of Origin (%)	Other Foreign (%)	Thai (%)
Japan	193	8,356	45.7	1.9	52.4	233	12,153	56.0	3.3	40.7	179	10,181	58.7	3.5	37.8
USA	79	3,261	38.4	8.5	53.1	88	3,868	37.3	10.2	52.5	54	2,559	50.1	19.6	30.3
UK	57	3,623	18.5	5.5	76.0	69	4,089	20.8	6.8	72.4	33	1,896	30.1	14.6	55.3
Taiwan	123	3,352	15.3	7.3	77.4	144	3,923	20.0	7.6	72.4	153	3,738	46.8	4.6	48.6
Hong Kong	70	2,843	29.5	10.6	59.9	87	4,112	32.2	10.8	57.0	54	1,590	38.6	12.7	48.7
Singapore	32	1,883	20.8	23.8	55.4	39	2,240	19.3	25.5	55.2	34	1,939	26.9	28.5	44.6
S. Korea	6	90	41.0	5.8	53.2	6	90	41.0	5.8	53.2	12	282	78.5	5.1	16.4

Note: Figures for firms in operation are questionnaire returns. Figures for firms with certificates are from project proposals.
Source: BOI.

and those that received promotional certificates but were not yet in operation in 1982 was 39.7%. In 1987 and 1988, there was a sharp rise in the ratio. As a result, the Japanese shareholding ratio among their joint ventures in 1988 was over 57.2% in terms of both firms in operation and those not yet operating.

In terms of industry, there is a special feature regarding the structure of ownership. Ordinarily, the average shareholding ratio by Thais is more than 50%. But foreigners, with the exclusion of Taiwanese, owned the majority of capital in their ventures in the machinery and electrical equipment industry, as shown in Table 19. Taking the example of Japanese ventures, Japanese hold 74.1% share in terms of firms in promotion, and other foreigners hold 5.1%, while the Thai shareholding ratio is only 20.8%. These figures reflect the predominance of foreign firms in the machinery and electrical equipment industries.

Table 19. Average Shareholding Ratio of Original Investors by Country and by Industry (1960 through December 31, 1988) (%).

	Japan	USA	UK	Hong Kong	Taiwan	Singapore
A. Firms in operation						
1	37.7	33.7	14.0	27.0	28.3	16.3
2	36.7	32.1	11.4	9.3	5.0	16.6
3	37.8	51.6	15.7	18.1	18.3	15.0
4	74.1	63.4	64.0	87.2	37.0	51.2
5	54.7	36.8	23.6	23.8	31.3	17.1
6	30.5	11.1	34.5	35.7	15.9	15.0
Subtotal	56.0	37.3	20.8	32.2	20.0	19.3
B. Firms with certificates but not yet in operation						
1	85.0	31.1	40.1	18.3	36.3	10.8
2	67.7	31.9	1.0	20.4	37.6	—
3	48.1	25.3	13.4	36.9	43.8	18.9
4	65.1	72.7	93.2	94.0	80.0	44.9
5	45.7	47.8	16.2	42.6	44.8	17.2
6	19.8	0.2	36.2	17.5	5.0	17.9
Subtotal	58.7	50.1	30.1	38.6	46.8	26.9
Total	57.2	42.4	23.8	33.9	33.1	23.5

1. Agricultural products and commodities.
2. Minerals, metal, and ceramics.
3. Chemical and chemical products.
4. Mechanical and electrical equipment.
5. Other products.
6. Services.

Source: BOI.

Industries That Attract Investors

Table 20 compares the number of Japanese investments as well as their amounts classified by industry. At the end of 1982, machinery and electrical equipment ranked first, followed by other types of manufacturing. Other types of manufacturing include the textile industry which employed as many as 30,000 workers. At the end of 1988, 143 firms were engaged in other types of manufacturing, 3.8 times as many as in 1982. This was followed by machinery and electrical equipment in which 133 firms were engaged, 2.7 times as many as there were six years previously.

Table 21 contains data on the number of BOI-approved projects in 1988 classified by industry. Japanese poured investment mainly into machinery and electrical equipment, while Asian NIEs invested mainly in light industries, which accounted for more than 50% of each of their total number of projects. The following industries attracted the largest number of projects from each country in 1988 in terms of the number of applications: from
⟨Japan⟩ electric and electronics parts (91), metal products (40), processed food (34), machinery and machine parts (29), plastic products (27), automobile parts (21), petrochemical products (15), sporting goods (12), and rubber products (11);
⟨the USA⟩ electronics parts (27), rubber gloves (17), metal products (11), petrochemical products (9), and chemicals (7);
⟨the UK⟩ electronics parts (6), toys and sporting goods (2), and jewelry and ornaments (3);
⟨Taiwan⟩ electric and electronics parts (54), rubber gloves (37), plastic products (36), toys and sporting goods (26), metal products (20), concentrated latex (19), sports shoes and accessories (13), processed food (11);
⟨Hong Kong⟩ rubber gloves (13), electric and electronic parts (12), toys and sporting goods (11), and plastic products (8);
⟨Korea⟩ toys and sporting goods (9), electric and electronic parts (6), and metal products (4).

DEVELOPMENT OF INVESTMENT POLICY

Development of Investment Policy Between 1988 and 1990

Amid the anticipation of high economic growth, there were active moves between 1988 and 1990 to review the nation's investment policy.

Table 20. Promoted Investment from Japan by Industry.

	1982			1988			
	No. of Firms	Total Investment (Mil. B)	No. of Employees	No. of Firms	Total Investment (Mil. B)	Registered Capital (Mil. B)	Japanese Shareholding (%)
Agricultural products and commodities	29	3,070	9,410	49	4,616	1,473	62.5
Minerals, metal, and ceramics	24	4,450	6,503	47	11,826	2,440	47.4
Chemical and chemical products	21	7,200	4,678	30	11,705	2,061	40.6
Mechanical and electrical equipment	49	10,500	15,182	133	42,123	8,970	69.7
Other products	38	8,590	33,947	143	21,818	7,009	50.2
Services	5	550	1,195	10	1,606	381	27.7
Total	166	34,360	70,915	412	93,694	22,334	57.2

Note: Combined figure of firms in operation and firms with promotion certificates but not yet in operation.
Source: Compiled from data of BOI.

Table 21. Approved Projects by Country and by Industry in 1988.

	Agricultural Products and Commodities	Minerals, Metal, and Ceramics	Chemical and Chemical Products	Mechanical & Electrical Equipment	Other Products	Services	Total
Japan	35 (13%)	21 (8%)	15 (6%)	101 (38%)	88 (33%)	4 (2%)	264
USA	24 (23%)	5 (5%)	7 (7%)	27 (26%)	39 (38%)	1 (1%)	103
UK	12 (28%)	2 (5%)	3 (7%)	4 (9%)	20 (47%)	2 (5%)	43
Taiwan	66 (22%)	18 (6%)	7 (2%)	53 (17%)	157 (52%)	2 (1%)	303
Hong Kong	22 (26%)	1 (1%)	5 (6%)	9 (10%)	48 (56%)	1 (1%)	86
S. Korea	3 (8%)	4 (11%)	1 (3%)	10 (28%)	18 (50%)	0	36

Source: BOI

Since a number of foreign firms are keen to invest in Thailand, it seemed like an opportune moment to revise the policy, utilizing tax incentives as a means of dispersing investment throughout the provinces and introducing foreign capital selectively into the field of industry, something which Thailand is in need of. The current guidelines for promoting investment targets include:

a) export-oriented industries;
b) industries that use local raw materials;
c) industries that expand the local industrial base through the development of supporting industries;
d) industries that contribute toward enhancing local technological capabilities; and
e) industries located in the provinces.

To attract foreign investment, the promotion policy in 1989 and 1990 can be summarized as follows:

1) dispatch of missions to attract investors from target countries;
2) selection of target industries for investment;
3) promotion of projects located outside the Bangkok metropolitan area;
4) increased participation of Thai capital in foreign-owned projects;
5) promotion of Thai investment abroad;
6) improvements in the institutional investment climate; and
7) setting targets for the number of projects and total investment.

When sending missions abroad, emphasis is placed on the USA and European countries in particular, weighting 70% to Europe and 30% to the USA. The objectives of this policy are as follows: attract investors from countries that import goods from Thailand in order to reduce trade barriers erected by the aforementioned countries in retaliation to Thai Government subsidization of promoted industries; offset the increasing influence of Japanese investment; and cope with the unification of the EC in 1992. Target industries are electronic parts and automobile parts, and the Japanese are expected to invest in these industries, aiming to increase exports to Japan.

There were changes in the criteria for promotion of investment in the provinces in September 1987 and January 1989. Table 6 shows the result of the changes in zoning. The proportion of projects located in Bangkok and Samut Prakarn decreased significantly, indicating the progress made in the distribution of investment among the provinces. The location of the projects undertaken by five foreign countries, in terms of the number of applications, are shown in Table 7. Compared with the total number of projects, most foreign investment tends to be located in the metropolitan areas, especially those of Japan and the UK. But the projects of these two countries are also located in Zone 3 with a rather high ratio. For example, in the Northern Industrial Estate in Lamphun, only 16 firms had reserved land in the estate by the end of 1988; however, by the end of October 1989, there were 52 firms, of which 19 were Japanese. The top five firms in terms of the size of investment are Japanese firms engaged in the manufacture of electronic parts and the processing of agricultural products. In contrast, Taiwanese firms tend to favor the central region.

Controversy Over the Role of the BOI

In 1989 and 1990, the role of the BOI became a source of controversy. Accordingly, the BOI set up a subcommittee to review its promotional policy in June 1989. The BOI is now concentrating its efforts on identifying industries that should be promoted.

In this regard, a major change can be seen from the arguments on the reduction of import duties on machinery. There were two main reasons for this requirement for reduction: first, considering the trade conflict that had been caused by the rapid growth of Thai industrial exports, it seemed necessary to abolish the reduction of import duties on machinery for BOI-promoted firms, and to levy these lower tariff rates equally. In this way it is possible to mute the accusations made by foreign trading partners that Thailand is subsidizing exports. Second, the abolishment of privilege and the reduction of tariff rates reduced the inequality between firms that receive promotional privileges and nonpromoted firms, thus creating fair competition in the private sector. The proposal also hopes to reduce industry's production costs. The tax on certain imported machinery and capital goods was reduced to a flat 5% rate in October 1990.

In the past, the BOI had been criticized for promoting foreign and large firms only. The BOI was instructed to take small- and medium-scale firms into account as well. In short, fair treatment means granting promotional privileges not only to large firms but also to small- and medium-scale firms; it is this kind of fair treatment that was frequently requested in the past. But during 1989 and 1990, there was a change of the view that fair treatment means abolishing the privileges given to only a small number of firms. What exactly is the background of this change?

Mainly, it is the result of the economic changes brought about by the investment boom the country has been experiencing since 1987. Given the momentum created by the large increase in foreign direct investment and the country's efforts to attain the status of an NIE, Thais are now confident of their economic performance. There is one line of thinking that asserts that the Thai economy is no longer at the stage where it needs to foster industry by attracting foreign investors with measures such as tax and duty privileges. In this context, the National Economic and Social Development Board recommended to the Council of Economic Ministers that BOI privileges be reviewed in June 1990.

The proposal made at the end of 1989 to abolish the BOI or to reorganize it as the Board of Export could be viewed as a logical follow-up to the aforementioned argument. The proposal was made by prominent economists, with full confidence in the performance of the Thai economy. They argued that Thailand had now reached a stage of development where it was able to attract foreign investment without offering privileges. In other words, foreigners are coming to invest in Thailand not because of privileges, but because it enjoys economic and political stability, the prerequisities for production, as well as necessary infrastructure. Since there is no need to give promotional privileges, the historical role of the BOI has come to an end. The Chatichai government also reportedly wanted to scrap the BOI.

With the cutting of duties on imported machinery and capital goods, and the planned but long-delayed replacement of business tax with a uniform value-added tax, BOI tax incentives lost their attractiveness to investors. Recently, the number of firms that do not apply for privileges is said to be increasing. Investors appear put off by the frequent changes in government policies. After the government's decision to reduce import duties on certain machinery, the BOI drew up a new promotional privilege policy with an emphasis on providing maximum benefits for regional and rural investment projects in 57 provinces. Although no dramatic change, such as dissolution of the BOI, can be expected in the near future because of strong opposition from business circles, privileges for investment will be more selective if the BOI's status remains unchanged.

Issues on Transfer of Technology

The most important mode of acquiring foreign technology in Thailand has been direct investment, which is a package of technology assistance, including transfer of technology and management know-how, importation of machinery that embodies new technology, manpower training, and linkage with local industries through subcontracting. According to a survey in 1982 on technology importation contracts, the number of contracts made by joint ventures consist of about 80% of the total. Tables 22 and 23 indicate the increasing trend of remittance payments

Table 22. Payments for Imported Technology by Category 1972-1988 (million Baht).

Year	Royalty	Trademark	Technical Fee	Management Fee	Total Technology Transfer Payment	TT Payment as % of GDP
1972	108.05	1.33	32.63	n.a.	142.01	0.08
1973	158.57	1.22	40.48	n.a.	200.27	0.09
1974	196.93	1.30	28.30	n.a.	226.53	0.08
1975	245.67	0.12	51.10	n.a.	296.89	0.10
1976	261.52	4.82	95.86	n.a.	362.20	0.10
1977	367.36	1.40	94.43	41.50	504.72	0.13
1978	347.34	12.82	149.28	34.43	543.87	0.11
1979	461.28	19.20	189.21	53.50	723.19	0.13
1980	581.52	4.44	275.38	75.26	936.60	0.14
1981	812.30	3.84	429.53	85.52	1331.19	0.18
1982	861.31	9.85	390.11	181.42	1442.69	0.18
1983	887.10	46.52	468.55	163.67	1565.84	0.17
1984	1123.36	37.85	722.59	109.61	1993.41	0.20
1985	1202.40	35.45	723.88	83.11	2044.84	0.20
1986	1192.9	69.0	669.0	128.4	2089.3	0.19
1987	1381.6	71.9	807.8	121.6	2382.5	0.19
1988					3441.1	0.23

Source: Technology Transfer Center, Ministry of Science, Technology and Energy; World Bank, *Technology Strategy and Policy for Industrial Competitiveness: A Case Study in Thailand*, April 1990.

Table 23. Payments for Imported Technology by Industry and Country (million Baht).

	1983	1984	1985	1986	1987
(1) Industry					
Agriculture, hunting, forestry, and fishing	0.3	1.2	1.7	3.6	6.7
Mining and quarrying	0.4	37.6	25.3	50.4	—
Manufacturing	1427.3	1770.2	1806.1	1609.0	1853.2
Construction	27.4	53.9	46.5	44.4	58.0
Service business	75.6	108.4	123.9	248.8	315,2
Other industries	39.6	22.6	35.1	132.6	149.7
(2) Country					
Japan	571.1	751.9	789.5	803.3	1033.3
USA	418.9	463.8	434.8	466.0	495.5
Switzerland	86.2	141.5	152.2	186.7	193.4
UK	162.6	146.1	217.9	135.3	168.2
Netherlands	100.5	131.1	86.5	121.7	154.6
Hong Kong	82.8	99.0	102.5	114.8	102.9
Other	148.3	260.5	261.7	261.5	235.0
(3) Total	1570.4	1993.8	2044.8	2089.3	2382.9

Source: Technology Transfer Center.

for the transfer of technology, in which Japan is the biggest technology resource country, followed by the USA, the UK, Switzerland, Germany, the Netherlands, and Hong Kong.

Until recently, the government was not aware of the growing importance of foreign direct investment to ensure the transfer of technology. But now new investment projects are likely to slow down in view of the fact that the country will lose its comparative advantage as a result of higher land prices and labor costs. Thailand's comparative advantage in labor costs is estimated to disappear within the next five years. Labor-intensive industries such as garments, toys, and sports shoes will have to adjust themselves. Furthermore, the critical shortage of engineers and technicians, and the insufficient infrastructure, have led some overseas investors to move to other Asian countries.

This is why the government has been planning to emphasize the transfer of technology and manpower training in order to strengthen the competitiveness of Thai industry and to sustain high economic growth in the 1990s. In the field of science and technology, in February 1989, the BOI issued criteria for promoting research and development (R&D)-related projects. A policy regarding the transfer of technology from foreign firms was also drawn up. It included measures for the BOI to monitor contracts on transfer of technology to ensure that the Thais derive maximum benefit from them and to remove restrictive clauses and unfair terms; however, the proposal was turned down by the government due to the complicated procedures which would have caused delays in the import of technology. Local manufacturers also do not want intervention by the government.

The Seventh Economic and Social Development Plan, starting in October 1991, will try to improve the efficiency of technology transfer from foreign countries by reviewing the policy on controversial intellectual property rights, providing the information on acquiring technology in terms of quality, price, and conditions, and encouraging the subcontracting system between large firms and small and medium firms. Furthermore, in order to put pressure on private companies to develop their ability in technological innovation, the government has adopted a policy to promote industrial competition by lowering import duties on capital equipment. Thus, the BOI is expected to play a more active role by giving greater importance to technology transfer when considering investment promotion.

References

Chiasakul, Samart and Mikimasa Yoshida (eds.). 1990. *Thai Economy in the*

Changing Decade and Industrial Promotion Policy. Tokyo: Institute of Developing Economies.

Japanese Chamber of Commerce. 1989. Recent trend of direct investment in Thailand, Bangkok, April 1989 (in Japanese).

Taniura, Takao (ed.). 1990. *Industrialization in Asia and Transfer of Technology*. Tokyo: Institute of Developing Economies.

World Bank. 1990. *Technology Strategy and Policy for Industrial Competitiveness: A Case Study in Thailand*. Washington, D.C.: World Bank.

9 Japanese Firms with Direct Investments in China and Their Local Management

Jian-An Chen

Fudan University

INTRODUCTION

Since the implementation of the open door policy by China in 1978, a large number of Japanese firms have made direct investment in the country, running joint ventures, cooperative enterprises, or wholly Japanese-invested enterprises. Most of them are presently operating smoothly, although some problems exist. Some of those problems arise from imperfections in the Chinese investment environment; a lack of mutual understanding between Chinese and Japanese partners is another major factor. The process of establishing Chinese-Japanese joint ventures means that two different cultures and value systems come into direct contact, naturally giving rise to problems and conflict. The key to the success of such an enterprise, then, is for the partners to seek common ground in problems and conflicts, eliminate misunderstandings derived from differences in culture, and promote mutual understanding.

In 1989-1990, we conducted an investigation and questionnaire survey of both Chinese and Japanese top managers of approximately 100 enterprises with Japanese investment in China, and visited some of them to interview their Chinese and Japanese general managers, in an effort to ascertain the difficulties they have in managing, the different expectations of direct investment by the Chinese and Japanese parties, and the problems in the Chinese investment environment. We were attempting to seek economic and cultural common ground and to find solutions to problems. We also went to Japan to visit the parent firms. The following is a report based on the questionnaire and the investigation, which gives a survey of the trends of Japanese firms' direct investment in China, the problems in management of such joint ventures, and both the Chinese and Japanese parties' views on some problems.

TRENDS OF JAPANESE FIRMS' DIRECT INVESTMENT IN CHINA

Japan started to expand its direct investment in China in 1984-1985. According to statistics issued by Japan's Ministry of Finance, there were only 25 investment projects in total with a total amount of US$70 million by the end of March 1984. But in fiscal 1986, the number increased by 85 investment projects with an investment value of US$226 million. The investment expansion reached its climax in fiscal 1988, with the addition of 170 investment projects amounting to US$296 million. By the end of March 1990, the aggregate number of investment projects totalled 691, with total invested capital reaching US$2,473 million (Table 1).

Table 1. Japanese Direct Investment in China.

Fiscal year	No. of projects	Amount (million US$)
1979	1	14
1980	6	12
1981	9	26
1982	4	18
1983	5	3
1984	66	114
1985	118	100
1986	85	226
1987	101	1226
1988	170	296
1989	126	438
Total for 1979-1989	691	2473

Source: Financial Statistics Monthly, Ministry of Finance, Japan.

The majority of investment projects take the form of joint ventures. As a result of changes in China's policies to attract foreign investment, the number of exclusively Japanese-funded enterprises has increased, although they account for a small proportion of the total. Compared with other countries, Japan invests particularly in tertiary industry, such as hotels and leasing, with a low share in manufacturing. Japanese firms have altered their management strategy due to the appreciation of the Japanese yen since 1987, and their investment in manufacturing has

Table 2. Distribution of Japanese Direct Investment in China(total for FY 1979-1988).

	No. of Projects	Amount (million US$)	Proportion (%)
Total in manufacturing	304	349	17.1
Food	65	38	1.9
Fibers	45	23	1.1
Wood, paper pulp	17	8	0.4
Chemicals	30	31	1.5
Iron and steel, nonferrous metal	22	24	1.2
Machinery	25	20	1.0
Electric machinery	39	154	7.6
Transport machinery	5	6	0.3
Other	56	45	2.2
Total in nonmanufacturing	254	1,624	79.8
Agriculture, forestry	16	6	0.3
Fishery, aquatic products	29	36	1.8
Mining	3	6	0.3
Construction	11	3	0.1
Commerce	54	43	2.1
Banking, insurance	1	1	0.1
Services	106	417	20.5
Transportation	9	8	0.4
Real estate	21	88	4.3
Other	4	1,015	49.9
Affiliates	8	54	2.7
Real estate	1	8	0.4
Total	567	2,036	100.0

Source: Financial Statistics Monthly, December 1989, Ministry of Finance, Japan.

grown (Table 2).

Table 3 shows the relevant statistical figures released by the government of China. Judging by the number of direct investments and the amount of money from different countries and regions, we see that Hong Kong and Macao stand in the first place, and the USA and Japan rank second and third, respectively.

FEATURES OF JAPANESE-INVESTED ENTERPRISES

Small Proportion in Manufacturing but Large Proportion in Nonmanufacturing

The proportion of Japanese direct investment in manufacturing is small, which is one of the features characterizing Japan's postwar foreign

Table 3. Direct Investment (Negotiated Investment)* by Country (Region) in China.

(US$)

	1979-1983 total		1984		1985		1986		1987		1988	
	No. of projects	Amount	No. of projects	Amount	No. of projects	Amount	No. of projects	Amount	No. of projects	Amount	No. of projects	Amount
Hong Kong, Macao	(482)	431,919	1,870	217,545	2,631	413,432	1,155	144,937	1,785	197,353	4,771	358,318
USA	(32)	85,981	62	16,518	100	115,202	102	52,735	104	34,219	269	37,040
Japan	(52)	95,491	138	20,304	127	47,068	94	21,042	113	30,136	237	27,579
Singapore	(6)	5,447	25	6,256	62	7,551	53	13,741	53	6,979	105	13,663
Italy	(7)	10,292	10	1,006	5	2,445	2	5,565	3	618	15	1,064
Canada	(7)	6,558	1	2	5	873	13	8,806	6	2,554	31	3,953
Germany	(4)	3,657	18	10,524	7	2,025	6	4,296	11	13,262	22	4,714
UK	(17)	32,140	4	1,262	8	4,428	8	4,280	12	2,470	21	4,159
Australia	(8)	8,697	10	420	8	1,406	8	3,154	10	4,526	20	1,740
France	(4)	21,221	3	34	15	4,922	6	485	8	6,358	12	2,303
Total	(638)	745,246	2,166	287,494	3,073	633,321	1,498	283,434	2,233	370,884	5,945	529,706

* Including compensatory trade before 1985.

Source: Yearbook of Chinese Foreign Trade, 1983-1989.

direct investment. This feature is also noticeable in its direct investment in China. By the end of March 1989, Japanese foreign direct investment worldwide was only 26.7% in manufacturing, but 70.8% in nonmanufacturing, while in Asia the figures were 38.4% in manufacturing and 59.8% in nonmanufacturing. In China, however, Japanese direct investment made up only 17.1% in manufacturing, but as much as 79.8% in nonmanufacturing.

Few Large-scale Investment Projects

Compared with the USA and European countries' direct investment in Chinese manufacturing industry, Japan's average investment project in this area is relatively small. Among the 82 Japanese-invested enterprises that gave detailed answers to the questionnaire, the investment value of 61 enterprises was less than US$4 million, which accounts for 74.4%. A calculation of the figures in Table 2 shows that the average amount for each investment project is only US$1.15 million. There are few large-scale investment projects; most of the investment enterprises are medium or small-sized ones.

Trading Companies (Banks) Involved in Many Joint-venture Projects

It is a unique international management strategy that Japanese trading companies (banks) are involved in foreign direct investment with firms. Japan's foreign direct investment by manufacturing firms is usually associated with trading companies (banks), hence the joint-venture form "three people with four feet," i.e., the firm, the trading company (bank), and the local enterprise. Of the 392 Japanese-invested enterprises we know in China, at least 109 are financed by trading companies (banks). Their investment ratio usually ranges from 10% to 20%. They are not interested in the operations of the ventures, but in their importation of materials and components and export of products. With acquisition of experience in the field of commodity circulation, there appears a tendency for both Chinese and Japanese manufacturing enterprises to separate from trading companies (banks).

Combining with Hong Kong's Capital (Local Legal Bodies)

The combination of Japanese with Hong Kong capital (local legal bodies) and jointly making direct investments in China is another feature of Japanese-invested enterprises. Of the above-mentioned 392 enterprises, at least 26 are financed jointly with Hong Kong capital (local legal bodies). There are few such cases among the US- or European-invested enterprises. The reasons given by the Japanese parent firms are: 1) it is cheap and convenient to obtain materials and components from Hong Kong; 2) it is easy to export products via Hong Kong; 3) it is possible to raise funds in Hong Kong when in urgent need; and 4) because the Hong Kong partners are familiar with the management approaches prevailing in mainland China, investing jointly with Hong Kong firms helps to avoid conflicts between the Chinese and Japanese parties which may arise from differences in their management approaches.

A SURVEY OF JAPANESE FIRMS' MOTIVES FOR MAKING DIRECT INVESTMENTS IN CHINA AND CHINA'S MOTIVES IN ACCEPTING

As our investigation indicated, the major motives for Japanese firms to make direct investments in China are: 1) China's potential market; 2) invitation from Chinese enterprises or authorities; 3) availability of inexpensive Chinese labor; 4) establishing the image of the enterprise; 5) availability of abundant, cheap material in China; 6) policies adopted by Chinese authorities to protect foreign-funded enterprises favoring local production; 7) following suit when other firms do; and 8) favorable taxation rates.

The major motives for China to accept direct investments are: 1) to import Japanese technology; 2) to use Japanese capital; 3) to meet the needs of the domestic market; 4) to make use of Japanese export channels; 5) to help export products to Japan; and 6) to use components from Japan.

Both China's and Japan's market motives are strong. The fundamental expectation of Japanese direct investment is to enter the Chinese market, while the ultimate expectation of China is to promote exports for more foreign exchange earnings through the import of Japanese technology and capital. If the two parties are not fully aware of their contradictory market motives, and lack mutual understanding, it is inevitable that problems and conflicts will arise in operations. They should, therefore, coordinate their market motives and handle their relations appropriately, which is a prerequisite to the success of a joint or cooperative venture. It does not help cooperation if each side thinks only of its own interests without considering the other side's expectations.

PROBLEMS IN CONTRACT NEGOTIATION AND APPROVAL

Causes of Delay in Contract Negotiation and Approval

For some of the Japanese-invested enterprises we investigated, contract negotiation and approval took too much time. According to the Japanese partners, the major causes are: 1) the complex approval procedures and poor working efficiency of the Chinese administrative authorities; 2) difficulty in carrying out feasibility studies; 3) lack of mutual understanding between the Chinese and Japanese partners; 4) changes in China's policies when negotiations are in process; 5) different interpretations of the same laws by the Chinese administrative authorities at different levels; and 6) Japan's lack of experience in foreign investment. According to the Chinese partners, the major causes are: 1) the complex approval procedures and poor working efficiency of the Chinese administrative authorities; 2) overcaution of Japanese firms; 3) lack of mutual understanding between the Chinese and Japanese partners; 4) difficulty in carrying out feasibility studies; and 5) inappropriate understanding of joint or cooperative ventures by the Chinese.

Obviously, both Chinese and Japanese investors think that the principal cause of delay in contract negotiation and approval is the complexity of approval procedures and the poor working efficiency of Chinese administrative authorities. In recent years, however, the investment environment in China has been greatly improved. In most cities and provinces, special organizations have been set up to offer services for foreign-invested enterprises, approval procedures have been simplified, and relevant laws and decrees have been further strengthened. Both Chinese and Japanese partners think positively of these measures. Certainly, China's investment environment needs to be improved as compared with that in Southeast Asian countries. Thus it is not surprising that Japanese firms take a cautious attitude toward investment in China. But the Chinese likewise think that it is necessary for them to reassess the improving Chinese investment environment. If overcautious, they will lose good investment opportunities.

Due to differences in the social systems and cultural backgrounds of the two countries, promotion of mutual understanding is the key to the success of their cooperation.

Appraisal of Material Assets

In a large number of the Japanese-invested enterprises we investigated, the Chinese partners invested material assets (land, factory buildings, and equipment), whereas the Japanese partners invested capital and industrial property. One-third of the Japanese investors complained that there were disputes over assessment of material assets, mainly because their Chinese partners could produce no proof of the purchase dates, prices, and depreciation of the equipment and building costs. But the Chinese partners argued that the Japanese parties tend to underappraise the material assets. It could also be general behavior for them to overappraise their material assets. This is short-sighted behavior indeed without considering the long-term interests of both sides, because the overassessed part will certainly be shifted to production costs, which will in turn reduce the competitiveness of their products. We learned in our investigation that some enterprises have already reconsidered their past behavior in this regard.

In addition, the Japanese partners of some enterprises hold that land is state-owned in China, it should thus have no price tag, and there is no reasonable standard for appraising if it is to be priced. There is consequently much disagreement on the value of land and the charges for use. It should be pointed out that foreign investment has brought into the Chinese planned economic system some element of a market economy, where value measurement should be based on the principles of a market economy, i.e., all the means of production have a price, including land. Its appraisal should hinge on the productive rate of land with reference to land values in countries at the same development level as China. It does not conform to the principles of a market economy to under- or overappraise or even deny land value, and it will not contribute to the development of Sino-Japanese ventures.

Technology Transfer

Of the enterprises we investigated, there were only a few to which the Japanese parties had technology to transfer. The disagreement on technology transfer mainly centers on the evaluation and applicability of the technology transferred. In recent years, as is widely acknowledged by the Japanese investors, the Chinese have had a better understanding of the value of intellectual property and have recognized the value of patented technology and technical know-how as well as technology itself. But the Japanese think that the Chinese still tend to undervalue the technology transferred, which dampens their enthusiasm for transfer of technology. The Chinese, however, think that some Japanese firms charge too much for technology transfer and try to control the operations of the enterprises technologically. As for the applicability of technology transferred, the Japanese partners complain that some Chinese partners insist on importing the most advanced technology without considering China's level of productivity and ability to apply new technology, and the imported technology cannot be efficiently applied as a result. Meanwhile the Chinese partners think that the Japanese are too conservative in transferring technology and are not willing to transfer key technology in particular.

It appears that the Chinese must further improve their understanding of the value of intellectual property and try to distinguish and evaluate technology and acquire relevant information about technology on the international market. It is also hoped that the Japanese partners will give full consideration to the joint or cooperative ventures' potential and their future production capacity and take measures to, for example, associate technology transfer with compensatory trade. Meanwhile, the Chinese partners must rectify the tendency of concentrating on the introduction of the latest technology only, and take into consideration whether they have the ability to digest it and whether it is applicable when importing technology. It should also be noted that China has acquired the ability to import and digest the world's most advanced technology in some areas. We hope that the Japanese will dispel their doubts and lend their cooperation.

PROBLEMS IN MANAGEMENT

Fund Raising

Generally speaking, when making foreign direct investment and establishing a subsidiary in a foreign country, a transnational firm usually follows the financial policy of raising as much capital as possible in that country and contributing as little of its own money as possible to reduce the risk to its capital.

As the questionnaire indicated, the Japanese partners raise funds from the following sources (arranged in order of the numbers of enterprises and their percentage of the total): 1) 30 (40.5%) from their parent firms in Japan; 2) 27 (36.5%) from China's financial institutions; 3) 11 (14.9%) from Japan's domestic financial institutions; 4) 4 (5.4%) from other sources; and 5) 2 (2.7%) from a third country's financial institutions. According to the Chinese partners: 1) 38 (45.2%) from China's domestic financial institutions; 2) 19 (22.6%) from their responsible departments; 3) 17 (20.2%) from Japan's financial institutions; 4) 8 (9.5%) from other sources; and 5) 2 (2.4%) from a third country's financial institutions.

Through investigation of the Japanese parent firms, we learned that even the bulk of funds raised directly by them is from Japan's domestic or a third country's financial institutions. The share of investment from the parent firms is very small. It was not expected that the number of enterprises raising funds from China's domestic financial institutions would be so large, however. It appears that the Japanese partners try every means possible to make use of local funds in China, especially for the working capital of enterprises. It is apparent that the Japanese firms have adopted the financial policy of making use of the Chinese financial market to the full extent in the process of expanding direct investment in the country. The Chinese partners of some joint ventures have questioned whether China sets up joint ventures to use Japanese capital or lets Japanese firms use China's. The Chinese parties raise funds mainly from domestic financial institutions or their responsible departments. Because of the guarantee problem, it is rather difficult to raise funds from financial institutions abroad, including Japan. The Japanese partners have similar complaints.

In late 1988, China adopted an economic retrenchment policy, which had an unfavorable effect on Japanese-invested enterprises. Due to the shortage of capital, some of them had difficulty in expanding their production; some could not even run at full capacity. What is more, the bearish market, overstocking of products, and heavy debts among enterprises made working capital tighter. We believe that China had no alternative but to adopt the retrenchment policy, and that its impact on the Japanese-funded enterprises was unavoidable. It is hoped that the Japanese parties can understand this, and take, with the Chinese partners, effective measures to alleviate or solve these problems. China is presently considering taking special measures to provide credit in an effort to help overcome the temporary shortage of funds. It is also hoped that the Japanese partners will give full play to their capability to raise funds abroad and take other measures as well to help the enterprises overcome the present difficulties.

Procurement of Materials and Components

The procurement of materials and components is the most acute problem that Japanese-invested enterprises presently face in management. Both Chinese and Japanese parties agree that there exist four problems in the supply of materials and components from Chinese domestic sources:

Quality
Both Chinese and Japanese partners of 90% of the Japanese-invested enterprises think that although the quality of Chinese-made materials and components has been much improved due to special guidance given in recent years, there is still a gap as compared with international quality standards, which makes it difficult for them to export their products.

Delivery
Most Chinese and Japanese partners complain that those Chinese enterprises who cooperate with them have no sense of responsibility, have very faint consciousness of fulfilling contracts, and often shift the responsibility onto others with the excuse that other cooperative enterprises fail to deliver on time. Because materials and components fail to arrive on time, some Japanese-invested enterprises' production and exports are adversely affected.

Price
China's shortage of materials in recent years has resulted in a sharp rise in their prices, A majority of the Japanese-funded enterprises are not able to procure materials at parity prices (official fixed prices), and can only buy them in the free market at negotiated (high) prices, which consequently increases production costs of the enterprises.

Stability of Supply
Although prices are rising, the supply of materials and components in the free market is by no means stable. In order to meet urgent needs, enterprises want to import from abroad, but imports are restricted by the balance of foreign exchange.

Although there are no quality or delivery problems if materials and components are imported from abroad, sometimes imports do not arrive on schedule or arrive shortweighted due to complex customs formalities and backward transportation conditions in China. In addition, some Japanese partners are dissatisfied with the rough classification of commodities and the unclear customs tariff rates. The Chinese parties, however, complain that some Japanese partners maintain control over the import of materials and components and raise prices at will.

As for the issue of producing components domestically in China, both Chinese and Japanese partners admit that it is difficult to raise substantially the proportion of domestically produced components in the near future because the quality cannot reach world standards. In the meantime, however, a number of Chinese partners think that the

Japanese parties show no interest in raising the proportion of Chinese-made components and overemphasize the use of products from their parent firms.

It appears that materials will continue to be scarce and that their prices will continue to rise for quite a long period. This will have an impact not only on Japanese-invested enterprises but on Chinese domestic enterprises as well. Both Chinese and Japanese partners should understand that. We hope that China will make greater efforts to upgrade the quality of the domestically produced products, make deliveries on schedule, and adopt a more flexible policy on imports and tariffs. We also hope that the Japanese partners will help China's cooperative enterprises to upgrade the quality and raise the proportion of their components, and use the import and export channels of their parent firms to extricate themselves from the present difficult situation of material shortages.

Obligations to Export and Balance of Foreign Exchange

China's relevant regulations require that joint or cooperative ventures fulfill their obligations to export, which reflect its market motive of attracting foreign direct investment in order to raise the capability to export for more foreign exchange income. Because this motive is different from that of Japanese firms for entering the Chinese market, there are quite a few disputes resulting between the two parties. Fortunately, however, there are no rigid, inflexible rules governing such obligations in most places in China. An export ratio clause is sometimes written into a joint-venture contract only because both parties wish the foreign exchange to be balanced.

Some of the Japanese-invested enterprises we investigated are not able to fulfill their export quotas. Both the Chinese and Japanese parties share the view that the principal causes are: 1) the quality is inferior; 2) prices are not competitive; 3) products are not marketable in the world market; and 4) there are losses with export. Additionally, the Japanese partners think that it takes time for the products to be come competitive in the world market after the enterprise goes into operation. The Chinese partners, however, argue that the Japanese partners are not enthusiastic about exports; some even exercise control over the export channels and lower the prices of the products, which results in export losses. These factors add to the difficulties in fulfilling export quotas.

Of the Japanese-funded enterprises we investigated, one-third could not balance their foreign exchange (most are in the manufacturing industry). Now they are trying to solve the problem in three ways: 1) receiving foreign exchange assistance from the responsible Chinese departments in a given period (limited only to enterprises with advanced technology); 2) raising foreign exchange at the foreign exchange adjustment center; and 3) receiving assistance from the parent firms in Japan (mainly in the form of selling joint-venture products to the parent firm).

Exports and the balance of foreign exchange is a major managerial concern in enterprises with Japanese investment. Neither the Chinese nor the Japanese have made efforts to coordinate their different market motives. In our opinion, the Chinese parties should not set export ratios as obligations, but let the enterprises decide them instead. The Chinese authorities concerned should take measures to assist those enterprises with their balance of foreign exchange before their products become competitive on the world market. It is worthwhile in the meantime to recommend measures taken by the Japanese partners in some enterprises: 1) the parent firms in Japan buy some of their products to sell at home or in a third country; 2) the parent firms purchase other commodities worth the same amount as their profits in China to sell at home or in a third country; and 3) the Japanese parties reinvest profits in other industries which may earn them foreign exchange to achieve a comprehensive foreign exchange balance.

Personnel and Labor Management

A large number of Japanese-invested enterprises feel that there are not sufficiently close contacts between Chinese and Japanese managerial staff. The major causes are: 1) a lack of mutual understanding; 2) a language barrier that makes it difficult to communicate; and 3) the Chinese and Japanese do not mix well with each other in or outside the enterprises. When conducting the present investigation, we inquired into the secret of some enterprises' success. Both the Chinese and Japanese in successful joint ventures said unanimously that they had understanding partners. This emphasizes the importance of improving mutual understanding. On the other hand, some Japanese partners reported discontent with their Chinese partners' practice of holding separate meetings or communicating internal regulations in a separate group, while some Chinese parties complain about their Japanese partners' practice of only informing them after the fact of management policies decided by the parent firms. In fact, these are manifestations of misunderstanding. Some meetings attended separately by the Chinese or Japanese partners have nothing to do with enterprise management. In joint ventures, both parties must be fully aware of their mutual responsibility and ask each other's opinions before a decision is taken, not after.

When recruiting workers in joint ventures, it is very common for workers from Chinese investment enterprises to be employed first. This has brought about a series of problems, such as difficulties in dismissing unqualified workers, low worker morale, and unavailability of qualified personnel from outside. Recently, more enterprises have exercised the right to recruit staff and workers from the public, especially those newly established Japanese-invested enterprises that generally give public notice of vacancies to be filled. There are still some difficulties in recruiting technical personnel due to the personnel system presently followed by Chinese enterprises, however.

There is great disagreement between the Chinese and Japanese parties on staff wages. Some Japanese partners have already raised such questions as: Why must the enterprises pay their staff and workers housing subsidies, social insurance, and social welfare expenses in addition to wages? Why must the enterprises pay Chinese managerial personnel at the same rates as Japanese managerial staff while the Japanese cannot receive the full amount? The answers, based on our understanding, are as follows:

In China, both state-owned enterprises and collectively owned enterprises must pay staff and workers housing subsidies, social insurance, social welfare expenses, and other necessary expenses in addition to salaries and wages, while all these expenses are included in salaries and wages in Japan. Equal pay for equal work is the principle of Chinese enterprises, and this should be applied to foreign-invested enterprises as well. The Japanese partners should talk with their Chinese partners to make explicit, apart from wages, other expense items and their amount. The Chinese partners should take into consideration the difference in living standards and expenses between China and Japan when deciding wage levels for managerial personnel. It should also be noted that, judging by the factor of labor productivity, labor in China is not cheap, which has a direct effect on the attraction of the Chinese investment market. Therefore, efforts must be made to bring increases in nominal wages under control so that wages do not surpass the growth in labor productivity.

CONCLUSIONS

Among Japanese management approaches, "showing respect to people" and "showing respect to worker initiatives" can be applied, to some extent, in China, a formerly Confucian country. But approaches that reflect egalitarianism such as the “seniority system,” “bottom-to-top decision-making,” and “heart-to-heart within the group” all appear difficult to apply in China. Since China and Japan take different management approaches, problems and conflicts occur without the causes being realized. Both Chinese and Japanese partners should be fully aware of the difficulties in operating joint ventures due to the different systems and values of the two countries, and make efforts on this basis to overcome problems and establish relationships of mutual understanding and interdependence which will be beneficial to the development of both sides.

Note

Financial Statistics Monthly, December 1989, published by the Ministry of Finance, Japan.

Appendix A
Japanese Foreign Direct Investment

The figures in this Appendix are based on data compiled by Shigeki Tejima of the Research Institute of Overseas Investment (RIOI), Export-Import Bank of Japan (EXIM Bank), and published by the EXIM Bank in the following publications: "Japanese Foreign Direct Investment in the 1980s and Its Prospects for the Early 1990s" (Figs. A-1 through A-3) and "Report on the Results of FY 1990 Foreign Direct Investment Survey" (Figs. A-4 through A-7).

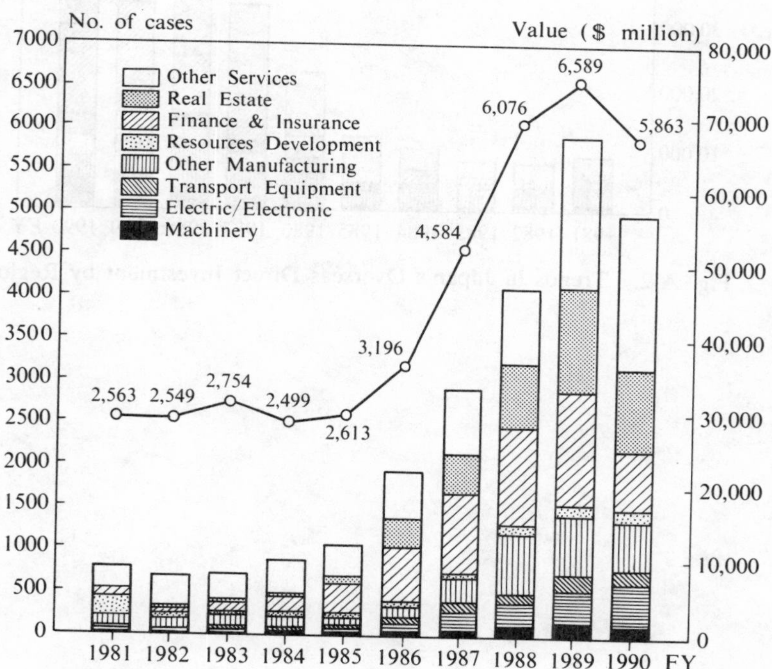

	1981	1982	1983	1984	1985	1986	1987	1988	1989	1990	
Manufacturing	2,305	2,076	2,588	2,505	2,352	3,806	7,832	13,805	16,284	15,486	($ million)
Total	8,932	7,703	8,145	10,155	12,217	22,320	33,364	47,022	67,540	56,911	($ million)

Fig. A-1. Trends in Japan's Overseas Direct Investment by Industry

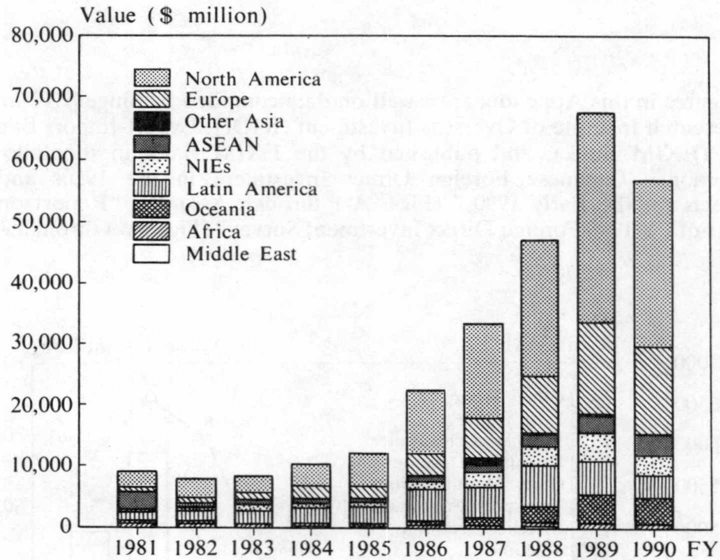

Fig. A-2. Trends in Japan's Overseas Direct Investment by Region

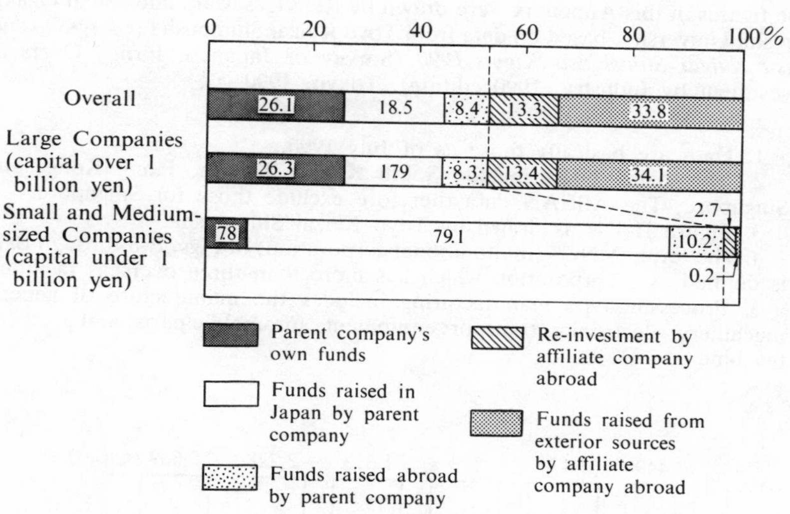

Fig. A-7. Funding for FY 1991

Appendix B
Japan-Based Manufacturing Firms and Japanese Processing-Type Multinationals' Overseas Operations

The figures in this Appendix were drawn by Rei Ogasawara and Eiichi Ozaki, Kyushu University, based on data from Toyo Keizai Shimposha (ed.), *Gyoshubetsu Kaigai Shinshutsu Kigyo 1990* (Survey of Japanese Firms' Overseas Investment by Industry, 1990 edition), Tokyo, 1990.

Notes:

1. Data are basically those as of July 1990.
2. The Asian NIEs include South Korea, Taiwan, Hong Kong, and Singapore, The ASEAN data therefore exclude those for Singapore.
3. Figure B-4 is as drawn by Toyo Keizai Shimposha.
4. The term "MNC" (multinational corporation) in Figs. B-8 through B-10 is defined as a corporation which has more than three overseas facilities.
5. Processing-type manufacturing includes the manufacture of general machinery, electronics, transport equipment, automobile parts, and precision machinery.

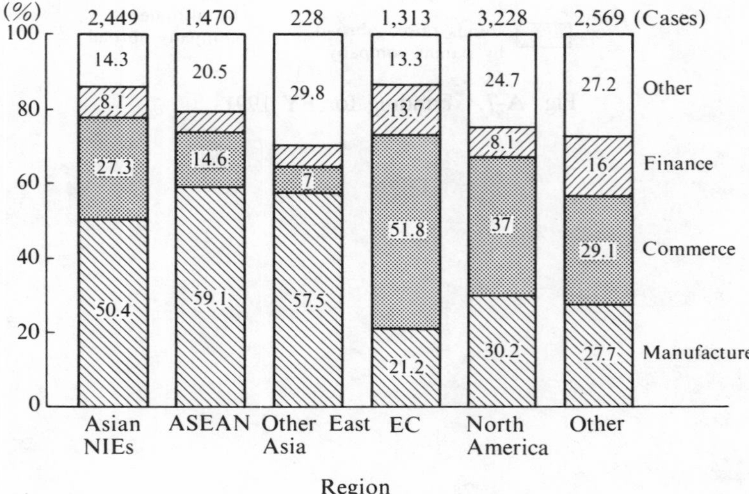

Fig. B-1. Overseas Facilities by Region and by Industry, July 1990

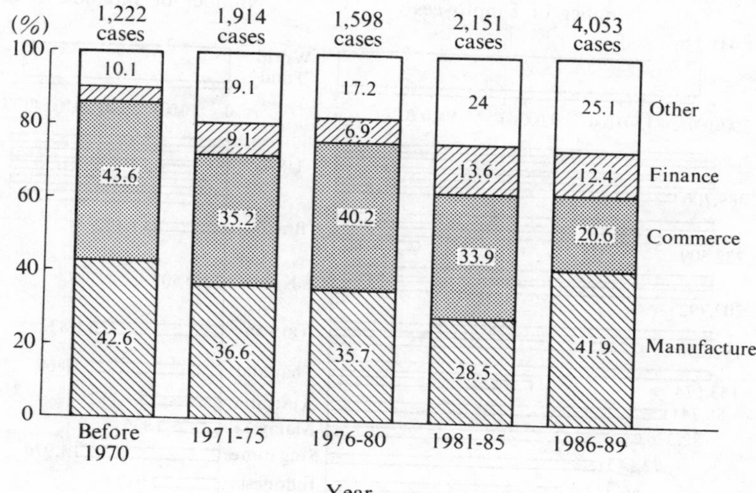

Fig. B-2. Overseas Facilities by Industry

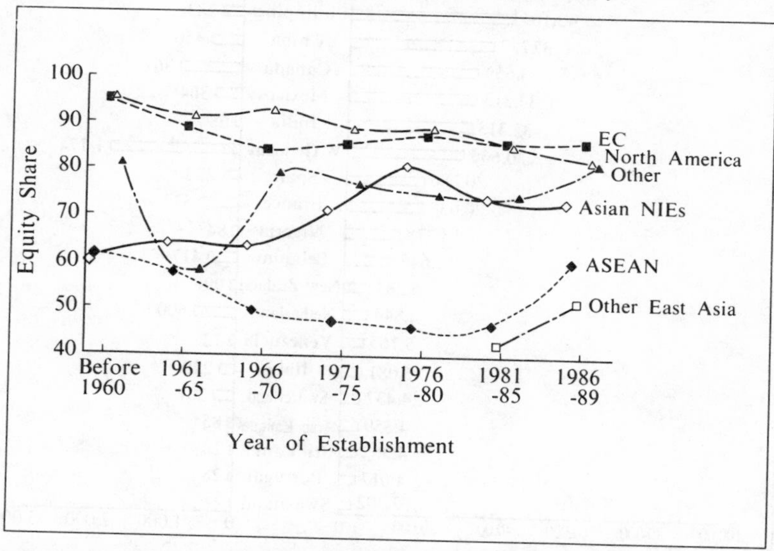

Fig. B-3. Trends in Average Equity Share of Japan-Based Manufacturing Firms

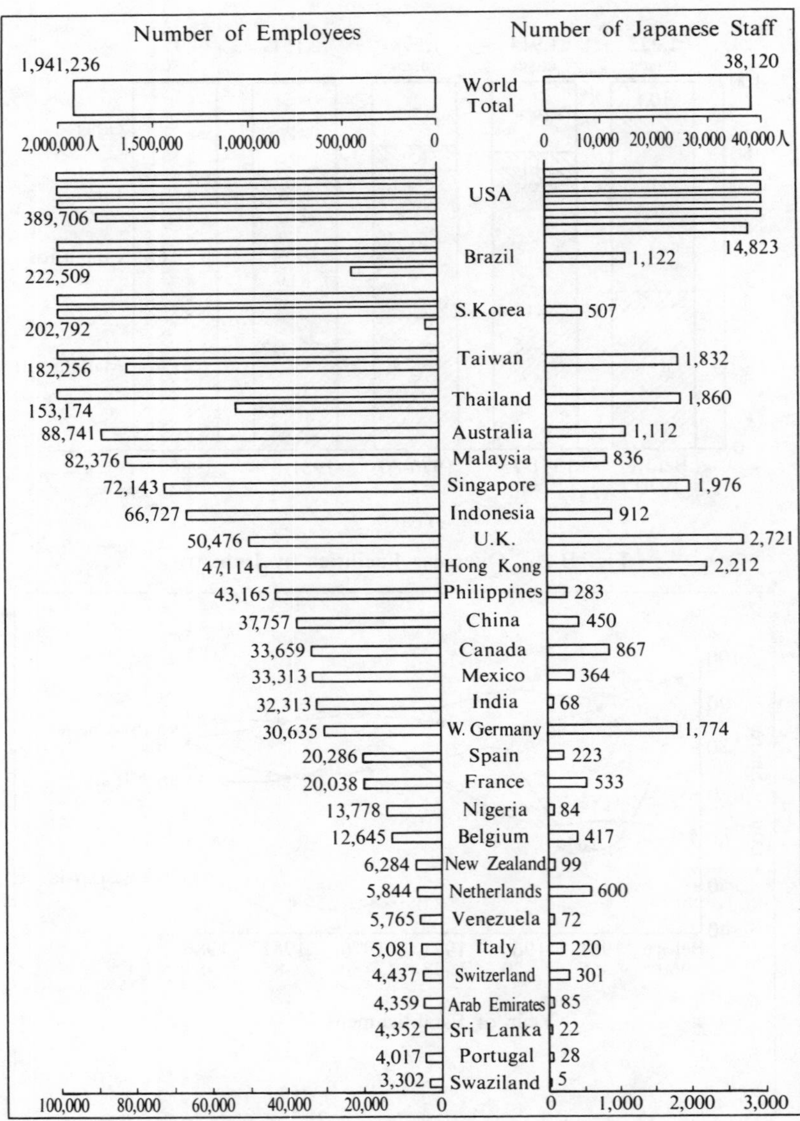

Fig. B-4. Numbers of Employees of Japan-Based Manufacturing Firms in 30 Countries Overseas (as of the end of July 1989)

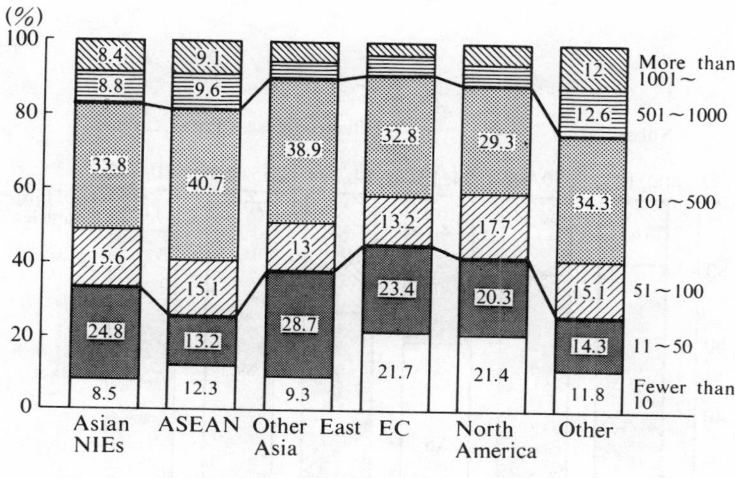

Fig. B-5. Size of Japan-Based Manufacturing Firms in Terms of Number of Employees, as of July 31, 1990

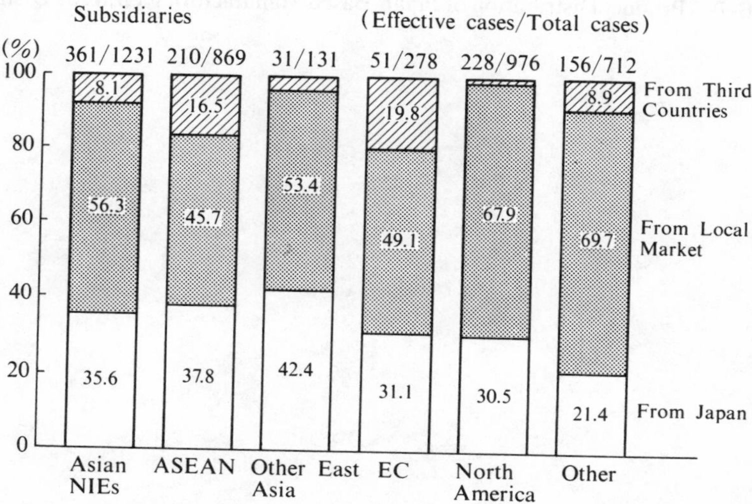

Fig. B-6. Purchases of Japan-Based Manufacturing Firms by District (% share)

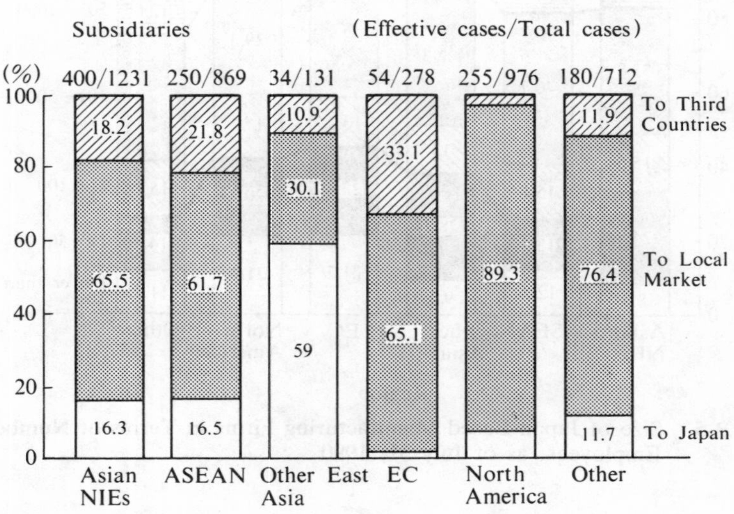

Fig. B-7. Product Distribution of Japan-Based Manufacturing Firms by District

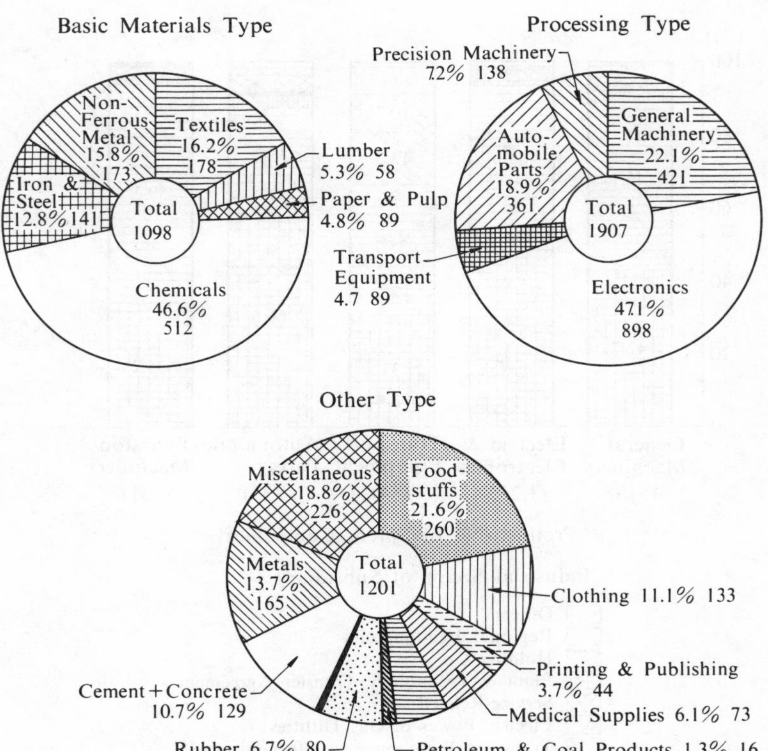

Fig. B-8. Classification of Japan-Based Manufacturing Firms

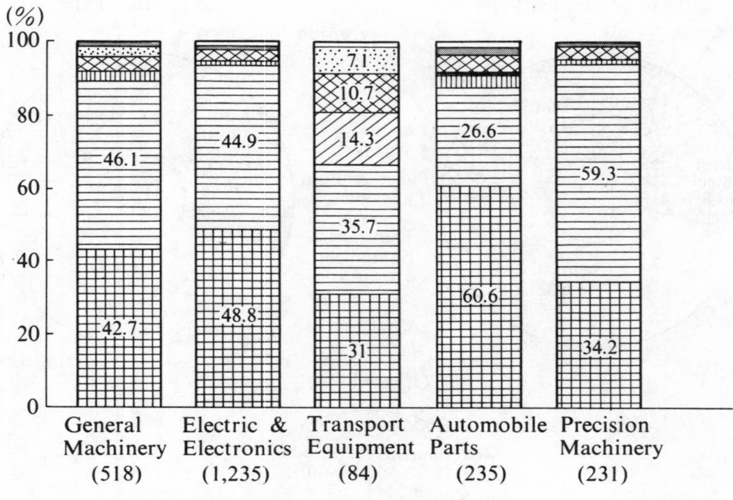

Fig. B-9. Overseas Subsidiaries Established by Japanese Processing-Type MNCs

Fig. B-10. **Overseas Business Operations by Japanese MNCs' Subsidiaries, Relative to Parent Companies' Capital**

(A) Location

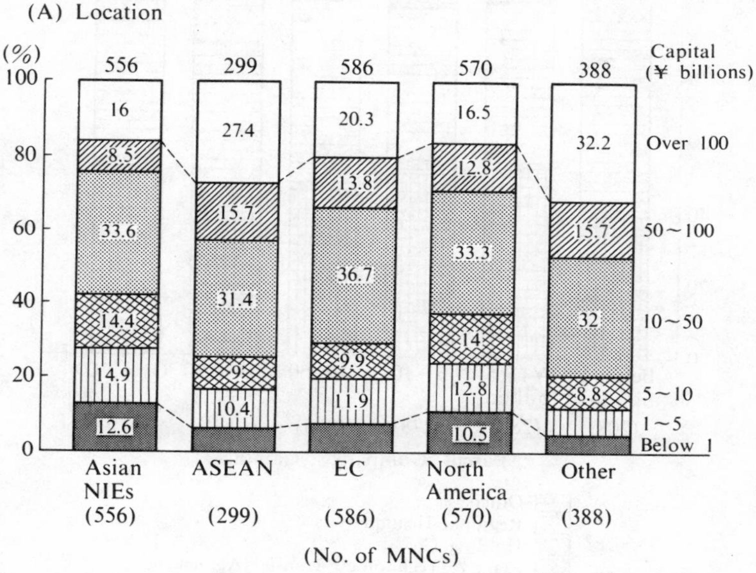

(B) Industrial Sectors of Subsidiaries

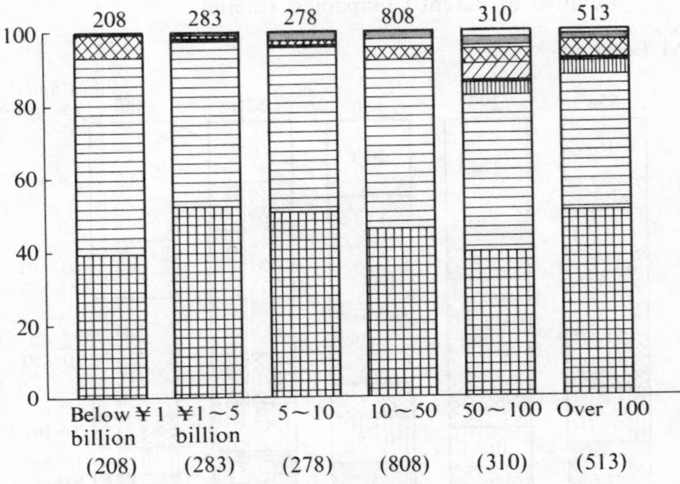

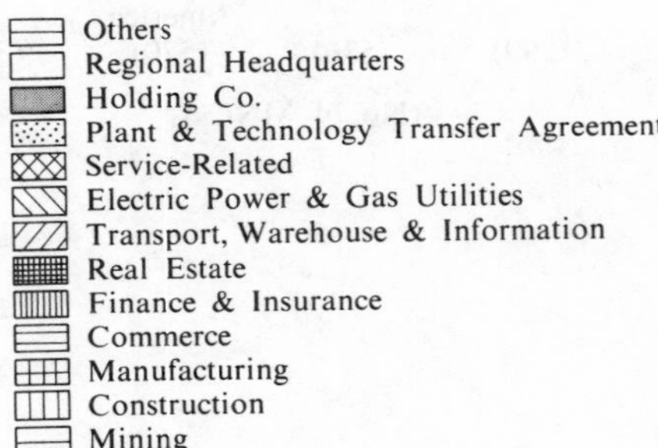

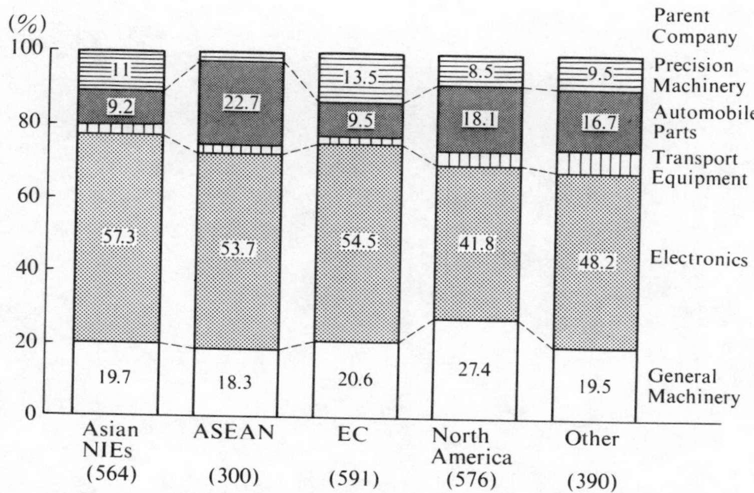

Fig. B-11. Location of Japanese Processing-Type MNCs' Subsidiaries

Index